DATE DUE			

324891090165

331.88   Bruns, Roger.
BRU

Cesar Chavez and the
United Farm Workers
movement

DISCARD

**PEIRCE ES
CHICAGO PUBLIC SCHOOLS**

573011 02450   35490A   0003

Cesar Chavez and the
United Farm Workers Movement

Recent Titles in
Landmarks of the American Mosaic

Wounded Knee
Martin Gitlin

Abolition Movement
Thomas A. Upchurch

The Chinese Exclusion Act of 1882
John Soennichsen

Cesar Chavez and the United Farm Workers Movement

Roger Bruns

Landmarks of the American Mosaic

GREENWOOD

AN IMPRINT OF ABC-CLIO, LLC
Santa Barbara, California • Denver, Colorado • Oxford, England

Library of Congress Cataloging-in-Publication Data

Bruns, Roger.
  Cesar Chavez and the United Farm Workers movement / Roger Bruns.
    p. cm. — (Landmarks of the American mosaic)
  Includes index.
  ISBN 978-0-313-38650-3 (hbk. : alk. paper) — ISBN 978-0-313-38651-0 (ebook)
1. Chavez, Cesar, 1927–1993. 2. United Farm Workers—History.
3. Agricultural laborers—Labor unions—United States—History—
20th century. 4. Grape Strike, Calif., 1965–1970. I. Title.
  HD6515.A292U543 2011
  331.88'13092—dc22   [B]   2011007433

ISBN: 978-0-313-38650-3
EISBN: 978-0-313-38651-0

15 14 13 12 11   1 2 3 4 5

This book is also available on the World Wide Web as an eBook.
Visit www.abc-clio.com for details.

Greenwood
An Imprint of ABC-CLIO, LLC

ABC-CLIO, LLC
130 Cremona Drive, P.O. Box 1911
Santa Barbara, California 93116-1911

This book is printed on acid-free paper (∞)

Manufactured in the United States of America

Contents

Series Foreword, vii

Introduction, ix

Chronology, xiii

ONE   The Forgotten Workers of the Fields, 1

TWO   The Education of Cesar Chavez, 5

THREE   The Community Organizers, 9

FOUR   Creating a Union for Farm Workers, 19

FIVE   The Delano Grape Strike and the Great March to Sacramento, 29

SIX   Strikes, Boycotts, Fasts, and the Politics of Nonviolence, 51

SEVEN   Wielding Political Power: The Agricultural Labor Relations Act of 1975, 91

EIGHT   Cracks in the Foundation, 95

NINE   The Continuing Fight, 109

Biographies of Key Figures, 119

Primary Documents, 127

Glossary, 169

Annotated Bibliography, 173

Index, 179

Series Foreword

THE LANDMARKS OF THE AMERICAN MOSAIC series comprises individual volumes devoted to exploring an event or development central to this country's multicultural heritage. The topics illuminate the struggles and triumphs of American Indians, African Americans, Latinos, and Asian Americans, from European contact through the turbulent last half of the twentieth century. The series covers landmark court cases, laws, government programs, civil rights infringements, riots, battles, movements, and more. Written by historians especially for high school students on up and general readers, these content-rich references satisfy more thorough research needs and provide a deeper understanding of material that students might only otherwise be exposed to in a short section in a textbook or superficial explanation online.

Each book on a particular topic is a one-stop reference source. The series format includes

- Introduction
- Chronology
- Narrative chapters that trace the evolution of the event or topic chronologically
- Biographical profiles of key figures
- Selection of crucial primary documents
- Glossary
- Bibliography
- Index

This landmark series promotes respect for cultural diversity and supports the social studies curriculum by helping students understand multicultural American history.

Introduction

REVERED LEADERS AND their deeds often spring from improbable roots and circumstances. Today across America there are streets, buildings, monuments, and many educational programs that carry the name of Cesar Chavez. His picture hangs on the walls of many households; his name is invoked in speeches and testimonials that talk about accomplishing the impossible against enormous odds, about standing up to injustice, about fighting for equal rights, and about making a difference.

For Chavez it was, indeed, an unlikely road. Born into a supportive but poor family of Mexican Americans in a small town outside Yuma, Arizona, burdened with an early life doing hard labor as a migrant farm worker in the harvest fields across California, without money or influence, Chavez took on a personal crusade that seemed a foregone failure. He would attempt to organize a labor union of farm workers.

Mostly Mexican American, the men, women, and children in those fruit and vegetable fields faced grueling days in the heat, worked in painful positions with inferior tools that made back injuries routine and lasting, were paid little in wages, had no benefits such as health insurance, often had no toilet facilities or access to running water, and lived mostly in shacks and other makeshift accommodations. They were American society's misfits and throwaways.

This is the story of how one of those young workers, Chavez, with little more than steely determination and uncommon instincts of leadership, took on American agribusiness and formidable political enemies, and, with the help of extraordinary allies such as Dolores Huerta, made real what seemed to most observers a fanciful dream—the United Farm Workers of America.

It is a story that springs from the profound upheaval and discontent of the 1960s—from the searing protests of the Vietnam War, political assassination, the civil rights movement, and the drive of Mexican Americans and other Latinos to gain equality and respect.

It is a story of young people and old thrust into situations demanding exceptional bravery and dedication; of marches, labor strikes and boycotts, of jailings and fending off violent attacks; and of putting into action the organizing techniques that could bring together people without power in order to enable them to achieve it.

The farm workers movement to establish a union had a profound national impact. The sparks of protest lit by Chavez in the tiny town of Delano, California, showed to the world the plight of the farm worker. The union's boycott calling on consumers not to buy grapes produced by growers who exploited farm workers, for example, raised the awareness of the issue to such an extent that millions of Americans stopped buying grapes in support of Chavez's call.

For Chavez, *La Causa* or "The Cause" was never a typical union. It was a movement for dignity as well as higher pay; it was for Latino self-identity as well as for bargaining rights. Chavez, Huerta, and other leaders of the movement remembered not only the sordid conditions they had faced themselves in the harvest fields but also the social barriers of contempt and discrimination because of their ethnic backgrounds. Through the formation and work of the union, Chavez could envision a new day for Latinos, a time when they could claim their well-earned place in an American society always resistant to change.

A half century after the first strike of Chavez's farm workers union, the debate in the United States about illegal immigration, border security, and undocumented workers rages, affecting even state legislation. Throughout its history, the UFW has wrestled with the immigration issue. Ironically Chavez himself fought against the importation of illegal workers from Mexico because those workers, who could be paid extremely low wages, were used by growers to replace members of Chavez's union in the fields. The UFW policy on immigration has since changed. But in the story of the UFW are the dilemmas and contradictions of a seemingly intractable issue that continues to defy solution.

As some of the union activists prominent in the formation of the union reach their elder years, many have written reminiscences, articles, and even books about their own experiences. Organizations have gathered together letters and other documents about the strikes, boycotts, and marches, about the strategies and tactics employed and discarded, and about some of the inner turmoil plaguing the union. We can see now more clearly the missteps and even imperious actions of Chavez along with his triumphs. After all, many of Chavez's closest advisors left the union or were forced out in the midst of bitter internal quarrels and disagreements. Much of this first-person testimony and original documentation is now available. We can now see much more clearly the driving forces behind the movement and the leadership qualities and limitations of many of the major figures.

Although farm workers in California and in other agricultural areas of the West and Southwest continue to labor under poor working conditions and although the actual numbers of members of the UFW are far lower than in earlier years, the movement produced astonishing accomplishments. Cesar Chavez and those who marched with him made indelible marks on American cultural and political history. Many reformers, activists, and other Americans committed to various causes trace their work and drive to the farm workers movement. They and their children and others newly inspired carry on their own march with Cesar.

Chronology

March 31, 1927   Cesar Estrada Chavez is born in Yuma, Arizona, on the small farm that his grandfather homesteaded in the 1880s.

1942   The United States signs the Bracero Treaty with Mexico to begin legal importation of Mexican laborers to work temporarily on contract to U.S. growers and ranchers.

1947   The Community Service Organization (CSO) is founded by Fred Ross and Edward Roybal to teach grassroots organizing techniques to help Latinos advance political and social programs.

1952   Chavez meets Father Donald McDonnell in San Jose, California. The priest, sent from San Francisco to work with farm laborers, introduces Chavez to papal encyclicals on labor, books on labor history, and a biography of Mahatma Gandhi. Chavez is recruited by Fred Ross to be an organizer for the CSO.

1955   Dolores Huerta is recruited by Ross to join the CSO.

1958–1959   Chavez works for the CSO to combat the effects of the Bracero program that had depressed wages and reduced jobs for local Mexican American field workers.

March 31, 1962   Chavez resigns from the CSO after the group refuses to commit to organizing farm workers into a union. He moves his family to the small Central California farm town of Delano to begin work to form a union.

September 30, 1962   The National Farm Workers Association (NFWA) holds its first convention in an abandoned movie theater in Fresno, California. The union unveils its new flag featuring a black Aztec eagle on a white circle in a red field, emblematic of pride and dignity. The union adopts the motto "*¡Viva la causa!*" or "Long Live the Cause!"

1964 NFWA has 1,000 dues-paying members and 50 locals. The union launches a newspaper called *El Malcriado*.

September 1965 The Agricultural Workers Organizing Committee (AWOC), mostly Filipino Americans, strike against Delano-area grape growers and ask the NFWA to join the walkouts.

September 16, 1965 NFWA, with 1,200 member families, votes to join the strike with the AWOC. Thus begins the five-year Delano grape strike.

Fall–winter 1965 The grape strike attracts widening support from labor, church, and civil rights groups. United Auto Workers president Walter Reuther comes to Delano to support the strikers.

December 1965 The NFWA calls a boycott against Schenley Vineyards, a major grape grower.

March 1966 U.S. senator Robert F. Kennedy, in hearings of the Senate Subcommittee on Migratory Labor, castigates law enforcement agencies in the Schenley strike area for arresting peaceful picketers.

March 17, 1966 Chavez leads strikers on a 340-mile march from Delano to the state Capitol steps in Sacramento. The rally at the end of the march on Easter Sunday, April 10, draws 10,000 people and much national attention. It also prompts Schenley Vineyards to negotiate an agreement with NFWA, the first genuine contract between a grower and farm workers' union in U.S. history.

August 22, 1966 The NFWA and the Filipino American AWOC merge to form the United Farm Workers Organizing Committee (UFWOC). It would later be renamed the United Farm Workers of America (UFW).

1967 The UFWOC strikes and boycotts Giumarra Vineyards Corp., California's largest table grape grower. For three years, hundreds of union volunteers and supporters fan out across the United States and Canada to organize an international grape boycott.

February 14, 1968 Chavez begins a fast to encourage a stop to violence among picketers in the Giumarra strike. For 25 days, he rededicates the movement to the principles of nonviolence practiced by Gandhi and Martin Luther King Jr. King sends a message of solidarity to Chavez.

March 10, 1968 Joined in Delano by Senator Robert Kennedy (D-NY) who, at the time, was running for the presidential nomination, Chavez breaks his fast.

April 4, 1968 Dr. Martin Luther King Jr. is assassinated in Memphis, Tennessee.

Spring 1968 The UFWOC works feverishly to help Robert Kennedy's campaign in the presidential primary in California.

June 5, 1968 Shortly after a victory speech in the California primary, Robert Kennedy is assassinated in the Ambassador Hotel in Los Angeles. Dolores Huerta and Cesar Chavez were in the hotel at the time.

May 10, 1969 The UFWOC announces plans for a worldwide boycott of California grapes. The beginning of the boycott features a march through the Coachella and Imperial valleys to the U.S.-Mexico border to protest use by California growers of undocumented workers from Mexico as strikebreakers.

Spring–summer 1970 The California grape boycott gains momentum as most grape growers in the state sign UFWOC contacts, including Giumarra.

Summer 1970 As a strategy to keep the UFWOC out of California lettuce and vegetable fields, some Salinas Valley companies sign contracts with the Teamsters Union that give the growers much more favorable conditions than those negotiated by Chavez's union. The UFWOC responds with a strike and calls for a nationwide boycott of nonunion lettuce.

July 29, 1970 Grape growers assemble at the union hall at the UFWOC field office on the Forty Acres west of Delano to sign their first union contracts after facing five years of strikes and a three-year international grape boycott.

December 4, 1970 Chavez is jailed in Salinas, California, for refusing to obey a court order to stop a boycott against Bud Antle, Inc., a major lettuce grower. Coretta Scott King, widow of Dr. Martin Luther King Jr., and Ethel Kennedy, widow of Robert Kennedy, visit Chavez in the Salinas jail.

1971 The UFWOC moves from Delano to new headquarters at *La Paz* in Keene, California.

1972 The UFWOC is chartered as an independent affiliate by the AFL-CIO and becomes the United Farm Workers of America (UFW).

May 11, 1972 Chavez fasts for 25 days in Phoenix over an Arizona law essentially banning the right of farm workers to strike, boycott, or organize.

Spring–summer 1973 When the UFW's three-year grape contracts with a number of California wineries come up for renewal, growers, including the E & J Gallo Company, sign deals with the Teamsters, as many lettuce and vegetable growers had done. The actions spark a bitter strike by grape workers in California's Coachella and San Joaquin valleys that results in several incidents of violence. Chavez calls off the strike and begins a second grape boycott across the country.

September 25, 1974 Cesar Chavez meets with Pope Paul VI during a European visit to encourage labor leaders to support the boycott.

January 13, 1975 After intense lobbying by the UFW, the California Supreme Court takes up *Sebastion Carmona et al. vs. Division of Industrial Safety*, a case relating to the dreaded *el cortito*, or short-handled hoe, a tool farm workers had long been forced to use in the fields that caused severe, long-term back injuries. The court outlaws the use of the short-handled hoe, an enormous victory for the UFW.

February 22, 1975 UFW members begin a 110-mile march from San Francisco to Modesto, California, headquarters of the E & J Gallo winery.

June 1975 Democrat Jerry Brown, an ardent supporter of Chavez, becomes California governor. In response to the strikes, boycotts, and political pressure from Democratic politicians, California enacts the Agricultural Labor Relations Act, guaranteeing California farm workers the right to organize, vote in state-supervised secret-ballot elections, and bargain with their employers.

July–August 1975 Chavez begins a 1,000-mile, 59-day march from the Mexican border through California to educate farm workers about their newly won rights. Thousands of farms workers march and attend rallies.

September 8, 1975 Workers at the Molera Packing Company, a California artichoke ranch, vote unanimously to join the UFW. It is the first election under the state's new farm labor law.

Mid- to late 1970s The UFW establishes schools at its *La Paz* headquarters to train farm workers and union staff to become negotiators and contract administrators.

1977 The Teamsters Union signs a "jurisdictional" agreement with the UFW and agrees to leave the fields.

January 1979 In an effort to improve wages and benefits, the UFW strikes a number of major California lettuce and vegetable growers.

February 10, 1979 Grower foremen shoot to death Rufino Contreras, a 27-year-old striker, in an Imperial Valley lettuce field.

July 31, 1979 The UFW begins a march from San Francisco to Salinas to dramatize the lettuce strike.

September 1979 After a strike and boycott, the UFW wins its demands for a significant pay raise and other contract improvements from Sun-Harvest, the nation's largest lettuce producer.

Early 1980s The number of farm workers protected by UFW contracts grows to the mid-40,000s.

Summer 1980 Thousands of garlic workers in Santa Clara and San Benito counties join UFW strikes and vote for the union in state-conducted elections.

1982 Republican George Deukmejian is elected California governor with $1 million in grower campaign contributions, an enormous political setback for the UFW. During his administration, Deukmejian stops enforcing California's farm labor law and thousands of farm workers lose their UFW contracts.

September 21, 1983 Rene Lopez, a worker at Sikkema Dairy near Fresno, is gunned down by company agents shortly after he votes in a union election.

1984 Chavez announces that the UFW is launching a new grape boycott and emphasizes the issue of pesticide residues on the fruits as a grave danger to the workers.

1986 Chavez launches a "Wrath of Grapes" campaign to draw public attention to the pesticide poisoning of grape workers and their children.

July–August 1988 Chavez, age 61, conducts his last and longest public fast for 36 days in Delano to call attention to farm workers and their children stricken by pesticides.

May–September 1992 Arturo Rodriguez coordinates UFW support for grape workers walking off their jobs as part of the largest vineyard demonstrations since 1973 in the Coachella and San Joaquin valleys. Grape workers win their first industry-wide pay hike in eight years.

April 23, 1993 Cesar Chavez dies near his birthplace in Yuma, Arizona, while defending the UFW against a lawsuit brought by a large vegetable grower.

April 29, 1993 Some 40,000 mourners march behind Chavez's plain pine casket during funeral services in Delano.

May 1993 Veteran UFW organizer Arturo Rodriguez succeeds Chavez as union president.

April 1994 On the first anniversary of Cesar Chavez's death, Rodriguez leads a 343-mile Delano-to-Sacramento march retracing the steps of the pilgrimage of the UFW in 1966. Some 20,000 farm workers and union supporters greet the marchers at the steps of the state Capitol in Sacramento.

1995 The UFW launches a major strike on behalf of 20,000 California strawberry workers. The strike results in two union contracts, including Coastal Berry Co., the nation's largest direct employer of strawberry workers.

March 1996 The UFW organizes marches in New York City, San Antonio, San Francisco, Los Angeles, and Chicago to demand workplace rights for California strawberry workers. In the front line of the marchers in New York and San Francisco were familiar faces from the early days of the farm worker movement, such as Jerry Brown, former governor of California, and Richard Chavez, brother of Cesar.

2001 The UFW signs a contract protecting the Ventura County field laborers at Coastal Berry Co., the largest U.S. employer of strawberry workers.

2001 The California Legislature passes and Democratic Governor Gray Davis signs UFW-sponsored laws seeking to end some of the worst abuses farm workers suffer from growers and farm labor contractors.

October 2002 Following strong support from the UFW, including a 150-mile march from Merced to Sacramento, Democratic Governor Gray Davis of California signs a binding arbitration and mediation law, the first major amendment to the Agricultural Labor Relations Act since its passage in 1975.

2003 The UFW and the nation's agricultural industry help negotiate an AgJobs bill, compromise federal legislation that would allow undocumented farm workers in the United States to earn the legal right to stay in the United States by continuing to work in agriculture. The bill eventually fails to muster 60 votes in the U.S. Senate to overcome a filibuster. The UFW continues to fight for the bill's reintroduction and passage.

August 2005 California Governor Arnold Schwarzenegger issues emergency regulations to help protect farm workers from heat deaths.

2005 The UFW mounts a major organizing drive among Central Valley table grape workers resulting in a summer election at Giumarra Vineyards, America's largest table grape producer. The company does not vote in favor of the UFW, a result that union officials charge was tainted with fraud.

2000–2010 The UFW increasingly makes use of the Internet to solicit mass grassroots participation in union organizing, boycott, legislative, and political campaigns. Nevertheless, its membership remains numerically stagnant and the struggles of the workers in the fields remain enormous.

ONE

The Forgotten Workers of the Fields

This I remember. Some people put this out of their minds and forget it. I don't. I don't want to forget it. I don't want it to take the best of me, but I want it to be there because this is what happened. This is the truth, you know. History.

—Cesar Chavez as told to Studs Terkel, *Hard Times: An Oral History of the Great Depression*

In the intense sun along the rows of crops, the migrants, mostly from Mexico, bent over in painful contorted positions and labored from early morning until the sun began to lower in the sky. In the grape orchards, lettuce fields, and other harvest areas of the American Southwest and California, they worked a grueling routine, day after day, men and women alongside young boys and girls.

They slept in cramped, rundown shacks and tin huts that had no water or electricity. Families shared dirty outhouses and water from nearby irrigation ditches. Always without enough food, faced with constant danger of disease or accident, a field worker in California made less than a dollar an hour. Their average life expectancy in the mid-1960s was 49 years. By the time most of the children were 12 years old, they joined their parents in the fields and attended school only when there was no work.

Isolated in the fields, the workers had no choice but to stay in those rundown shacks; no choice but to buy food and other supplies from makeshift stores owned by the companies that also charged outrageous prices; no power to stop unscrupulous labor contractors hired by the companies to skim off a portion of their salaries for the opportunity to work.

Novelist and screenwriter John Gregory Dunne saw firsthand the conditions under which grape pickers in California worked in the 1960s: "The workers hunch under the vines like ducks. There is no air, making the intense heat all but unbearable. Gnats and bugs swarm from out under the leaves. Some workers wear face masks; others, handkerchiefs knotted around their heads to catch the sweat" (Dunne [1967] 2007, 16).

For over a century and a half, the Mexican migratory worker has been vital to American agriculture production in the Southwest, especially as fruit production increased in California in the mid-1800s. Mexican workers also helped build railroads, worked as miners and on cattle ranches. But it was in the harvest industries of growing American agribusiness that labor from Mexico became indispensable during the harvest seasons.

For many decades, small groups, including Filipinos, Anglos, and Mexicans, had attempted to organize farm workers. None were ultimately successful, thwarted by the power and influence of growers and ranchers who were backed by political allies and local law enforcement.

The entry of the United States into World War II produced damaging labor shortages in many areas of the economy. The war especially affected agriculture production and the necessary workforce to move crops from the harvest fields. Faced with farm worker shortages, the United States and the Mexican governments, on August 4, 1942, created the Bracero program.

Designed to provide temporary work to thousands of impoverished Mexicans and also to produce a vital source of labor to agricultural businesses during harvest, the program operated through contracts controlled by independent farmers associations and the Farm Bureau. When the contracts expired, the braceros were required to turn in their permits and return to Mexico.

Most braceros were experienced farm workers from regions such as Coahuila and other lush agricultural regions in Mexico. From their rural villages and towns to recruitment centers in such Mexican cities as Chihuahua and Monterrey, the men came to be registered, medically screened, given an identification card, and shipped to the U.S. border. Often they felt like cattle. Cecilio Santillano, an ex-bracero, remembered the trip to the United States. "They brought them in trucks and some in trains and not passenger trains but cargo trains . . . like sheep, up to El Paso" (Santillano).

At the border, where they underwent more registration procedures, medical exams, and fumigation, they signed work contracts and were shipped to farms across the United States, mostly in the American Southwest.

They picked lettuce, cotton, tomatoes, asparagus, grapes, and other agriculture staples, enabling extraordinary growth in agribusiness, especially in California. At first a wartime measure, the Bracero program was codified into law and expanded, especially in California where farm worker shortages continued to plague growers.

Children of Mexican farm workers, 1940s. Driven by the need for temporary agricultural laborers during World War II, the U.S. and Mexican governments created the Bracero program designed to provide work in the United States for thousands of Mexican field workers. Created in 1942 and first administered by the Farm Security Administration (FSA), the Bracero program opened up opportunities for Mexican laborers but also led to exploitation—substandard housing, racial discrimination, and low wages. These children of migrant workers pose at an FSA camp. (Library of Congress)

The Bracero program also became an effective weapon that growers used to discourage the unionization of farm workers. Braceros simply became scab labor.

While bracero workers were supposed to return to Mexico at the end of their contracts, not all did. Many, who did return, later immigrated to the United States.

At the end of World War II, the federal government began decreasing the number of Mexican laborers imported under the Bracero program. By the 1960s, the problem with Mexican farm laborers had turned from a shortage to an overflow and an increasing number of poor Mexicans crossed the border as "illegal aliens." The Bracero program was thus ended.

Whether working as American citizens or illegal aliens, the lot of the farm worker remained one of grinding labor, inhumane work conditions, and ethnic prejudice. Concerned individuals would attempt to help these workers find a better life. They would dedicate their own lives to stop the injustice, discrimination, and mistreatment directed toward those with the least power and influence. Many would make a difference.

One of those was a young Mexican American who had labored in the fields with his family for much of his early years, following the harvests picking apricots, prunes, walnuts; taking any jobs available from the contractors; living in various labor camps or under bridges; and often facing humiliation. He remembered the words on signs at many establishments— "White Trade Only" or "We Don't Sell to Dogs or Mexicans"; the time in Indio, California, when his father was turned away from a small restaurant along the road when he tried to buy coffee; and the time in Brawley, California, when, as a youngster, he tried to get hamburger at a diner and was told to go to "Mexican town," and the many other times.

He later described those stooped in the fields as "the human beings who torture their bodies, sacrifice their youth and numb their spirits to produce this great agricultural wealth, a wealth so vast that it feeds all of America and much of the world. And yet the men, women and children who are the flesh and blood of this production often do not have enough to feed themselves" (Grossman 2002). That man was Cesar Chavez, and he would indeed make a difference.

References

Dunne, John Gregory. (1967) 2007. *Delano: The Story of the California Grape Strike*. New York: Farrar, Straus & Giroux. Reprint, Berkeley: University of California Press. Citations refer to the University of California Press edition.

Grossman, Marc. 2002. "Chavez, Steinbeck: The Ties That Bind." *Sacramento Bee*, October 2. http://www.ufw.org/_page.php?menu=research&inc=history/14.html.

Santillano, Cecilio. "Bittersweet Harvest: The Bracero Program 1942–1964." Smithsonian Institution, National Museum of American History. http://american history.si.edu/exhibitions/small_exhibition.cfm?key=1267&exkey=770&page key=778.

TWO

The Education of Cesar Chavez

Born near Yuma, Arizona, on March 31, 1927, Cesar Chavez was the second of six children of Librado and Juana Chavez. His fraternal grandfather, Cesario "Papa Chayo," had crossed the border into Arizona from Mexico in 1888, settling on a farm in the North Gila Valley desert, along the Colorado River. It was here that the extended family, including Librado and Juana Chavez, worked the land, cared for horses and cows, and opened a small grocery store.

Centered in a Roman Catholic faith, Chavez's family, especially his grandmother, taught the children the rituals and trappings of religious life. He was baptized in the Immaculate Conception Church in Yuma. Throughout his life, Chavez would look to those teachings and his own religious impulses for guidance.

Unable to make tax payments on their farm, the Chavez family left Arizona in 1937. Cesar was 10 years old. Loading their few possessions in a dilapidated car, the family joined other Depression-era families on the road to California to its harvest lands and the faint promise of work.

From valley to valley, from harvest to harvest, the Chavez family kept moving. For a time, Brawley, California, became a home base. Traveling northward each spring from job to job, they gained knowledge about the rotation of crops and the successive harvests and the better job opportunities. They picked peas, lettuce, tomatoes, figs, prunes, grapes, and apricots. And, as other Mexican Americans, they faced the constant reminder that they were a minority race and culture. From his earliest childhood days, Cesar, as did other Hispanic children in the United States, learned limitations rather than possibilities.

Chavez later remembered an early labor uprising that fizzled almost as soon as it began: "When I was 19 I was picking cotton in Corcoran. A car with loud speakers came around," he said. "The speakers were saying: 'Stop Working. You're not making a living. Come downtown to a rally instead.'

My brother and I left, with many others. 7000 cotton pickers gathered in a little park in the center of Corcoran. There was a platform and a union leader got up and started talking to all the workers about 'the cause.' I would have died right then if someone had told me how and why to die for our cause. But no one did. There was a crisis, and a mob, but there was no organization, and nothing came of it all. A week later everyone was back picking cotton in the same field at the same low wages. It was dramatic. People came together. Then it was over. That won't organize farm workers" ("*Viva la Causa*" 1964).

In 1943, the Chavez family settled in Delano, California, in the center of the crop-rich San Joaquin Valley. The young Chavez began to sport the pachuco or "zoot suit" look—a flowing coat, tapered pants, and a broad, flat, wide-brimmed hat, and long, ducktail hair. Nurtured in Los Angeles, the style was of rebellion, anger, and frustration of Mexican American youth.

Cesar's father joined the National Farm Labor Union. Organized by Ernesto Galarza, a Mexican American sociologist and labor organizer, the union organized a number of strikes in the 1940s but they were short-lived and relatively ineffective. Nevertheless, Cesar admired the union's purpose—to face indignities and injustice against long odds.

Cesar Chavez, eighth-grade graduate. Born in Arizona to migrant farm workers from Mexico, Chavez spent his formative years in migrant camps in California, attending various public schools as his family moved from job to job. In 1942, he posed in a suit and tie for his eighth-grade graduation. He would now work full-time in the fields. (Wayne State University/Walter P. Reuther Library)

He fought back at racism. At a movie house in Delano with a young woman named Helen Fabela, Chavez refused to stay on the right side of the theater, which was reserved for Mexicans, and instead sat down in the Anglo section. "The assistant manager came," Chavez recalls. "The girl who sold the popcorn came. And the girl with the tickets came. Then the manager came. They tried to pull me up, and I said, 'No, you have to break my arms before I get up.'" Chavez was hustled off to the jail for a lecture from the chief of police on proper behavior in a segregated place of business ("The Little Strike" 1969, 205).

In 1946, Chavez enlisted in the Navy. After his enlistment ended in two years, he returned to Delano. On October 22, 1948, he married Helen Fabela. They would eventually have eight children. He was 21 at the time of his marriage—thin, five feet six inches tall, with a shock of jet-black hair, his body muscled from years of grinding work in the fields. But like most farm workers, he was plagued by back pains, the result of daily stooped labor.

In 1952, Chavez moved with others of his family into a barrio in southeast San Jose with the uninviting name of *Sal Si Puedes* ("Get Out If You Can"). As California's agricultural areas grew, new Mexican American barrios emerged as laborers such as the Chavez family became settled. *Sal Si Puedes* was one of those barrios.

When a young Catholic priest named Father Donald McDonnell traveled to *Sal Si Puedes* to help establish a community organization among the farm laborers, Chavez soon became a close friend. A graduate from St. Joseph's College in Menlo Park, California, in 1950 and from St. Patrick's Seminary in 1956, McDonnell was ordained in San Francisco. Sensitive to social issues and injustices, he asked to be assigned to the poorest parish.

McDonnell admired the principles of justice enunciated by Pope Leo XIII in his 1891 encyclical *Rerun Novarum*. Pope Leo's document affirmed the Catholic Church's position on the rights of workers in the wake of industrialization, declaring that one role of the church is to speak out on social issues and that workers should be able to make free agreements with employers regarding wages or other working conditions. For Father McDonnell, that charge by the church, made nearly a century earlier, was a call for social justice that should apply to farm workers in the 1960s.

Chavez remembered the priest sitting with him late at night "telling me about social justice and the Church's stand on farm labor and reading from the encyclicals of Pope Leo XIII in which he upheld labor unions." Chavez said, "I would do anything to get the Father to tell me more about labor history. I began going to the bracero camps with him to help with Mass, to the city jail to talk with prisoners" (London and Anderson 1970, 143–144).

The two were nearly the same age, both excited about working for change. McDonnell gave Chavez various books. Later, it was not unusual for Chavez to quote Winston Churchill. He even obtained the transcripts of a current hearing in the U.S. Senate chaired by Robert LaFollette (D-WI) on agriculture, strikes, and the tactics of big business in busting those strikes. Chavez intently took it all in, developing his own perceptions of the social order and how to challenge its injustices.

For Chavez, it was coming together, now—the lessons from his father about not accepting as fate the conditions in which you found yourself and about working with others in unions to improve those conditions; the teachings of his grandmother about spirituality and the elements of Catholicism that inspired one to reach out to help those in need; and also the example of his mother, who, on many occasions, asked her children to go out by the railroad tracks and ask a hobo to come for dinner.

He read biographies of individuals whose leadership made a difference such as labor organizers John L. Lewis and Eugene V. Debs. He read about Mahatma Gandhi, the Indian politician and spiritual leader who had passed away in 1948, the revolutionary who preached and practiced the philosophy of nonviolent social change. He was particularly struck by the power unleashed strategically by campaigns of civil disobedience and even the spiritual ritual of fasting to unleash the power of redemption. Chavez studied the writings and the histories of civil rights leaders such as Martin Luther King Jr. and their own strategic use of nonviolence grounded in theological terms to promote social change.

He was young and poor but had in him a fire to make something happen to change the lot of his family and the thousands of others who worked painstakingly in the fields. He decided to become a community organizer.

References

"The Little Strike That Grew to *La Causa*." 1969. *Time*, July 4, 20.

London, Joan, and Henry Anderson. 1970. *So Shall Ye Reap*. New York: Thomas Y. Crowell.

"*Viva la Causa*: Cesar E. Chavez, Interviewed by Wendy Goepel." 1964. Originally published in *Farm Labor* 1, no. 5 (April). http://www.sfsu.edu/~cecipp/cesar/lacausa.htm.

THREE

The Community Organizers

The Roots of Community Organizing

In Chicago's tough, crime-ridden neighborhoods of the 1930s, Saul Alinksy, a graduate of the University of Chicago with a doctorate in archeology, a man who had grown up in the city's Jewish ghetto, began his life's work of helping ethnic groups, unions, and others to organize themselves to take on governments and corporate interests that had wielded power over them. In 1936 Alinsky cofounded the Back-of-the-Yards Neighborhood Council (BYNC), his first effort to build a neighborhood citizen reform organization. In the South Side, largely Irish Catholic community near the famous Union Stockyards, Alinsky's group was able to apply enough pressure on Chicago's city hall to gain significant assistance in restoring a rapidly declining neighborhood. Allied with the United Packinghouse Workers Union, BYNC was instrumental in helping tens of thousands of packinghouse workers to improve their standard of living and gain the dignity that comes with union recognition and collective bargaining.

In 1939, aided by the Marshall Field Foundation, Alinksy established the Industrial Areas Foundation to help reform other declining urban neighborhoods. His approach was to unite ordinary citizens around immediate grievances and stir them to vigorous protest—to enable them to organize effectively for reform. He taught them techniques such as house meetings and organized protest meetings and marches and communication strategies to help them become effective forces in bringing about solutions to their problems, whether those problems stemmed from racial and religious bigotry, poverty, homelessness, or just the lack of streetlights in a slum area.

Alinsky inspired the organizing methods of numerous groups. He forged his techniques in city after city, modifying his own approaches to fit the situations. Other organizations traced their own strategies to Alinsky's work and made fundamental modifications of their own. One of those groups was the Community Service Organization (CSO).

Fred Ross and the CSO

Born in San Francisco in 1910, Fred Ross graduated from the University of Southern California with a teaching credential. Unable to find a teaching job, he became a case worker for the state relief administration. Later, he took a position with the Farm Security Administration (FSA), one of President Roosevelt's most notable New Deal programs. It was with the FSA that Ross began his community service outreach.

When the acclaimed novelist John Steinbeck wrote *Grapes of Wrath* in 1939, a story of the tribulations of the Joad family, a group of migrants from Oklahoma who traveled west to California looking for a way out of destitution, he modeled the setting in the novel from a federal farm labor camp at Arvin, California, near Bakersfield.

Shortly after Steinbeck left the area, it was Ross who became the camp's director. At Arvin, Ross earned the trust and respect of the laborers by instituting a form of self-government for the camp. Every day he went from cabin to cabin encouraging residents to band together as a large force to help improve the conditions and to fight for concessions from those who held power. He prodded people to speak up for their interests, to fight through the fear of confrontation, and to be heard.

Ross later joined with social activists in helping blacks and Mexican Americans fight against segregation in housing and education. In Arizona, he helped Yaqui Indians acquire medical facilities, streets, and other basic needs.

In 1947, Ross, Edward Roybal (later a U.S. congressman), and others founded the CSO, a Latino civil rights group that became highly successful in registering new voters and in establishing citizen involvement in social issues. By building Mexican American voter strength, Ross believed, politicians would have to pay attention, would be forced to improve services, streets, parks, sewage systems, garbage removal, and, especially, schools. Learning Spanish from flash cards, Ross met small groups of Mexican Americans in their homes. The groups then branched out into the community, creating new groups, and establishing footholds.

Ross once wrote, "To carry on a hard-hitting program of civic action and militancy, you must have people who are of a certain temperament, who just cannot live with themselves and see injustice in front of them. They must go after it whenever they see it, no matter how much time it takes and no

Fred Ross Sr., 1988. One of the nation's foremost community organizers, Fred Ross helped found the Community Service Organization (CSO) in 1947, a group to promote Latino citizenship drives and voter registration. It was Ross who recruited both Cesar Chavez and Dolores Huerta for the CSO and helped with the organization of the farm workers union. Ross, shown here with Chavez in 1988, was a lifelong and tireless supporter of the union. (Wayne State University/Walter P. Reuther Library)

matter how many sleepless nights of worry." In 1952 Ross found such a man in San Jose. He was Cesar Chavez. (Levy 2007, 95).

Deeply distrustful of Anglos, Chavez hesitated when the lanky Ross, in wrinkled clothes, driving a beat-up car, walked up to Chavez working in the fields and asked if he could have a house meeting with him and some of his friends. A dubious Chavez agreed but almost as a lark. "I had hatched a plan with some of my Pachuco buddies to scare him away. At a prearranged signal from me, they'd start insulting him; that way, we thought, Fred would leave" (Chavez 2008, 227).

The plan never worked because Chavez never gave the signal. Instead, he began listening carefully to the things that Ross said. When one of the friends in the room interrupted, Chavez demanded silence. This was the beginning of a remarkable friendship and a historic collaboration.

Ross saw immediately in Chavez the burning desire to change the plight of farm workers. For two months, Chavez showed up at the meetings Ross held for the workers, displaying the kind of urgency and determination that Ross had not seen in others.

As a young boy, Chavez had worked alongside other family members in the harvest fields of Arizona and California and felt the sting of injustices meted out to his own family and others. After returning to the fields after his stint in the Navy, he now burned with a determination to do something to change the conditions under which the farm workers had to toil—the agonizing, stooped labor for a pittance of wages, the deplorable living conditions and lack of sanitation facilities provided by the growers, the absence of leadership and total lack of political muscle of an entire group of American workers. "I kept a diary in those days," Ross said later. "And the first night I met Cesar, I wrote in it, 'I think I've found the guy I'm looking for'" (Levy 2007, 102).

Chavez agreed to help organize a voter registration drive in San Jose. Still working as a field laborer to make ends meet, he conducted house meetings at night, talking with fellow field workers about their constitutional rights, and showing them how to register to vote. Chavez recruited friends from the barrio to help with the work and by the end of the campaign he had signed up several thousand new voters.

In joining in the CSO voting drive, Chavez had entered a rough fighting ground of partisan politics. These new voters that Chavez and his team signed up were going to vote Democratic in an area now controlled by Republicans. Startled by the advent of a new Mexican American voting bloc in its midst, the local Republican organization decided to challenge first-time Mexican American voters at the polls. Republicans showed up on election day charging that many of the first-time Mexican Americans were actually illegal aliens or suggesting they had criminal backgrounds.

So infuriated was Ross at the tactics that he wired the U.S. attorney general in Washington asking that the federal government investigate this voter intimidation. Chavez added his name to the letter. For the Department of Justice and the Federal Bureau of Investigation, however, this letter was less an alarm against voter fraud than a signal that this group in San Jose might be tied to some kind of communist conspiracy.

Indeed, in Bakersfield, California, a young congressman from California was organizing hearings concerning labor walkouts, believing that labor protestors were more than likely connected to anti-American subversion. The congressman was future president Richard Nixon.

And now, alerted to the labor unrest in California, the FBI sent agents to follow the activities of this young activist Chavez and his comrades. Who was this new face of protest and what were his links to communism?

It was not long before they rounded up Chavez. "The FBI agents took me in their car for a meeting with members of the Republican Central Committee which turned into a shouting match," Chavez later remembered. "That's the first time I started shouting at Anglos, shouting back at them."

The confrontation became the subject of a newspaper story and suddenly Chavez was the talk of the area. The press fueled any stories of communist subversion, Chavez said, and "Everywhere I went to organize they would bluntly ask, 'Are you a Communist?' . . . Later I found out that when they learned I was close to the church, they wouldn't question me so much. So I'd get priests to come out and give me their blessing" (Levy 2007, 106).

The file on Cesar Chavez at the FBI grew larger over the years, filling up with information about his friends, work, speeches, philosophy, and family. As the FBI tracked Chavez with increasing intensity, it found no evidence of his implication in communist activities. Instead, the massive file filled up with evidence of Chavez's remarkably strong commitment on behalf of Latino farm workers.

Ross and the CSO decided to hire Chavez as a full-time organizer. His pay was $35 a week. In his entire career, he would never earn more than $6,000 a year.

Chavez's single-minded purpose and drive was evident to all those small groups of people he gathered in the house meetings, the fellow workers he recruited from the fields, many of whom would stay with him and his cause for years. In the 1950s, Chavez organized more than 20 new CSO chapters in such California towns as Madera and Hanford. During his years with the CSO, the young organizer met a whole range of public and private authorities who were involved with labor issues and social problems involving Mexican Americans. To worker after worker, Chavez intently listened to their problems. To him they came singly or in groups; for them he wrote letters to government agencies and intervened in misunderstandings with the police or with physicians or with welfare departments.

As other Mexican American community organizations, or *mutualistas*, the grassroots CSO, through the use of many volunteers, promoted self-reliance and provided a variety of services including low-cost medical care and job referral. It fought for better education for the children of Mexican descent, worked for civil rights issues, and campaigned for voter registration. It was work to which Chavez, at least for the moment, was totally committed.

Dolores Huerta

In the mid-1950s, Chavez befriended Dolores Huerta. She, too, was a recruit of Fred Ross.

Born in New Mexico and raised in Stockton, California, Huerta barely knew her father who left the family when she was very young. Nevertheless, he proved to be an inspirational figure. A migrant farm worker and miner, he joined a number of political and labor groups that sought to improve the lives of those who worked the land and who had been systematically treated as little more than cattle. Dolores managed to attend Stockton College after graduating from high school. She married and began to raise two daughters, but the union soon ended in divorce. After leaving Stockton College with a degree and teaching certificate, she began working in the classroom. Frustrated and disillusioned by attempting to help students who did not have enough clothing or food, she decided to move her life in a different direction.

Impressed by Huerta's passion and outspoken nature, Ross immediately envisioned her as a dynamic addition to his organization. Huerta was soon sold on the CSO, an organization, she thought, that could actually make a difference at the grass roots, one into which she could pour her energy and passion. Huerta later remembered the excitement of learning about the health clinics that the CSO had helped build in the city and by the fact that a number of local Hispanic leaders had actually entered the political arena.

She agreed to help Ross organize a Stockton chapter and to run a CSO civic and educational program. She also began to take an active political role for the organization. Attractive, gregarious, Huerta would be an especially effective representative for the CSO in face-to-face meetings with local government leaders and with potential donors. Huerta also took on lobbying efforts with members of the California legislature in Sacramento for such issues as the expansion of state disability assistance to agricultural workers.

Huerta had heard of Chavez, heard about his extraordinary energy and his ability to gather people together to work for the CSO cause. In her mind, Huerta had imagined a powerful figure with gifted abilities as an orator. Yet, when she met him in person, she was surprised. He seemed shy in conversation, almost retiring in manner. Yet, she began to realize that he was, indeed, a special individual with keen intelligence, a fiery disposition, and, especially, a firm determination to make a difference in the lives of farm workers. At a meeting in 1957 in Stockton, she marveled at the way he answered questions directly, precisely, and without pretension. He was, she concluded, a special messenger and activist for the cause of the workers.

In the summer of 1958, Chavez was in Oxnard, a town north of Los Angeles, to establish a local office of the CSO in one of the leading citrus-growing areas of the state. Early on in his work to help farm workers, Chavez realized that the Bracero program, the federally funded means by which workers from Mexico were brought to the United States for temporary work in the fields, was fraught with problems for local workers. Because of the financial advantages that the Bracero program afforded the growers, many of the local California Mexican American workers and other migrant laborers frequently went without jobs. By the late 1950s, Mexican American field workers had been to a large extent replaced by the braceros. Signs declaring "No Pickers Wanted" increasingly greeted those looking for work.

Although sympathizing with the plight of the Mexican workers brought into the United States in the harvest seasons and then sent back, Chavez realized that the system severely jeopardized the wages of Mexican American workers already in the country. Not only were the braceros used by the growers as strikebreakers, the low wages they received and the conditions under which they worked set a standard of wretchedness that gave Chavez sleepless nights. The growers were treating these guest workers like the lowest peons outside of slavery, and it was all being undertaken under a government-sanctioned program.

The dilemma was extraordinary. Mexican American workers could not protest wages or working conditions for fear of losing jobs to braceros. The braceros, on the other hand, could not protest their treatment for fear of being returned immediately to Mexico.

Chavez had carefully studied the nonviolent but aggressive tactics used by Martin Luther King Jr. and others in the civil rights movement that had gained momentum in the American South. He read about the sit-ins at lunch counters, the bus boycotts, had talked with veterans of various marches and acts of civil disobedience, and had gained invaluable insight into ways that powerful interests can be challenged through nonviolence. He saw in the civil rights movement the same kind of philosophy that he had read about in the books given to him years earlier by Fred Ross and Father McDonnell. The strategies worked. They could work, he believed, for the farm workers.

Chavez and his lieutenants doggedly rallied the farm worker community to his cause, gathering more than 1,500 workers. By the end of 1959, they had set up at a local CSO headquarters a so-called hiring hall from which many of the growers agreed to find workers. Chavez had essentially turned the local CSO in Oxnard into a union hall. So encouraged was Chavez in his early successes that he began to envision something much broader than a hiring hall in one local agricultural area. It was in Oxnard that Chavez began to see clearly in his mind the exciting potential of organizing the farm workers of California into a union.

Encouraged by the backing of the 1,500 workers at Oxnard, he proposed to the CSO that they found a union. The proposal was turned down. The organization, the CSO Board of Directors insisted, was by nature a social service program organization, not a union.

Both Chavez and Huerta tried to convince their mentor, Ross, that the organization should take its work beyond urban areas to the field workers. Three months before the CSO's annual convention set for Calexico, California, in the spring of 1962, Chavez again asked CSO's board members if he could establish a pilot project to organize a union of farm workers. He would take no salary from the CSO, he said, but would accept funds from the workers themselves.

Although Ross and others at CSO shared the belief that some kind of activism was necessary to improve the lot of the field workers, they did not agree to take the CSO in a direction that might adversely affect the work they were already undertaking. After all, the possibility of forming

With flashing personality and seemingly inexhaustible energy, Dolores Huerta, co-founder with Cesar Chavez of the National Farm Workers Association (later the United Farm Workers), organized marches and picket lines, negotiated contracts, and rallied farm workers for decades to fight for their rights. Here she signs up new members for the union at its founding convention in Delano, California, in 1962. (Wayne State University/Walter P. Reuther Library)

a successful union of such diverse, oft-moving, and unskilled workers seemed fanciful at best.

Ross agreed to have the Chavez proposal presented at the convention to the full membership. The vote lost. When the vote was announced, Chavez quietly rose in the hall and said that he had an announcement. It was two words—"I resign."

The Chavez resignation shook the convention. Many stunned members tried to persuade Chavez to reconsider. He did not back down. "It took me six months," he said later, "to get over leaving CSO" (Ferriss and Sandoval 1997, 62).

He had little money, no property, and no job. What he did have was a burning wish to form a union and a determined will to succeed. He soon asked Huerta to join him. She accepted.

"I had some ideas of what should be done," he said later. "No great plans; just that it would take an awful lot of work and also that it was a gamble. If I can't organize them to a point where they can carry on their own group, then I'm finished, I can't do it, I'd move on and do something else" (Chavez 2008, 7).

On his 35th birthday, Chavez cleared out his desk at the CSO headquarters in Los Angeles. With Helen and the children, he drove to the small beach town of Carpinteria, near Santa Barbara. They talked of their plans. They would go to Delano, California, to start a union. A town of 12,000 in 1962, Delano was in the center of the nation's table grape industry. It was Helen's hometown. Two of her sisters lived in Delano, and two brothers were nearby. It was also the town that Chavez's brother, Richard, had made his home. After filling the tank of their beaten-up Mercury, they headed north.

References

Chavez, Cesar. 2008. *An Organizer's Tale.* Edited by Ilan Stavans. New York: Penguin Classics. http://www.farmworkermovement.org/essays/essays/Gringojustice.pdf.

Ferriss, Susan, and Ricardo Sandoval. 1997. *The Fight in the Fields: Cesar Chavez and the Farm Workers Movement.* New York: Harcourt Brace.

Levy, Jacques E. 2007. *Cesar Chavez: Autobiography of* La Causa. Minneapolis: University of Minnesota Press.

FOUR

Creating a Union for Farm Workers

Soft-spoken, with jet-black hair, liquid-like, heavy brown eyes, and, often-times, a wry grin, Chavez was almost boyish-looking at 35 years old when he arrived in Delano with his family in the spring of 1962. He had a natural instinct to gather around him many loyal friends. However unlikely it seemed, Cesar Chavez was a determined man ready to make his dream a reality.

Chavez knew that an effort to create a full-scale union was a daunting prospect, nearly impossible. Most labor union leaders around the country believed that organizing farm laborers presented overwhelming hurdles. Mostly poor, many illiterate, and divided culturally from mainstream America, farm workers usually did not remain very long in one locality, making stability and communication highly dubious. They had little economic power, no experience either in unions or in carrying out strikes and other activities in which unions engaged. If they refused to work, growers could replace them with cheaper bracero labor or illegal immigrants from across the Mexican border.

As he began his adventurous, if unlikely, dream, to build a union, Chavez had about $1,200 from gifts and loans. Helen began to earn extra money by returning to work in the fields. As he made the rounds of Delano and nearby fruit-growing areas, he avoided using the term "union" because to most of the workers that meant "strikes," through which some of them had already suffered. From one labor camp to another, he canvassed the San Joaquin Valley. He talked about the potential strengths of a social movement or *movimiento*, the idea that to gain real power the workers must consolidate and use whatever nonviolent muscle they had.

Chavez also brought with him to the new organizing adventure another of the CSO workers with whom he had come in contact—Gilbert Padilla. One of nine children, Padilla had migrated throughout the harvest fields of California from his earliest days, although managing to attend schools into the seventh grade. After serving in the U.S. Army during World War II, he

Cesar Chavez, 1972. By 1972, Cesar Chavez, seen here delivering a speech, and his colleagues had turned an unlikely dream of a farm workers union into a full-fledged organization that had won contracts from growers and was providing various services to its members. So successful had been the advent of the union that the national AFL-CIO offered it a full charter as the United Farm Workers of America. (National Archives)

opened a dry cleaning business with his brother. In 1955, he returned to the agricultural fields as a foreman for a labor contractor, and, then, in 1957 he met Chavez. Drawn to the mission of the CSO, Padilla joined the local chapter. When Chavez mentioned his seemingly quixotic quest to form a union of farm workers, Padilla decided to join him. He would be among the vital core that carried on the cause, one of those who would tie his own fortune to that of Chavez.

One of the men later said, "Here was Cesar burning with a patient fire, poor like us, dark like us . . . moving people to talk about their problems, attacking the little problems first, and suggesting always, suggesting never more solutions that seemed attainable. We didn't know it until we met him, but he was the leader we had been waiting for" (Meister 1968, 90).

Recruits and volunteers arrived in California from various backgrounds and locales. Chris Hartmire moved to California from New York in 1961 when he was named executive director of the National Farmworker Ministry. For more than 30 years, the farm worker cause was his life's work.

For most of the members of the families of Chavez's team, their lives were defined by the demands of the work. John Hartmire, son of Chris, later wrote, "During those years my father was gone a lot, traveling with, or for, Cesar. I 'understood' because the struggle to organize farm workers into a viable union was the work of a lifetime, and people would constantly tell me how much they admired what Dad was doing. Hearing it made me proud. It also made me lonely. He organized the clergy to stand up for the union, went to jail defying court injunctions and was gone from our house for days on end, coming home, my mother likes to say, only for clean underwear. . . . It's no wonder Dad missed my first Little League home run" (Hartmire 2000, 12).

At first, the growers and the rest of the community were totally skeptical of any attempts to rally farm workers as a group. After all, it had never been done successfully. Workers knew their place, the growers believed, and would never be able to muster the coordination or commitment to endanger the system in place. The workers had endured the injustices so long and knew the reprisals that had been dealt to others who had challenged the system that they expected the treatment and the system to continue. In addition, all the local institutions, from the police to business owners and political leaders, could be expected to react defensively, protecting the status quo.

But Chavez and Huerta settled in Delano to try to make American labor history. With the help of friends and relatives, they continued to travel from house to house setting up small meetings with farm workers and their families, attempting to interest them in the idea of union. Gradually, their earnest and enthusiastic arguments won over an increasing number of laborers who suddenly found an outlet for their frustrations, a hope in bettering their condition, and a way in which they could fight back at farm labor conditions both unjust and brutal.

In the first six months, Chavez crisscrossed the San Joaquin Valley in a 1953 Mercury station wagon that, like Chavez himself, never quit. The car lasted for more than 300,000 miles. For a time, he and his family lived on food given to him by people in Delano and on the road.

On Sunday, September 30, 1962, in an abandoned theater in Fresno, California, nearly 300 workers gathered to show their solidarity and celebrate a new union. They called the new organization the National Farm Workers Association (NFWA). They adopted a union motto: "*¡Viva la causa!*" or "Long Live the Cause!" They also waved a new flag bearing the organizational symbol—an Aztec eagle, emblematic of pride and dignity. A white circle in the flag signified the hopes and aspirations of the farm laborers;

the black of the eagle represented the plight of the workers; and the red background stood for the hard work and sacrifice that the union members would have to give. The flag was designed by Chavez's brother, Richard, and sewn by his cousin, Manuel Chavez. When they showed off the flag at the meeting, Manuel Chavez leaped to his feet and shouted, "When that damn eagle flies, the problems of the farm workers will be solved" (Altman 1994, 64).

Chavez talked to the new recruits of the NFWA about the possibilities of growing so powerful that they might force growers to engage in collective

At rallies and marches, the symbol of the United Farm Workers was often emblazoned on flags carried by demonstrators. The symbol was an Aztec eagle, emblematic of pride and dignity. (Wayne State University/Walter P. Reuther Library)

bargaining as other organizations had been forced to do by labor unions. He spoke about the possibilities of gaining enough political leverage that they might be able to lobby the governor and the state legislature for a state minimum wage for farm workers and the right to unemployment insurance. He talked about forcing growers to provide better working conditions. He talked about plans for an association-run credit union and a hiring hall to help workers locate jobs. This, he enthusiastically predicted, would be the first successful farm workers' union in history.

At a Constitutional Convention held in Fresno on January 21, 1963, Chavez became president of the new organization; vice presidents were Dolores Huerta, Gilbert Padilla, and Julio Hernandez, a field worker from Corcoran, California. The preamble to the NFWA Constitution that Chavez drafted at a table in his garage made clear the abuses against which the movement would march:

We the Farm Workers of America, have tilled the soil, sown the seeds and harvested the crops. We have provided food in abundance for the people in the cities, and the nation and world but have not had sufficient food to feed our own children. While industrial workers, living and working in one place, have joined together and grown strong, we have been isolated, scattered and hindered from uniting our forces. (Altman 1994, 64)

Chavez, Huerta, and Gilbert Padilla gathered together a close-knit set of "co-fanatics," as they called themselves, including Jim Drake, a graduate of Occidental College and Union Theological Seminary and a director of the California Migrant Ministry, an organization made up of Protestant ministers dedicated to helping the farm workers. Drake, a newly ordained minister of the United Church of Christ when he joined the California Migrant Ministries in the early 1960s, raised money to pay rent and buy food for strikers and recruited new members. Drake said of Chavez, "His consistency and perseverance really shook me. . . . A disability case, a worker injured on the job—he would stay with that worker day and night, day and night, until he could locate an attorney who would take the case for nothing, or find some way of settling it that was of benefit to the worker. That's how his union was built: on plain hard work and these very personal relationships. It was a slow, careful plodding thing; the growers didn't even know he was in town. Even when the strike started they had no idea who Cesar Chavez was, but the workers did" (Matthiessen 1969, 54).

Although their relationship was sometimes contentious given their mutual headstrong beliefs and self-confidence, Chavez and Huerta worked closely together. Chavez stayed mainly at the union's headquarters in Delano; Huerta worked often in Stockton; and both fanned out across the rich agricultural valleys of California to spread the word and recruit new supporters and volunteers.

Early on, the NFWA gradually, painstakingly added members. Chavez and other leaders held house meetings wherever they could get the space and draw a few workers. Huerta began to take charge of various administrative matters. Gilbert Padilla and others continued working in the fields while secretly passing out literature to the workers. But even when workers agreed to sign up, some would soon change their minds; others simply moved to other areas and lost interest. For the leaders of the union, the formative months and years were a challenge not only to enlist new supporters but to find ways to keep their families afloat financially.

By 1964, through arduous and often frustrating months of work, Chavez, Huerta, and other lieutenants had signed up more than 1,000 families.

Often, Chavez would be on the road in the middle of the night heading for work sites. Chavez's own children, as well as his nephews and nieces, all pitched in to help as the registration drive mounted. On some occasions he would squeeze his eight children into his battered station wagon and try to make the trips a family outing.

Chavez and his lieutenants looked forward to the time when the union could seriously challenge the growers with a strike. Nevertheless, they did not feel that the time had yet arrived. Chavez, Huerta, and other leaders of the infant union knew well the tactics they would face from the growers as soon as they called a strike. The owners would approach the courts for rulings to prevent the union from boycotting or picketing. They would hire "goons" and thugs from other parts of the valley to come in and beat up strikers. They would bring in undocumented foreign workers to help to replace picketing workers. They would enlist the efforts of police to arrest picketers and protesters for causing mayhem. They would plant stories in the media that the strikers were violent, un-American, and probably communists.

They also knew how difficult it would be to embolden strikers to stand tough against these kinds of threats and intimidation, against actual assaults, and against the loss of wages during the protests. They knew that for the workers to stand up to the roughhouse methods and to be nonviolent in response they would need outside support, solid commitment, and a dedication to a cause that would overcome hardship.

Small Steps in Asserting Union Power

By 1964, the NFWA had signed up more than 1,000 families. For the first time, Chavez could go on a salary from union dues. The organization had not only launched a credit union, run by Helen, but also other community service programs such as immigration counseling and assistance with voter registration.

The organization also began publishing its own newspaper called *El Malcriado* ("The Unruly One"). Following the cartoon figure Don Sotaco, readers kept abreast of job openings and issues relating to work conditions.

In the spring of 1965, Chavez and his union engaged in its first small-scale, localized strike actions—a wage protest by rose grafters in McFarland, California, and a rent increase at a labor camp.

Rose grafters were skilled workers whose job entailed many rigorous physical demands. Crawling on their knees for miles, the grafters slit mature rose bushes and inserted buds. If the workers were careless, many of the bushes could be ruined. For this labor, the workers had been promised $9 for a thousand plants. They had not received their full wages. Instead, they had received less than $7 per thousand plants. The largest company, Mount Arbor, employer of nearly 100 workers, became the union's first target.

On a Sunday prior to the strike, the workers gathered in a formal ceremony, with Dolores Huerta holding a crucifix, and pledged not to break the strike. Early Monday morning, Chavez and Huerta drove around the camps watching for any of the workers who might have changed their minds. Only a few had balked and were gently persuaded from heading off to the fields. When a couple of workers decided to go to work later in the week, Huerta was in front of their house in her green truck and refused to move.

The strike was not entirely successful. The company brought in a group of Mexican workers as scabs. Nevertheless, the company did agree to increase the wages of the workers for the remainder of the season.

At about the same time, the Tulane County Housing Authority, located in nearby Porterville, California, decided to raise the rents in two farm labor camps, whose facilities lacked running water and whose tin shacks, that had been built during the Great Depression, had broken windows and doors. Jim Drake of the California Migrant Ministry and Gilbert Padilla persuaded the workers to strike for lower rental costs. Through the summer of 1965, joined by about 20 students from California college campuses, the new union protested. Chavez later remembered that it was at the Tulane

Front page of an edition of *El Malcriado*. In 1964, Cesar Chavez and Dolores Huerta founded a newspaper for the infant farm workers union. It was called *El Macriado* ("The Unruly One") and featured humor and biting satire aimed at unscrupulous growers, low wages, ill-suited working conditions, and other concerns of farm workers. A central cartoon figure in the paper was Don Sotaco, created by artist Andy Zermeno. Wily and resourceful, if often victimized, Don Sotaco represented a caricature with whom the average farm worker could identify. The issue pictured above featured a discussion of a farm workers medical plan established by the union in the name of Robert F. Kennedy, an ardent supporter of Chavez and his union. (Wayne State University/Walter P. Reuther Library)

strike demonstrations that the union's black eagle flag was first carried by picketers.

Unlike the rose strike, in which the union gained only a modest pay hike, the efforts at the Tulane labor camps gained the union its first notable gain. The summer-long picketing prompted the Tulane County Housing Authority to tear down the tin shacks and replace them with modest but livable cottages. Although the two small strike actions undertaken by Chavez and his associates were encouraging signs, could the new union successfully undertake larger enterprises? Although Chavez was not aware of it, he and his union would soon face the test.

References

Altman, Linda. 1994. *Migrant Farm Workers: The Temporary People.* New York: Franklin Watts.

Hartmire, John. 2000. "At the Heart of a Historic Movement." *Newsweek*, July 24, 12.

Matthiessen, Peter. 1969. Sal Si Puedes: *Cesar Chavez and the New American Revolution.* New York: Random House.

Meister, Dick. 1968. "*La Huelga* Becomes *La Causa*." *New York Times Magazine*, 52, November, 90.

FIVE

The Delano Grape Strike and
the Great March to Sacramento

As the summer of 1965 drew to a close near Delano, California, and grapes ripened on the vines, farm workers began moving through the rows of the harvest fields expecting to make 90 cents an hour plus 10 cents a basket. But members of a mostly Filipino group called the Agricultural Workers Organizing Committee decided to go on strike. They demanded higher wages.

The Filipino farm workers, many of whom were single men in their fifties, had lived most of their adult lives in ranch housing along back country roads east of Delano. After joining the strike en masse they were evicted. Led by Larry Itliong (a friend of Dolores Huerta), Andy Imutan, Ben Gines, and others, the Filipinos realized that any success they might have in Delano depended on an alliance with Cesar Chavez's new labor union.

Although the Farm Workers Association had made substantial progress by 1965, Chavez was not yet planning a major strike. At the time the union had been founded in September 1962, he had figured that it would take at least five years of organizing before it would be ready to take on the growers. After all, the power of the growers and affiliated companies represented a formidable adversary and most of the union members were especially poor and had very little or no experience in union activities.

In an interview early in 1964 Chavez said, "I figure . . . that even if we had a 50–50 chance of carrying off a successful strike, the gamble would still be too great. You stand always to lose more than you gain. . . . Thirty men may lose their jobs as a result of a strike. You lose thirty members, and you gain thirty 'disorganizers.' So we must work on immediate goals— helping the members get a little living through using the facilities of the association, through getting what they are entitled to, through learning how to participate more fully in social life. And the hard work of gaining official recognition, including strikes if necessary, will come." The union

had approximately 2,000 members, almost all of whom were totally unfamiliar with union strikes and the demands and commitment they demanded. "You cannot organize a strike, or build a union," Chavez said,
"until the members who must do the real work understand what all this
means, what kind of activities are involved. They must, first, be able to ar-
ticulate their own hopes and goals" ("Preliminary Report" 1966).

But after several discussions with the Filipinos and with his own associates, Chavez decided to ask the members of the union to join the strike.
The unique opportunity and the personal alliances with the Filipinos were
forces too great to resist. Dolores Huerta recalled later: "I had worked
with Filipino leaders like Larry Itliong for a while before we went on
strike. When our Filipino brothers went on strike in Coachella the union
only had $70 in its account. . . . I still recall the evening when we gath-
ered and found out about the Coachella strike. We knew we had to support it. Yet I had seven kids to feed and Helen and Cesar had eight. As we
discussed the situation all eyes turned to Helen and without a blink of an
eye she said, 'Well, we have to support the strike!'" (United Farm Workers 2005).

On Mexican Independence Day, September 16, 1965, the mostly Latino
membership of the National Farm Workers Association met in the hall
next to Our Lady of Guadalupe Catholic Church in west Delano. Chavez and
others put up their huge union flag and posters of Mexican leader Emilio
Zapata along with Jack London's famous labor writing, "Definition of a
Strikebreaker."

Into the pews and balconies wedged more than 500 workers and their
families. Chavez had sent out word through local disk jockeys on Spanish radio and in the union's paper that something big was in the works.
Dressed in an old sport shirt and work pants, Chavez sat next to Fred Ross
and Larry Itliong and others. He stepped up to speak to the large gathering, some of whom had never before seen or met him, although his name
was fast becoming known throughout the migrant communities of central California. In a halting and somewhat shaky voice, he rallied the men
and woman to what he called *La Causa* ("The Cause"). Chavez invited
other farm workers to tell their personal stories. An older worker who had
been around when some migrants had gone on strike years earlier said, "I
saw two strikers murdered before my eyes by a rancher. There was nothing to eat in those days, there was nothing. And we're in same place today,
still submerged, still drowned" (Levy 2007, 185).

At the meeting was Wendy Goepel, who had majored in sociology at
Stanford and briefly worked for the California Department of Health and

who had also been a consultant to Governor Pat Brown on the antipoverty VISTA program. She joined Chavez as a close volunteer in the early days of the union. "I was his eager student," she wrote, "his community-organizing skills were of a unique bent and his ability to facilitate meetings was useful in every other project I was working on. During the meetings, I was mesmerized by the passionate stories about injustice that the farmworkers told, and by the evolving strategies for righting wrongs" ("The Story of Wendy Goepel Brooks").

The meeting, Goepel said, was "a bit frightening and quite amazing. Something big was happening here on September 16, 1965. For the first time, I could imagine what it was like to be in the south with Martin Luther King, Jr., or out in the middle of nowhere in the Peace Corps, or picketing to protest the war. Suddenly I was part of that group of freedom fighters. My mind raced and my body numbed" ("The Story of Wendy Goepel Brooks").

The union voted unanimously to go forward with the strike that night at the church. The cry was now "*¡Viva la Huelga!*" ("Long Live the Strike!"). Chavez appealed for nonviolence. Cheers of approval roared. Personally, Chavez remained cautious. The union had little money or experience. But it had the spirit, he felt, to join with the small Filipino group in a strike against Delano table and wine grape growers.

On September 20, 1965, UFWA workers joined a winding picket line in the dawn's fog alongside a farm east of Delano. As workers pulled up to go to work, picketers challenged them to join the strike. Many responded. Soon, foremen in trucks sped along the dirt road throwing dust in the faces of the strikers, demanding that they leave the area. The protestors remained.

In the chaos of the first days of the strike, the workers stayed disciplined and controlled. At the headquarters, Chavez worked with other staff amidst a few typewriters, cheap paper, and a blackboard. At the entrance hung a banner that said "The Hottest Fires in Hell Are Reserved for Those Who Remain Neutral in a Moral Crisis." Through the headquarters in the days following scurried picket captains, field workers seeking to learn about the union, reporters alerted to this phenomenon getting underway in tiny Delano, police, church groups and ministers, children of the staff members, and many curious spectators.

Esther Uranday, one of the workers who went on strike, later remembered the first meeting in the town hall where Chavez had told the Latino workers about the Filipino union and its strike. "It was at that moment," she said, "that imminent had become reality." That reality was the picket line and Esther Uranday was there. "Our first encounter was with the John

Pagliarulo & Son farm. From there we headed off into several other farms, picketing and showing our demands. I am sure it must have been quite a sight for all those growers to see these farm workers waking them up at 3 A.M., ready to do battle with them. It must have been quite a wake up call" (United Farm Workers 2005).

On October 16, 1965, Kern County sheriff LeRoy Gallyen issued an announcement that picketers who called out to the scab workers over loudspeakers would be arrested. It did not take long for the NFWA to take on the threat. The following day, after the Reverend David Havens read Jack London's "Definition of a Strikebreaker" over a loudspeaker, he was arrested and hustled off to jail. Two days later, the strikers decided on a strategy of mass arrests. After alerting the press to their plans, and with camera crews gathered at the strike site, Helen Chavez led 8 women and 11 clergymen in chanting "*¡Huelga!*" They were promptly arrested. Chris Hartmire later remembered the scene: "The sheriff grabbed me and threw me in the car, right while I was talking with Harry Bernstein from the *L.A. Times.* [Bernstein] was totally offended that this guy interrupted the conversation. The sheriff was just used to having the power and doing what comes naturally." Bernstein soon wrote a piece for the *Times* that gained national attention. And Hartmire now realized "that calling from Delano was like calling from Selma, from the front lines" (Ganz 2009, 136).

Wendy Geopel later wrote, "The line between intimidation and violence was always a very thin line. Early in the strike, a lone picketer had been ordered at gunpoint to hand his picket sign over to a grower's son-in-law, who shot the sign full of holes and then burned it. The terrified picketer ran half a mile back to the NFWA office, but he did not fight back. The growers hired guys we called 'Rent-A-Fuzz' to brandish shotguns and mock police badges. These guys would walk along the row of picketers and look menacing, just inside the ranch property" ("The Story of Wendy Goepel Brooks").

In 1967, Luming Imutan, a Filipino farm worker, spoke of the difficulties facing picketers from those unsympathetic to the strike: "One of the hardest parts about being on strike," he said, "and being on picket lines is taking the insults that people give you . . . people would ask, 'Why don't you go to work?' There were many people who called us a disgrace to the public" (Rose 1990, 284–285).

Huerta seemed born for such clashes. Tough-minded, focused, she coordinated the picket lines, entreating those who grew tired to keep up the pressure. In the Delano strike, Huerta would join workers in jail for violating local ordinances and orders from police. It would be the first of more than 20 arrests over the course of her career. She would see the arrests as badges of honor.

Writer John Gregory Dunne, who witnessed events in Delano, said that growers tried all methods of intimidation: "Some growers would move their workers from the roadside to the middle of a vineyard so they would not see the pickets. Others drove down the edge of their property line with spraying machines shooting insecticide and fertilizer on the pickets, or gunned over the roadside in tractors, raising dust to choke the strikers. Growers played radios at top volume to drown out the pickets' shouts of 'La Huelga' or else placed a line of automobiles between the picket line and their workers so that the strikers could not see the field help" (Dunne [1967] 2007, 25).

On October 19, 9 clergymen joined Helen Chavez and 34 strikers in going to jail for shouting "*¡Huelga!*" on the picket line. On December 13 and 14, 11 national religious leaders, Protestant and Catholic, visited Delano. It was not long before Protestant denominations across the country struggled over whether and how deeply the church should be involved in the events unfolding in the fields of California.

More important, small religious groups and individuals were pulled into the battle by the strikers. Many people opened their homes to house meetings, joined picket lines in front of grocery stores, leafleted neighborhoods, joined in prayer vigils and rallies, and pulled stunts such as filling shopping carts in the stores and then leaving them in checkout lines. To many in the community, the protestors were nuisances at best and leftist fellow travelers at worst. To others, the protest struck nerves, convinced people that the cause was worthwhile. Sometimes they went to jail for disturbing the peace.

Chavez recruited LeRoy Chatfield, a young teacher from Bakersfield who had earlier visited Delano to see what the farm worker movement was all about. Chatfield was studying at USC for his PhD. Chavez asked Chatfield to change his plans. Would he join Cesar to help raise funds and supplies to support the families on strike? He agreed.

Chatfield would be a lifelong admirer of Chavez and would, indeed, shape his career around the interests of farm workers. He later said that when a farm worker joined the union, "You invested in the dream that someday, perhaps not in your life time but in the life time of your children you would belong to a union that would be strong enough to meet with the growers and successfully negotiate: better wages, access to bathrooms in the fields, drinking water available on the job, rest breaks, an end to stoop labor with the short handle hoe, medical benefits, pension benefits, and unemployment benefits" (Chatfield 1991).

From the outset of the strike, Chavez preached the message of nonviolence. He had seen Martin Luther King Jr. and other black civil rights leaders use the tactic successfully.

Dolores Huerta said later of the concept of nonviolence: "It's very ingrained in the organization. Nonviolence really strengthens the individual. There's a whole transformational process about it. When you use nonviolence to win, you have to involve other people, build relationships with other people, and become more dependent on other people. It makes the organization stronger." She spoke of the spiritual quality inherent in the movement and the dynamic of faith that it builds in the group. "In order to work with nonviolence, you have to have a lot of faith. It builds the foundation and strengthens your belief that something can happen" (Drake 2000, 37).

King himself sent a telegram to Chavez commending the labor and civil rights activist on his "commitment to righting grievous wrongs forced upon exploited people." King wrote, "We are together with you in spirit and determination that our dreams for a better tomorrow will be realized" (Bogater 2009).

Also, like King, Chavez was deeply religious. The union often held religious services and Chavez surrounded himself with Christian religious leaders from various denominations. Many Christians, both clergy and lay, worked for *La Causa*: giving money to help buy necessities for strikers' families; giving time to be on the picket lines; writing letters to politicians and newspapers denying that Cesar Chavez's movement was communistic; and documenting the farm workers' heroic nonviolence, especially in the face of the goon squads hired by some growers.

The catalyst for the clerical involvement in the beginnings of the Chavez's work was unquestionably the California Migrant Ministry, and its leaders Chris Hartmire and Jim Drake. Speaking to synods, conventions, assemblies, and other kinds of religious gatherings, they clearly laid out in terms understandable to both clergy and laity the origins of the farm workers' movement, its deep connections to ideals of Christian charity, and the religious impulses that drove Chavez in his quest for social justice. Later, Chavez said that the union might well not have survived had it not been for the CMM.

Chavez had met Hartmire during Chavez's time with the CSO. In 1950, Hartmire had attended Princeton University on a scholarship to be a civil engineer but later turned to the ministry. He attended Union Seminary in New York, was ordained a Presbyterian minister in 1960, and served on the staff of the East Harlem Protestant Parish in New York. With his work at the parish and its ministry to the poor, Hartmire then accepted an offer become the director of the CMM. Arriving in Los Angeles in 1961, he inherited a ministry that had been launched in New Jersey in the 1920s and in California during the Great Depression.

By the 1950s, the CSO had had migrant ministry programs in 38 states that provided nursing care, educational and recreational activities, day care, and other services. When the NFWA joined the AWOC on September 20, Chavez asked Chris Hartmire for help in staffing, donations of food, and delegations of church members to go to Delano and join the picket lines.

Hartmire saw the struggle in Delano as crucial in exemplifying how a drive for social justice could succeed. "The organization [UFW] is focused in California, but the future of all farm workers is tied to Cesar Chavez and the pioneer workers with him in Delano," Harmire said. "If the Delano strikers can succeed, then energy and hope will be released to workers throughout the nation" (Wells).

Chavez was emotionally moved by the relationship of these ministers to the farm laborers. He often used the example of Hartmire and his group to persuade other religious organizations, including the Catholic Church, to send more representatives to the fields and barrios.

"His integration of faith and action was reflected in the manner in which he led the movement," commented Cardinal Roger Mahony of Los Angeles, a longtime supporter of the farm workers' cause. "Rallies began with the celebration of mass; marches were conducted under the banner of Our Lady of Guadalupe while the rosary was prayed; and his speeches and writings frequently referred to gospel values as he quoted the church's documents on human rights and justice. Cesar Chavez truly understood his Christian vocation to build up the kingdom of God in this world" ("Champion of Farm Workers Dies" 1993).

Luis Valdez and El Teatro Campesino

Luis Valdez and Cesar Chavez had similar backgrounds. Both were born in Arizona to farm worker parents; both moved to California. By the age of six, Luis joined his nine brothers and sisters in the fields of the San Joaquin Valley picking cotton, cherries, grapes, peaches, plums. Moving from harvest field to harvest field, they lived for a time on the Chagrin Ranch in San Jose. Like Chavez, he was in and out of schools in various towns.

Valdez became interested in plays and acting at an early age and earned a scholarship to attend San Jose State College and developed a special interest in the work of Bertolt Brecht, the German dramatist who developed a theory of theater that attempted to inspire audiences to go out into the world to correct its ills. Brecht's plays were akin to political meetings. Actors directly engaged the audience in conversation. A Brecht play would often include exaggerated characters and even placards to explain events and roles.

Valdez joined the San Francisco Mime Troupe after his graduation. But when Chavez began his union movement in Southern California, Valdez found a perfect vehicle for his political and social protest instincts. Two months into the strike, he joined Chavez in Delano.

Valdez later recalled: "One day I spoke to Cesar about expressing La Causa in artistic terms and he said, 'It's great, but there is no money, no actors, no theatre, no place to rehearse and no time to rehearse. Do you still want to do it?' Well, with an opportunity like that how could I refuse?" (United Farm Workers 2005).

Valdez created a theater company of actor-laborers not only to raise funds and to publicize the farm-worker strike but to energize the workers. On Friday evenings Chavez began to hold two-hour meetings to bolster the camaraderie of the strikers. With songs, testimonials from families and friends of the strikers, and presentations by guests from religious, social, and labor organizations, the meetings forged greater union. Singer and songwriter Augustin Lira led the group with renditions of "*Niños Campesinos*" and traditional union and civil rights songs such as "*Solidaridad Para Siempre.*"

And it was here in one of these Friday meetings that Luis Valdez included the first performances of *El Teatro Campesino.* It combined Mexican folk theater, comedy, and mime, offered comic reflections on laborers, bosses, and others in the world of the farm worker. The actors themselves were campesinos. The company created short skits that they performed not only at the Friday night gatherings but also on flatbed trucks at the strike sites. Starting at dawn, the group would drive from location to location, pull up at the sides of roads, and start performing. They later toured towns and cities to raise money for the union.

With rapid-fire intensity, the *Teatro*'s brief 10- to 15-minute performances aimed a volley of attacks and ridicule against the growers and their hired scabs and thugs. Using only a few props—a wine bottle or maybe some old pans—the actors made their points with stinging effect. They used armbands to identify characters; they hung signs around their necks. For the audiences of mostly farm workers, the performances were spellbinding and hilarious. They were morality plays brought to work sites.

El Teatro Campesino, 1966. In 1965, a young playwright named Luis Valdez, who had worked with the San Francisco Mime Troupe, joined Chavez in Delano to organize a theater group called *El Teatro Campesino*. On the road in marches and on picket lines, the group performed witty skits of political satire and slapstick in which actors, identified by placards hung around their necks, represented such figures as grape growers, scab laborers, and the archetype of the migrant workers, Don Sotaco, who also appeared in the pages of the union's newspaper, *El Malcriado*. (Wayne State University/Walter P. Reuther Library)

In addition to the presenting performances of *El Teatro Campesino*, the union strove in other ways to foster an unbreakable unity in the members. "*Huelga* Priests" held masses for the workers several times a week. Workers began to speak about their Latino culture, began to talk about Mexican history, and the relationship of this strike to other battles of the poor and dispossessed. They waved banners of the Virgin of Guadalupe, the patron saint of Mexico, and carried both the Mexican and U.S. flags. They chose an anthem. Instead of a militant labor protest song, they picked as their informal anthem "*De Colores*," a Spanish hymn.

> De colores, de colores se visten los campos en la primavera.
> De colores, de colores son los pajaritos que vienen deafuera.
> De colores, de colores es el arco iris que vemos lucir.

Y por eso los grandes amores de muchos colores me gustan a mi,
Y por eso los grandes amores de muchos colores me gustan a mi

In colors, in colors the fields in the spring dress up.
In colors, in colors the little bids come from far off
In colors, in colors the rainbow we see glistening
And that's why those big many-colored loves are what I like.
And that's why those big many-colored loves are what I like.
(Richmond 1999)

For most, all of this was a nearly delirious change in their lives, a sudden sense of belonging to a mutual cause, however improbable the outcome. For workers who heard Valdez's plays and sang the Mexican and labor songs, and shared the Friday evenings together, it was a refreshing addition to their lives.

The growers fought the new union with every weapon at their disposal. And they had a formidable arsenal. Company lawyers persuaded the courts to issue injunctions against picketers, restrict organizer's access to the fields, and evict strikers from their shelters at the labor camps. They could count on the local police to enforce those orders. Growers also turned to undocumented immigrants as scabs to fill the slots abandoned by the strikers, fully confident that the police would not interfere. The flow of undocumented workers across the border increased at the behest of growers, especially at times when strike actions threatened the harvest.

After absorbing the first round of volleys from the growers, Chavez decided to raise the level of the protest. He decided to employ a boycott. He would turn the Delano strike and the cause of the farm workers even more intensely into a national movement.

Boycotting Schenley Industries

In early December 1965, Chavez called a boycott of the large grape producer, Schenley Industries. From the outset, the coordination of boycott activities was a daunting undertaking for the new union. To make the boycott work, Chavez and his fellow leaders would have to raise money quickly, find union members willing to move temporarily to various parts of the United States with little or no financial reward, develop an instinct for achieving maximum media attention, anticipate countermeasures by the various companies under attack, and fend off the usual frustrations and challenges of any labor action, especially in the early days.

Recruiting additional volunteers from churches, community organizations, labor organizations, and universities, the union began to set up boycott centers in various cities across California. Soon, union volunteers would fan out across the United States to major cities. With little money, the volunteers hitchhiked to New York, Chicago, St. Louis, and other major cities, carrying signs imploring people not to purchase products produced by Schenley. Signs appeared urging the public to "Help Farmworkers—Do Not Buy Grapes." The protest thus moved from the fields to the urban areas. It also began to attract additional national attention.

Volunteers arrived ready to do social work battle. Young and old, Mexican Americans, other Latinos, whites—they arrived in Delano wanting to be a part of the fight. They went to work for no wages and for barely enough to eat. They took on various tasks. A youngster named John Shroyer jumped freight cars to keep track of where grape shipments were headed and then rode the rails back to Delano to report to Chavez and the other leaders. Others formed student groups to picket at universities and university towns and to organize rallies. Others worked from the union office in Delano writing thank you letters to donors, sending out donations of food and clothing to the families of workers on strike. Others babysat the youngest children while parents walked the picket lines and participated in boycott activities.

Many Chicanos in cities and towns across the country closely identified with the struggle of the farm workers. They followed the marches, strikes, and boycotts intensely, and many became politically motivated themselves. They joined the pickets in front of grocery stores in their own neighborhoods during the grape boycott and began to sing and chant the slogans of Chavez's campesino movement.

As news of the strike and boycott spread through the national media, Delano became increasingly the center of a major, unfolding drama. On December 13, 1965, a delegation of 10 church leaders—4 Roman Catholics, 1 Jewish, and 6 Protestants—arrived in Delano to meet the strikers and issue a statement of support: "The suffering of farm workers and their children cries to heaven and demands the attention of persons of conscience. Farm workers are worthy. Their labor is important to the agricultural industry. It is both natural and just that they should participate in the decision-making process about wages, working conditions, and automation. . . . [T]his basic right is being denied to farm workers in this valley" (Ganz 2009, 142).

As in the black civil rights movement, Christian clergy and laity became ever more omnipresent in the farm workers' struggle. They donated money, food, and other necessities during strikes; they participated in marches, meetings, and on picket lines. They recruited volunteers through their own ministries. They lobbied legislatures at all levels of government. And they gave to the movement a legitimacy that helped deflate rumors and innuendo that somehow Chavez and his allies were bent on violence and posed a threat to American values and way of life. It was difficult to charge Chavez with being a communist when he was surrounded by prominent Protestant and Catholic leaders.

On December 16, 1965, United Auto Workers president Walther Reuther visited Delano to pledge his support of the strike. Nearly 1,000 farm workers and others joined in a spirited rally. For Reuther to have made this visit to Delano was an enormous boost to Chavez at this critical time in the strike, giving powerful national visibility and endorsement to the movement. Reuther announced that the AFL-CIO and the UAW would provide a cash contribution for organizing activities and would also allocate $2,500 per month to support the strike.

It quickly became clear that Chavez was no ordinary leader, and this was no ordinary strike and boycott. This was more than a typical fight for wages and working conditions; this was a movement of ethnic identity and a quest for justice rooted in Catholic social teaching.

As the strike gathered increasing momentum and the boycott got underway, more outside organizations joined the effort. The American Friends Service Committee agreed to pay the rent and utilities for Delano striker families. Truckloads of food, clothing, and other donations rolled into Delano, provided by various organizations, enough that a distribution warehouse was set up to ensure that the donations reached the workers on strike.

This was a movement that elicited fear and contempt from California growers. One of the most vocal was Delano vineyard owner Bruce Dispoto. On December 22, 1965, shortly after Reuther's visit and the national attention lavished on Chavez and the farm workers and the derisive attacks against growers at the mass meeting, Dispoto lashed out, saying that the strikers "do not represent our workers. Our workers have rejected them for what they are, perpetrators of hate and deceit" (Federal Bureau of Investigation).

The pressure on the strikers increased. The local Delano sheriff and his deputies, inextricably tied to the owners, did their own part. At one point a decree went forth that picketers would no longer have the right to shout at scabs because it was disturbing the peace. Quieting the strikers was no small order, but it did add another annoyance to the labors of those on the lines. The no-shouting order, however, proved to be a near-perfect foil for Chavez.

In order to test the mettle of the sheriff, Chavez carefully created a special picket line filled with women and children. More than 40 mom protestors were hauled off to jail; Chavez asked his aides to take the 76 children of the incarcerated mothers to a nearby park where they ate and played games. The following day, a massive protest, including the children, surrounded the jail. On the third day, the American Civil Liberties Union posted bail and the strikers emerged to great cheering. The Delano sheriff and his men were now suitably tainted with the same kind of ignominy as the Birmingham, Alabama, police and others in the South who wielded hoses and thrust dogs at black demonstrators.

But the strikers persevered. When the scab laborers imported by the growers quit work and walked out the fields, they heard Mexican guitars serenading along the fields. If they came close to the music, they would also hear pleas from strikers to quit the jobs and support the farm worker cause. Some pickets were able to infiltrate the scab labor force to learn about the feelings of the workers in the fields. On occasion, strikers floated helium balloons with the word *Huelga* prominently displayed.

At a local railroad loading dock where growers brought their grapes for shipment, the union set up a 24-hour picket line. On one occasion a truck drove into the picket line, seriously injuring one of the protestors. Angered and frightened, the picketers nevertheless kept up the line day and night.

When the season ended, the growers claimed that despite the strike they had enjoyed a bumper crop, that the efforts of the union had been futile. However, the Federal Marketing Service Commodity Report told a different story. It showed one-half million fewer grapes sold in 1965 than in 1964. In truth, the California growers had suffered from the strike, and many were nervous about the future.

Alfredo Vazquez, one of the original picketers, remembered later, "We were insulted and provoked by the police. They tried to break us and humiliate us, yet they were not able to succeed. Cesar was very firm that we should not play in to their hands by fighting them because it would only make matters worse. For me that was the most excruciating time. Being battered and insulted just for wanting better working conditions seemed like an inhumane price to pay." Vazquez believed that the strike changed the course not just of the lives of people involved but of later generations of Mexican Americans. They had set an example. "It was during this time that I really learned the meaning of courage and standing up to those people without violence and not playing into their hands," he said. "We were able to gain a lot more sympathy from a lot of people by taking the non-violent route. We focused on the problem, which was workers rights, and not riots or violent uprisings. That is what I am most proud of" (United Farm Workers 2005).

Support from the Student Nonviolent Coordinating Committee (SNCC)

More than any other civil rights organization, the SNCC recognized early on that Cesar Chavez's efforts in behalf of Mexican American farm workers were strikingly similar to those efforts of Martin Luther King Jr. and others to combat racial and ethnic prejudice and to improve the lives of people living on the edge of America's capitalist system. Founded in 1960, SNCC, comprised primarily of college students, stood for multiracial equality, not just the equality of blacks and whites. Their support of Mexican Americans during the farm workers' movement thus set them apart from other civil rights organizations that were focused almost entirely on African American rights and causes.

The SNCC's strong belief in multiracial equality and cooperation made possible the first major coalition between a civil rights organization and the drive for Mexican American workers and civil rights. The SNCC was not only helpful in the farm workers' battle against Schenley but also encouraged other civil rights organizations to tie their own causes to those of the farm workers.

Mike Miller, head of the San Francisco SNCC office, pioneered the civil rights organization's activism on behalf of agricultural workers and persuaded SNCC to explore the idea of voter registration among Mexican farm workers in California. Chavez now had an inside connection with one of the country's major civil rights organizations.

Chavez asked officials of SNCC and the Congress of Racial Equality (CORE) to send some representatives to help the strikers overcome the natural instincts to lash back at the repressive tactics of local police and goons hired by companies to incite violence. Within a week, both organizations sent veteran civil rights workers to California. But it was SNCC that would lend support to Chavez through many struggles.

That SNCC was intimately involved in Chavez's first strike and boycott was not surprising to those who knew of Cesar's understanding of the philosophy and tactics of nonviolent protest movements. In areas such as direct action confrontation, the need to organize oppressed groups from within, and the appeal to religious symbols and message, Chavez approached the leaders of SNCC to broaden the work they had already done to include Mexican American workers. They responded.

One of the first SNCC representatives to arrive was Marshall Ganz from the San Francisco office. Born in Bakersfield, California, the son of a rabbi, Ganz had been a Harvard student who participated in the Mississippi Freedom Summer civil rights campaign in 1964. He dropped out of school to work in Mississippi and other parts of the South during the protest marches. When word of the new unionizing activities in the fields of California reached Ganz, he saw many parallels among the injustices suffered by blacks and by field workers—racial discrimination, intolerable working conditions, lack of political power, and the excesses of capitalist greed and disregard for the rights of working people. Fluent in Spanish, he joined Chavez in 1965 and became a chief strategist and organizer.

In December 1965, after a small delegation from SNCC including Stokely Carmichael visited Delano, Dickie Flowers, a staff member of SNCC from Greenwood, Mississippi, also arrived to work with Ganz. Flowers would later be especially effective in organizing farm workers in Bakersfield, an area where there was a concentration of African American workers.

One of SNCC's first contributions to the NFWA strikers was a supply of two-way radios. As the area of the strike expanded over hundreds of miles, the radios became effective in alerting leaders along the strike route of any new influx of scab labor and harassment and violence perpetrated against the workers.

In March 1966, the strike received unexpected and welcome publicity. The U.S. Senate Subcommittee on Migrant Labor, including Senator Robert Kennedy (D-NY), scheduled a visit to Delano to investigate conditions in the farm labor sector. At first Kennedy was skeptical about a long plane trip to California to discuss farm worker problems. Nevertheless, United Auto Workers president Walter Reuther and labor activists among his staff prevailed, and Kennedy went to see firsthand the working conditions under which laborers suffered at the hands of the agricultural forces in California.

The subcommittee toured the union offices with large numbers of curious farm workers trailing the group, with cameras flashing, and reporters taking down notes. At the jammed meeting hall, both supporters and opponents of the strike gathered as large numbers outside surrounded the building to get first word about the deliberations.

Angered by what he saw and mightily impressed by Cesar Chavez, Kennedy embraced the farm workers' movement. He would be a friend to which Chavez would turn and on whom he could rely. George Murphy, a one-time Hollywood song-and-dance man who had won a Senate seat from California, was at the hearings in Delano. Later, Murphy, who was not particularly an admirer of Chavez, spoke about the harsh interrogation of the growers by Kennedy. "Bobby had gone out to California to meet with Chavez and with Dolores Huerta, Chavez's second in command, and with the strikers," Murphy said. "And he supported Chavez's uprising with such conviction I felt it would work against him if he ever ran for president. He would be considered a revolutionary" (Heymann 1998).

Shortly after the visit from Senator Kennedy, Chavez announced a major plan that would, in the end, have historic consequences for *La Causa*. The NFWA would begin a 300-mile pilgrimage, or *Peregrinación*, from Delano to the state capital of Sacramento. The march, Chavez said, would end on the steps of the Capitol on Easter Sunday.

The Peregrinación

Chavez realized that the day-by-day grind of the strike and boycott was taking a toll on the union members. A stalemate was not acceptable, and he searched for a way to jolt the protest, to gain greater national publicity, and, most of all, to lift the spirits of the protestors to a new high. He decided to adopt another tactic that had been successful in the civil rights movement—a long march. It would cover a route from Delano to the state capital of Sacramento, through such towns as Madera, Fresno, Modesto, and Stockton.

Chavez was following a Mexican custom of walking to historic shrines to do penance during the season of Lent. Its theme would be pilgrimage, penitence, and revolution. The striking farm workers—the *huelgistas*— would march to do penance for the ills they might have committed during the strike. The march would help cleanse their feelings, Chavez felt, for any violent actions, either committed or planned.

Chavez wrote a brief explanation of what the event would represent: "In the march from Delano to Sacramento there is a meeting of cultures and traditions, the centuries-old religious tradition of Spanish culture conjoins with the very contemporary cultural syndrome of 'demonstration' springing from the spontaneity of the poor, the down-trodden, the rejected, the discriminated-against baring visibly their need and demand for equality and freedom." He said that in every religion "pilgrimage" has been an expression of penance and commitment. He talked especially about religious shrines in Mexico to which many of those among the farm workers had marched themselves in their lives. He talked about the Lenten penitential processions in much of the Spanish-speaking world in which the marchers often dressed in sack cloth and ashes. "Pilgrimage, penance and revolution. The pilgrimage from Delano to Sacramento," he wrote, "has strong religion-cultural overtones. But it is also the pilgrimage of a cultural minority who have suffered from a hostile environment, and a minority who mean business" (Chavez 1966).

On the morning of March 17, 1966, Chavez gathered the marchers in Delano to begin the *peregrinación*. A line of 68 chosen *peregrinos* began by walking east out of Delano onto Highway 99 toward Ducor, then Porterville, and other small towns in the rich agricultural areas in which they had worked.

Felix Ytom, a displaced Filipino grape worker, was among the first, along with Carolina Franco who had picketed from the beginning of the

The march to Sacramento, 1966. On April 7, 1966, striking grape workers triumphantly approach Sacramento, California, completing a 300-mile march from union headquarters in Delano. Chavez had called the march a *peregrinación*, from the Mexican custom of doing penance at historic shrines. The march convinced Schenley Industries to recognize the farm workers union and to grant wage increases, the first important contract won by Chavez and his allies. (AP/Wide World Photos)

strike. There was also Roberto Bustos, named by Chavez as one of the captains of the march. Bustos said later, "I'll always remember Cesar coming into the office one day and saying, 'We are going to go to Sacramento.' I was very enthusiastic about the idea and was already loading up my car with all my things, and then he gave me the harsh news that we would be marching from Delano to Sacramento! At that moment I thought the man had lost his mind. I looked at the map and saw that the journey was 245 miles." Actually, the distance to Sacramento would be longer than that because the march would detour to several towns and cities along the way, including Ducor and Fresno. Nevertheless, Bustos and the other *originales* who left Delano persevered. "We walked over 15 miles a day, every day," he said. "At times I thought we wouldn't make it. In fact, had we not been given new boots by a company in Porterville we probably wouldn't have" (United Farm Workers 2005).

As they marched, some carried pictures and waved banners of the Virgin of Guadalupe, the patron and symbol of Mexico, representing the fusion of the Aztec and Spanish cultures. According to Mexican legend, in 1531 the Virgin Mary, her skin brown, dressed in royal Aztec raiment, appeared to an Indian peasant named Juan Diego. The apparition asked that a church be erected so that Mexican Indians could come to her and tell her of their suffering. December 12, the feast day of the Virgin de Guadalupe, became one of the Catholic calendar's three most popular churchgoing days in heavily Mexican dioceses in the United States. Mariachis serenade her at dawn.

Chavez infused such religious symbols in the farm workers' movement from the beginning. When one of the marchers questioned the wisdom of such a heavily religious emphasis at one of the meetings, Chavez brought the issue to a vote. They voted overwhelmingly with Chavez. AFL-CIO organizer William Kircher remembered, "A crew of people walking along the highway carrying the banner of Our Lady, calling meetings at night which attracted farm workers out of the fields and towns, opening with 'De Colores' (a song about the colors of spring in the fields) maybe a prayer. The whole thing had a strong cultural, religious thing, yet it was organizing people." Our Lady of Guadalupe was a part of every UFW demonstration (Matthiessen 1969, 167–168).

As Catholic and Episcopal bishops voiced support for the strike and the peregrination and as rabbis appeared along the march route, it was clear that Chavez, now limping badly on his swollen feet and using a cane, had succeeded in framing the march in religious as well as cultural terms.

He had also succeeded in framing the strike, not as a labor action or a left-wing political maneuver, but as a fight for justice.

The journalist and writer Richard Rodriquez wrote: "Chavez cast his campaign for better wages and living conditions for farm workers as a religious movement. He became for many Americans, especially Mexican Americans (my parents among them), a figure of spiritual authority. I remember a small brown man with an Indian aspect leading labor protests that were also medieval religious processions of women, children, nuns, college students, burnt old men—under the banner of Our Lady of Guadalupe" (Rodriquez 2010).

Among the marchers there were members of the press, several FBI agents, and other onlookers. Soon, they began to pass some of the vineyards in which they had worked and against which they had organized pickets six months earlier. They carried banners and union flags. Some carried large crosses. Some wore Veterans of Foreign Wars hats.

At every stop the marchers were hosted by farm workers in the nearby towns. There were rallies and meals for the marchers, and nightly performances by *El Teatro Campesino* as well as mariachi bands and other musicians. And as the march reached new locations, it picked up additional participants: boys and girls on bicycles, elderly men and women who had been in the fields for decades, nuns and priests carrying banners, all of them joining in the chanting and the singing, a kind of festival of protest, marching north.

In an attempt to connect even further the union movement with the history and culture of Mexico, Chavez asked Luis Valdez to help write a "Plan de Delano" to be read in each town through which they marched. Valdez remembered the "Plan of Ayala," a document written by Emiliano Zapata and his supporters in 1911 during the Mexican Revolution. Calling for land reform and freedom, it became the rallying cry for the Zapatismo movement. Zapata himself was from a small southern Mexican state and was rebelling against the members of the wealthy class who had stolen land with impunity. The Plan of Ayala was designed to make clear to peasant groups the injustices of the Mexican government under the regime of Porfirio Diaz and called for radical land reform. The assassination of Zapata in April 1919 ended the hopes of his followers for his ascension as leader of Mexico, but the plan remained an iconic symbol of the aspirations of the poor and dispossessed.

The Plan de Delano would follow in the tradition of a leader fighting for the rights of native peoples against powerful landowners. It became yet another symbol around which the strikers rallied. It talked of a pilgrimage to seek an end to the suffering of farm workers; of their determination to be heard; and of their resolve to follow their God. It promised unity with people of all faiths and races; inclusion of all races and workers across the land; and a revolution for "bread and justice."

In every town, NFW members told farm workers about the progress of the strike and asked them to stop picking grapes. Luis Valdez carried "The Plan of Delano" to be read at each stop and signed by local workers. At each stop he read aloud: "WE SHALL OVERCOME. Across the San Joaquin Valley, across California, across the entire Southwest of the United States, wherever there are Mexican people, wherever there are farm workers, our movement is spreading like flames across a dry plain. Our PILGRIMAGE is the MATCH that will light our cause for all farm workers to see what is happening here, so that they may do as we have done. The time has come for the liberation of the poor farm worker. History is on our side. MAY THE STRIKE GO ON! ¡VIVA LA CAUSA!" ("The Plan of Delano").

"When I joined Cesar he was walking with a cane, his feet burning with blisters, one of his legs severely swollen. I hesitated to disturb him," one marcher said. "But he greeted me graciously, obviously pleased that a priest had connected with the march, his dark, fascinating eyes capturing me forever. He spoke of the pilgrimage as a way of spiritual training for himself and the other farm workers to prevail in the long, long struggle that by this time was all too evident" (Boyle 1993).

As the marchers neared Sacramento, with approximately a week to go before they would reach the edge of the city, Chavez answered a phone call. It was from a representative of Schenley Industries. Already stung economically and suffering from negative press attention, the company decided to limit the damage. A triumphant Chavez was now able to tell his troops on the march to Sacramento that the company had capitulated, that its owners would enter into negotiations with the union for a contract.

The company agreed to recognize formally the National Farm Workers Union. This was the first time in U.S. history that a grassroots, farm-labor union had achieved recognition by a corporation. Schenley agreed to a substantial increase of wages and to an improvement of working conditions. Anxious to settle before the marchers reached Sacramento and before the inevitable landslide of publicity that the event would produce, the company signed a preliminary agreement. Huerta drew up a full contract that would be finalized in 90 days. As the grape strike continued against other companies, Huerta would successfully negotiate more contracts for the farm workers. In some cases, she was able to secure health and benefit plans for farm workers, a nearly unheard-of achievement. She set up hiring halls for workers, administered the contracts, and worked on behalf of many workers on grievance procedures. Word spread among some of the growers that Dolores Huerta, as tough a labor negotiator as many had ever seen, was "The Dragon Lady."

On Saturday afternoon, the day before Easter, the marchers gathered on the grounds of Our Lady of Grace School on a hill looking across the Sacramento River and held a rally. They had covered more than 300 miles; some 51 *originales* had walked the entire distance.

On Easter Sunday, April 10, 1966, led by some supporters on horseback carrying the UFW flag and many others wearing sombreros, to the sound of trumpets and the rhythm of guitars keeping the beat, they crossed the bridge, paraded down the mall, and ascended the Capitol steps.

Several thousand gathered at the steps of the Capitol. Among the speakers was Huerta. She declared that California—and America—could no longer take Mexican Americans for granted, and that their presence at the capital that Easter Sunday embodied the long-denied quest for dignity and justice. She praised the example set by Chavez that farm workers themselves would be in the forefront of the battles ahead, that if they were to win, they would win through their own fortitude and courage. At the same time, she said, "We are not alone but are joined by many friends" (Wells).

Reverend Chris Hartmire, director of the California Migrant Ministry, followed Huerta to the podium. Hartmire spoke of the spiritual roots of his and the California Migrant Ministry's involvement with the United Farm Workers. "Farm workers suffer in this world, not just by accident but because some men live off the sweat of their brows and because too many of us are silent and complacent. Men live at the expense of other men in that real world. Important people lie in public and conspire in private to maintain their own privilege. . . . All is not bleak in that real world, and thank God for the hope of this glorious Easter morning" (Wells).

A weary but jubilant Chavez stood before the 10,000 supporters and told them that Schenley had bowed before the pressure of the union, before the will of the campesinos, many of whom had marched. His words were nearly swallowed in thunderous cheers.

References

Bogater, Jillian. 2009. "King, Chavez Shared Social Justice Spirit on Road to Change." MLK Symposium, University of Michigan. *The University Record Online*, January 22. http://www.ur.umich.edu/0809/Jan19_09/20.php.

Boyle, Eugene. 1993. "*Viva la Causa!*" *America*, 4.

"Champion of Farm Workers Dies." 1993. *The Christian Century*, May 12, 513.

Chatfield, LeRoy. 1991. "Meeting Cesar Chavez and Becoming a Disciple." Farmworker Movement Documentation Project. August. http://farmworkermovement.com/category/commentary/leroy-chatfield-recalls/.

Chavez, Cesar. 1966. "Peregrination, Penitencia, Revolucion." United Farm Worker Documents. March. http://farmworkermovement.com/documents.

Drake, Susan Daniels. 2000. "The Progressive Interview: Dolores Huerta." *Progressive*, September, 37.

Dunne, John Gregory. (1967) 2007. *Delano: The Story of the California Grape Strike.* Farrar, Straus & Giroux. Reprint, Berkeley: University of California Press. Citations refer to the University of California Press edition. Federal Bureau of Investigation. File on Cesar Chavez and the United Farm Workers, Part I. http://foia.fbi.gov/foiaindex/chavez.htm.

Ganz, Marshall. 2009. *Why David Sometimes Wins: Leadership, Organization, and Strategy in the California Farm Worker Movement.* New York: Oxford University Press.

Heymann, C. David. 1998. *RFK: A Candid Biography of Robert Kennedy.* New York: Penguin.

Levy, Jacques E. 2007. *Cesar Chavez: Autobiography of* La Causa. Minneapolis: University of Minnesota Press.

Matthiessen, Peter. 1969. Sal Si Puedes: *Cesar Chavez and the New American Revolution.* New York: Random House.

"The Plan of Delano." http://www.aztlan.net/plandela.htm.

"Preliminary Report on the Grape Strike." 1966. SDS Regional Newsletter, no. 5, January 24. http://content.cdlib.org/xtf/view?docId=kt600004n0&brand=calisphere&doc.view=entire_text.

Richmond, Michael. 1999. "The Music of Labor: From Movement to Culture." Legal Studies Forum. http://tarlton.law.utexas.edu/lpop/etext/lsf/richm23.htm.

Rodriquez, Richard. 2010. "Saint Cesar of Delano." *Wilson Quarterly* (Winter): 6–20.

Rose, Margaret. 1990. "From the Fields to the Picket Line: *Huelga* Women and the Boycott, 1965–1975." *Labor History* (Summer): 284–285.

"The Story of Wendy Goepel Brooks, Cesar Chavez, and *La Huelga.*" www.farmworkermovement.us/essays/essays/007%20Brooks_Wendy.pdf.

United Farm Workers. 2005. "Veterans of Historic Delano Grape Strike Mark 40th Anniversary with Two-Day Reunion in Delano and *La Paz.*" *El Malcriado*, Special Edition, September 17–18. http://www.ufw.org/_page.php?menu=research&inc=history/05.html.

Wells, Robert. "Cesar Chavez's Protestant Allies: The California Migrant Ministry and the Farm Workers." www.farmworkermovement.us/essays/essays/cec.pdf.

SIX

Strikes, Boycotts, Fasts, and the Politics of Nonviolence

Forty Acres

In the spring of 1966, Chavez and his team picked out a piece of land that would become the union headquarters. When a woman from Pasadena who had inherited a 40-acre parcel of land west of Delano put the property up for sale, LeRoy Chatfield and Richard Chavez hustled to the corner of Garces Highway and Mettler Avenue. They saw a barren piece of land overgrown with debris and weeds. The two men saw something else. "So we looked at it," Richard later remembered, "and it was forty acres. . . . This would be great . . . it was just far enough out of the city . . . [that] we could really build something" (National Historic Landmark Nomination).

"This place is for the people, it has to grow naturally out of their needs," Cesar explained as the property began to take shape a year later. "It will be kind of a religious place, very restful, quiet," he continued. "It's going to be nice here" (Matthiessen 1969, 27).

Chavez's vision was of a center where farm workers could find products and services normally hard to access for lower-income, Spanish-speaking migrants—a gasoline station with automobile repair and a grocery, a health clinic, a credit union and other banking services, legal services, and other necessities that would make life easier for those laboring in the fields. As Fred Ross, Chris Hartmire, and Chatfield garnered some funding to help make this vision a reality, Richard Chavez, a carpenter, became the property developer, the individual most responsible for turning this piece of land into what would be called "The Forty Acres."

Chavez enlisted Chatfield to develop his vision of a service center. The result was the nonprofit, tax-exempt organization called the National Farm Workers Service Center Inc. (NFWSC). It was to serve as the umbrella for the newly formed Farmworker Cooperative Inc. and any other programs that would develop in the farm worker movement.

The new service center leased a vacant Texaco station on Cecil Avenue, and the first farm worker coop gas station was launched. It sold "*Huelga* Co-op Gas." Soon, at Forty Acres, there would be a health clinic and a small retirement home for aging Filipino farm workers.

Boycotting DiGiorgio

In the spring of 1966, the union launched a boycott against DiGiorgio Fruit Corporation. Founded by Giuseppe DiGiorgio in 1920, DiGiorgio controlled vast citrus fields in California's southern San Joaquin Valley. By 1946 the company was the largest grape, plum, and pear grower in the world and the second-largest producer of wine in the United States. By the 1960s DiGiorgio had acquired S&W Fine Foods, TreeSweet Products, and the White Rose food distribution business in greater New York. The company was a major hurdle in the farm workers' union struggle.

Looking back on the events of 1965 and 1966 and the capitulation of Schenley, LeRoy Chatfield, who played a key role in Chavez's union organizing, later said that it worked successfully because of the simultaneous boycotts in the cities. When the strike began the union fought more than 30 growers over an area of greater than 400 square miles. As the growers began bringing in Mexicans by the truckload to break the strike, leaders of the union decided to broaden the attack. "Our solution was to take the fight to the cities," Chatfield said. "We would boycott the grapes and let people in the cities know what was happening in Delano. At first the boycott and the response were very slow. However, with time things began to pick up and eventually the momentum built and there was a lot of support. . . . The boycott could only work if the strike was taking place and vice versa" (United Farm Workers).

And now the union would go after DiGiorgio with the same tactics. In fighting the strike and boycott, DiGiorgio, known for its ruthless strike-breaking methods, tried a new strategy. DiGiorgio's officers turned to the International Brotherhood of Teamsters Union, whose leadership was open to the idea of incorporating farm workers among its membership. DiGiorgio knew that the Teamsters would be a much less demanding organization with which to deal than the upstart but spirited NFWA. The grape grower and the Teamsters would try to use each other to defeat Cesar Chavez and his union. DiGiorgio invited the Teamsters to organize company workers. The agreements would provide job security, seniority rights, and other benefits for which the NFWA was pledged to fight.

In the summer, the company reported the results of a hastily held election, announcing that the farm workers had chosen to be represented by the Teamsters. After reports of numerous cases of voter irregularity, an investigation by the California state government proved that the election had been rigged. The company agreed to a new election to be held on August 30, 1967.

A few weeks before the new election date, Chavez unexpectedly employed another effective strategic gambit. He agreed to merge the NFWA with the AWOC, the mostly Filipino union, with whom he had been working in the Delano strike. On August 22, 1966, the NFWA and the AWOC became the United Farm Workers Organizing Committee (UFWOC) under the umbrella of the AFL-CIO, the national labor federation. Chavez and his union would now receive organizing funds from the AFL-CIO.

As the new election among workers at DiGiorgio approached, Chavez turned to Fred Ross to head up the election drive. Ross had run Edward Roybal's winning campaign for a seat on the Los Angeles City Council in 1949. The first president of CSO, Roybal became the first Mexican American to win a Los Angeles city council election in more than 70 years. It was a milestone victory, one that infused many Latinos throughout California with a sense that perhaps political power could come through tough grassroots organizing, talented candidates, and the will to win. And now to the farm workers' cause, Fred Ross brought his experience in city political organization to the UFWOC's election hopes at the DiGiorgio ranch.

Ross employed a structured system: frequent meetings, scrupulous accounting, and strict reporting from the various coordinators to Ross and to Chavez. Former civil rights activist Marshall Ganz, who would devote 16 years of his life helping Chavez and his union, later wrote: "Organizers discussed themes, reviewed leaflets, tallied numbers, analyzed problems, and reconsidered approaches. . . . As the organizing team grew to include farm workers, students, clergy, and AFL-CIO organizers, this structure created a venue within which a diversity of views could enhance the NFWA's strategic capacity, rather than tearing it apart—as could quite easily have occurred" (Ganz 2009, 191).

As election day approached, Chavez travelled to Chicago to attend the AFL-CIO Executive Council meeting at which the merger of the NFWA and AWOC was formally approved. Congratulations on the merger poured in from various unions as well as from Senator Robert Kennedy. The news of the merger gave the union's struggle with the Teamsters and the upcoming election some needed national news.

But could this infant union pull it off, could it beat the established Teamsters? The Las Vegas betting line of Jimmy the Greek gave odds of 3–1 against the NFWA. Network predictions were likewise gloomy. And yet, on election day, August 30, 1966, the farm workers marched to the polls and voted overwhelmingly for Chavez's union. At the union hall in Delano, they celebrated long into the night. Soon afterward, the company agreed to sign a three-year contract.

For Fred Ross the result was not all that surprising. Teamsters, he said, like all powerful groups, had underestimated their opponents. "They believed the migrants had scattered like the sands of the desert, that we'd never be able to round them up. . . . They underestimated our willingness to work and to win" (Ganz 2009, 198).

Striking and Boycotting Giumarra Vineyards

Chavez, Huerta, and other union leaders now turned their sights on Giumarra Vineyards Corp., located north of Bakersfield, California, the largest producer of table grapes in the United States. The strike began on August 3, 1967. Led by Fred Ross, Eliseo Medina, Jessica Gove, Marshall Ganz, Marcos Munoz, and others, the organizing team prepared to tackle a strike operation that covered 12,000 acres.

Dolores Huerta told a newspaper reporter, "If we can crack Giumarra, we can crack them all." A Giumarra official dismissed the union as a "socialist-civil rights movement" aided by "do-gooder elements, beatniks, and socialistic-type groups" ("Farm Union Pins Its Hopes" 1967).

The early signs were optimistic for the union. But despite the fact that nearly all of Giumarra's workers responded to Chavez's call for a strike, many of them did not stay long on the picket lines. In addition, Giumarra responded with a well-coordinated effort to locate a large influx of Mexican labor from across the border. Also, the Kern County Superior Court issued an injunction restricting picketing to one person per hundred feet. The injunction also banned the use of bullhorns.

Chavez would respond to this particular setback by resuming the nationwide boycott on table grapes with even more intensity. The answer to the continuing roadblocks faced by the union, Chavez believed, was increased nationwide visibility.

In 1967, Chavez hired a young lawyer Jerry Cohen as general counsel. Although he had no background in labor law, Cohen did have a history of student organizing at Amherst and had been involved in the free speech, civil rights, and antiwar movements at Berkeley. He also worked briefly for the California Rural Legal Assistance program. Cohen would play a pivotal role not only in the strike and boycott but in numerous contract signings, battles with the Teamsters, and legal and political matters involving the California state legislature and various suits both filed by and defended by the union. As many other recruits to the cause, Cohen was new to the farm worker struggle. When he first talked with Chavez about the job, he later recalled, "I said, 'I don't know anything.' And he [Chavez] said, 'That's fine, we don't know anything either. . . . We'll just learn this together'" (Ganz 2009, 217).

Cohen played an invaluable role in the early legal struggles of the union. Daring, imaginative, he learned to anticipate Chavez's wishes and worked to define strategies that more often than not brought success. Early on, communication between the two sometimes failed. During the strike against Giumarra, Cohen first tackled the bullhorn prohibition. Cohen appealed the prohibition in court and won. When he told Chavez, Cesar was not overjoyed. He had intended to go out on the picket line, use a bullhorn, and get arrested, thus gaining publicity. Cohen later remembered. "We got some pretty straight communication pretty early in the game because when we struck Giumarra, . . . one of the things this one judge did was that he took away our bullhorns. Turns out, you know, you really can't *do* that. I mean, you have a right to use a bullhorn in rural California. . . . I thought. So I told Cesar I was going to take a writ. And he didn't have any faith in that. So he, without letting me know, was planning on just going out there and using the horn and getting thrown in jail. So I bop in one day, after going up to the appellate court in Fresno, and say 'I've got this writ of prohibition. We're getting our bullhorns back.' Chavez was not particularly pleased with the victory" (Gordon 2005).

In the late spring of 1967, as the Giumarra struggle continued, Gilbert Padilla led a strike of melon pickers in the Rio Grande Valley of Texas. When a group of Texas Rangers repeatedly roughed up the strikers, in one case fracturing the skull of a woman named Magdaleno Dimas, Cohen was dispatched to Texas to stir up legal action. Aided by counsels from both the ACLU and the UAW, Cohen sued the Texas Rangers. The suit began its long journey through a labyrinth process that would finally result in a favorable U.S. Supreme Court decision on behalf of the union.

In the meantime, however, Chavez decided that he needed to assert some kind of direct action to protect his picketers against the outrageous assaults by the Rangers. When Chavez arrived, he told Cohen, "We'll teach these bastards the power of prayer." Cohen watched with fascination Chavez's nonviolent attack: "The scene was right out of a western, names and all. In the afternoon around four o'clock the Rangers would leave the Ringold Hotel and walk across a dusty street to the Catfish Inn. On one such afternoon women related to Magdaleno Dimas were in front of the hotel on their knees dressed in black, praying for the Rangers' souls. TV cameras caught this image, and within a few days Governor [John] Connelly had pulled the Rangers out" (Cohen).

Meanwhile, J. Edgar Hoover's FBI continued its surveillance of the union's activities, looking for ties to subversive elements and communist connections. Despite the lack of incriminating intelligence, Hoover decided to infiltrate the Texas activity just to make certain it was clean of communism. Once again, Hoover and his agents came up empty—no communist ties, no antigovernment subversive motives, and no plots of violence. Indeed, one FBI informant who attended a meeting in El Paso recorded some of Chavez's words: "Chavez was asked about his position on violence, at which time he said he was against violence in Vietnam or any other war, was against violence in the streets or in any other shape or form. Chavez said it takes a lot of discipline to take his recommended course of action. He said people have to be 'militant' but they also have to be on the defensive because they should not hit back with violence. Chavez said that all they had were their lives, and that there was no reason for violence to take place between people" (Federal Bureau of Investigation).

Ironically, in October, when protestors were arrested for blocking a bridge spanning the Rio Grande River at Roma, Texas, to protest Mexican nationals serving as strikebreakers, one of those arrested was an FBI informant.

As the national media focused more intently on the farm worker struggle, as the stakes became higher, so did tensions and anger. Beset by hired thugs and with little or no money, the strikers became increasingly restive and barely able to continue their nonviolent methods. In a number of cities, fights broke out. In some cases, protestors roughed up a number of individuals suspected of being company spies.

Frank Bardacke, a one-time field worker who became a community activist and author, remembered a fellow worker named Roberto Fernandez during one of the strikes: "We were on a picket line together, trying to prevent a helicopter from spraying a struck field. We were with a group of other strikers, half-jokingly using slings to throw rocks at the helicopter as it flew past. Suddenly, Roberto ran into the field, directly at the oncoming helicopter, a baseball-size rock twirling in the sling above his head, screaming a warrior's roar. The rest of us were astounded; God knows what the pilot thought as he yanked the helicopter straight up and away from the kamikaze attack" (Bardacke 1993, 130–136).

The personal pressures on the strikers, many of whom were nearly impoverished and the target of increasing harassment and physical abuse, were enormous. They found it increasingly difficult to stand by their pledge to Chavez to remain nonviolent. By early February 1968, Chavez's concern about increasing attitudes of violence in the ranks of his own protestors reached, for him, a critical point.

The Expanding Grape Boycott

When Chavez and the NFWA decided to intensify the nationwide boycott of table grapes, many questioned whether they could muster the funds, the support troops, and the communications challenges inherent in such an undertaking. The organizers and strikers were concentrated in a limited farming area of California. How could they fund the travel, the living expenses, the money for pamphlets and posters and other necessities?

Early on, Chavez found enough individuals willing to take on the daunting task with little or no financial assistance from the union. Some did it by hitchhiking to their destinations and taking part-time jobs. They shared food, housing, and whatever savings they on hand. One group left for New York in old school buses.

Eliseo Medina led the boycott in Chicago. He was, as he often said later, scared. He was born in a small Mexican town called Huanusco to the son of a bracer. At age 10, he moved to Delano after spending nearly two years in the Mexican town of Tijuana waiting with his mother for official permission to enter the United States. Along with his mother and two older sisters, he joined his father in the grape fields. Conditions were stark—no toilets or easily available drinking water and often a long wait on Saturdays to get paid for the week's work.

It was then that Medina decided to see for himself this new union of farm workers and to see the leader of this movement in person. He remembered his astonishment at Chavez's small stature but was soon taken aback by the moral force of Chavez's bearing, his words, and how he interacted with the workers. Medina left a meeting of the UFW, managed to pull together $10.50 dues for three months, and joined. Soon, he was on a picket line.

The young worker made an immediate impact. He was on the cover of *El Malcriado* pictured as one of the union's "Young Tigers." It did not take long for Medina to take on a serious mission. Chavez asked him to run the boycott in Chicago.

Medina later talked about his leadership role in Chicago. Although he had talked to many involved in the union struggle about tactics, much of his strategy, he said, seemed to develop around the stories he had learned about the civil rights marches and the talks he had had with Chavez and others about nonviolent protest movements. "We would have rallies, fancy fundraisers, and then fundraisers in the Latino community," he said. "We did sit-ins in the stores, pray-ins etc. You always felt encouraged to think creatively about new strategies . . . we borrowed, we improvised, and in some cases we took it a step further. I learned to talk to everybody you can. Go out and talk, talk, talk, and then people will help you" (Ganz 2009, 222).

They enlisted civic groups, labor organizations, churches, and student and women's groups; they made speeches, printed out literature to be handed out on street corners and in front of grocery stores; and managed to get media attention. They began to have an impact. Many people across the country gradually refused to buy grapes.

Within a few months, he was nervously appearing on television, leading a "pray-in" at supermarket vegetable counters, enlisting the help of young activists, labor leaders, and building confidence in his own ability to make a difference. He raised thousands of dollars to support the UFW boycott.

Like the efforts of Medina in Chicago, the work to mount coalitions in the various cities would be painstakingly difficult. None of the boycott leaders had ever before undertaken such work. But mostly they seemed undaunted by the challenge, eagerly throwing themselves into the cause of uniting disparate elements in each city, from clergy to labor to other activists. As they mustered increasing numbers of volunteers, the bumper stickers, signs, buttons, petitions, and picket lines began to demonstrate undeniable progress. The national boycott was well underway.

Meanwhile, in Delano, Chavez and his staff worked mightily to bring new services to their dues-paying members. By 1967, the farm workers union numbered about 8,000 members. Chavez, as unlikely and unusual a union leader as the nation had ever seen, remained cautious yet exuberant in his early successes. The membership of the union had spread outside the boundaries of California and so had its influence.

From his tiny two-bedroom house in Delano, Chavez, Helen, and eight children lived on $10 a week from the union and on food from a communal kitchen in the nearby union headquarters. As the union began completely to dominate his time and energy, Chavez had almost given up casual socializing. He no longer smoked or drank alcohol. He liked Chinese food along with traditional Mexican food and low-calorie sodas. Invariably, for the large Chavez family, the union—its work and battles—was the central focus of their lives.

Fasting—February 1968

As the battles along the picket lines grew increasingly tense, Chavez was aware that a number of those engaged in the strike were beginning to doubt whether the tactic of nonviolence would work and whether the strikers themselves could find the courage to resist retaliation. Chavez later remembered that in 1968 there came a point when a "sudden increase in violence against us, and an apparent lack of progress after more than two years of striking" led some movement participants to conclude that "the time had come to overcome violence by violence. . . . There was demoralization in the ranks, people becoming desperate, more and more talk about violence. People meant it, even when they talked to me" (Daniel 1987, 369).

Profoundly disappointed by the reports of violence, Chavez, in mid-February, 1968, called a meeting in Delano to announce his decision to engage in a fast until union members recommitted themselves to nonviolence. For this student of Gandhi, the great Indian independence hero whose large portrait hung in Chavez's office, his reaction to these unfolding events was not totally surprising. It was what Gandhi had taught; it was what Gandhi himself had practiced. On February 14, 1968, Chavez stopped eating. At first, he told only a few of his closest friends. After a few days, the word spread quickly.

The fast, he believed, would emphasize the dimensions of his movement for social justice—nonviolent, spiritual, a willingness to sacrifice for the greater good. The fast, he said, was a form of prayer. Most of his fellow lieutenants, although very worried about the health of their leader, also saw that his extreme sacrificial gesture, religious in nature, was his own way to rededicate the cause to nonviolence.

As far as generating publicity and support, the fast gained remarkable attention. Chavez took Communion every day. From Martin Luther King Jr. and from Senator Robert Kennedy of New York, now in the race for president of the United States, came words of support. He asked that daily mass be held at union headquarters each day. His wife, Helen, became increasingly concerned about his health, and some his closest friends and supporters not only worried about his health but about the tactic itself.

Huerta, who was in close contact with labor leaders and organizers around the country, later said, "Well you can imagine what these tough, burly labor leaders from New York thought when we told them our leader, our president, was fasting. 'What's wrong with him? Is he crazy?' I mean they were just—they went ballistic. Because in New York, especially during that time, they'd go into a place and wreck it up. They would wreck it

all up to get a contract and here we had our leader who was *not eating.*
All he would do was take Holy Communion every day" (Veterans of Hope
Project).

Chavez always insisted that his fasting was not directed toward his opponents but toward his allies, to motivate and refocus their attention on
the movement, to remind them that the drive toward social justice must
always be nonviolent.

But the fast quickly became an organizing bonanza. Letters, some with
donations, began arriving by the fistfuls at union headquarters. Most important, the fast energized the workers who began to see again what the movement was all about. Only through a nonviolent course could they prevail.

Chavez did not know how long he would carry out the fast. As the days
wore on, Helen grew increasingly concerned about his ebbing strength.
Often, she would remind him that everything they were working toward—
the union, the betterment of the lives of the farm workers, the demand for
dignity toward Mexican American workers—would be jeopardized if he
lost his health and perhaps his life.

But as the fast continued and bulletins about his condition became daily
staples of news programs on television and radio and in the print media,
it was clear that the fast had become a dramatic organizing tool for the
union. As concern about Chavez's health increased, so did the echoes of his
message. Across the country, people from various backgrounds began to
voice support for union and its strike. More press representatives flocked
to Delano. Money arrived.

During the fast, Chavez said, "I am convinced," he wrote, "that the truest
act of courage, the strongest act of manliness is to sacrifice ourselves for
others in a totally non-violent struggle for justice. To be a man is to suffer
for others. God help us to be men" (Rodriquez 2010).

At one point during the fast, Chavez was forced into court to defend himself against an injunction. In many of its legal struggles with the growers,
the UFW often used the courthouses as stages to publicize the cause. Often,
UFW protestors and their supporters, much like the civil rights demonstrators in the South, surrounded courthouse proceedings with vigils, song-
fests, and pray-ins. Lead counsel Cohen recalled the scene after Chavez was
led into the courtroom as hundreds came to protest: "Workers all around
the building, workers lining every wall of the courthouse . . . workers were
singing softly, and they were praying. . . . We hadn't been having too much
luck in that courthouse before, because it's really the growers' courthouse.
But I think everybody that morning knew it was our courthouse." The lawyer for the grower, Cohen said, failed to convince the judge to remove the

workers. The judge's response: "If I kick these workers out of this court-house, that will be just another example of goddamn gringo justice. I can't do it" (Gordon 2005).

For 21 days, Chavez fasted, losing much weight and drawing dire warn-ings from his doctor. He finally decided to end the fast on March 10, 1968.

After making the decision, Chavez received word that Robert Kennedy would join him. Chavez had first met Kennedy in 1959 when Chavez was working for the CSO. In 1966, with Chavez's new union attempting to gain a footing, Robert Kennedy, at the time a Senator from New York, came out publicly for the rights of farm workers and the efforts of Chavez's union to secure those rights. "About the only people for us were ourselves," Chavez reminisced about those days in 1966. "Then Bobby came and did something heroic. He endorsed us, but in a clear cut manner" (Robert F. Kennedy Conference 2000).

And now, in March 1968, Kennedy, in the midst of his campaign for the presidency, came to break bread with his friend. With Kennedy's aides and bodyguards forming a shield around him, the people pressed close trying to get a glimpse of their friend. Some were able to touch him, shake his hand, and others waved and blessed themselves as he passed. Dolores Huerta, squeezing his arm, later said, "It was the most wild moment in my life. All these farm workers really loved Bobby. They called him brother and saw him as more saint than politician. The chants of 'Bobby, Bobby, Bobby' in the air, photographers and TV crews were swept aside. Everybody who could see him wanted a photo of Robert Kennedy or a personal greeting" (Robert F. Kennedy Conference 2000).

As a crowd of several thousand watched, Chavez sat with his wife and mother and Kennedy. At the open-air Mass, several priests and nuns dis-tributed bread to the crowd. Addressing the 8,000 onlookers, Senator Ken-nedy heaped praise not only on Chavez but on the workers themselves who had, through nonviolence, achieved profound victories in assert-ing the rights of Mexican Americans and of farm workers. Kennedy said, "And when your children and grandchildren take their place in America—going to high school, and college, and taking good jobs at good pay—when you look at them, you will say, 'I did this. I was there, at the point of diffi-culty and danger.' And though you may be old and bent from many years of labor, no man will stand taller than you when you say, 'I marched with Cesar'" (John F. Kennedy 1968).

With Chavez too weak to deliver a message to the supporters who gath-ered at union headquarters, Reverend Jim Drake of the California Migrant Ministry read his words. Chavez said the fast was "for non-violence and a

Senator Ted Kennedy signs the grape boycott petition, 1985. In 1984, as the Republican-controlled state government in California intensified its efforts to weaken the California labor laws that supported farm workers, Cesar Chavez called for another grape boycott. Just as his brother, Robert Kennedy, had done years earlier, Senator Kennedy publicly stood by Chavez's side supporting the union's fight. (Wayne State University/Walter P. Reuther Library)

call of sacrifice. Our struggle is not easy. Those who oppose us are rich and powerful and they have many allies in high places. We are poor. Our allies are few. But we have something the rich do not own. We have our own bodies and spirits and the justice of our cause as our weapons. When we are really honest with ourselves we must admit that our lives are all that really belong to us. So it is how we use our lives that determine what kind of men we are. It is my deepest beliefs that only by giving our lives do we find life . . . in a totally non-violent struggle for justice." The fast, he said, was for penance and hope and a further dedication to nonviolence as the only way that a movement of social justice could go forward (Goepel).

The union's counsel, Jerry Cohen, said later of the fast: "Cesar spent himself like coin in an effort to cement nonviolence into the Union's foundation. . . . The fast had put the Union on the map and was instrumental in forging the coalition of religious groups and Labor which led to the success of the grape boycott" (Cohen).

The Boycott Progresses

By early 1968, the UFWOC had placed organizers in 20 strategic cities. Their job was to gain cooperation from wholesalers and retail outlets, to picket those who were uncooperative, and to get publicity for the boycott in local news media.

When Marcus Munoz, one of the organizers in the Boston area, enlisted the aid of Boston mayor Kevin White, the Boston protestors decided to hold an event certain to draw media attention. Munoz recalled, "In an effort to copy the events of the Boston Tea Party, we emulated the event by dumping grapes arriving from California into the harbor instead of tea. Then Cesar suggested we leave some for Ronald Reagan, who was the California governor at the time and a huge supporter of the farmers. So we sent these smelly, rotten grapes back to California, to the governor's office" (United Farm Workers 2005).

In 1968 Huerta headed the New York City boycott and was instrumental in developing a model strategy for building community support. It reflected much of what she had learned from Fred Ross and the CSO years earlier. During the New York campaign she reported, "The students have volunteered to form a speakers bureau and we now have students who will be going to churches to speak on the boycott. After we cover churches and political groups, we hope to pick up enough speakers to approach each individual union shop. We are doing this by areas, though, and as we pick up people to help we refer them to the coordinator in their own town, or neighborhood. We hope to build a community neighborhood machine by this method for the boycott" (Shaw 2008, 29).

She later told a story illustrating the determination and commitment of the individual farm workers who joined her in New York despite the odds. "When I was in charge of the New York boycott," she recalled, "a farm worker called me. He had been picketing in front of a grocery store, all by himself, and he had just succeeded in bringing the store around. And he said, 'Señora Huerta, they took the grapes out of the store.' I said, "*¿Como se llama?*" ("What's the name of the store?") And he said, 'I don't know. I don't know how to read.' And I thought to myself, this farm worker, out of Delano, California, who'd never been out of Delano before, had gone all the way to New York City and got people not to shop at that store" (Huerta 2009, 36).

Fred Ross said later, "It's amazing the tremendous effectiveness of the boycott, considering the small size of the staff that was involved. We never had too many full-time people on it. That first busload to New York had about forty farm workers and ten young volunteers, students, and ex-students. We all were paid five dollars a week and room and board" (Levy 2007, 268).

The boycott spread to other cities such as Los Angeles and Detroit. Jessica Govea and Marshall Ganz launched a boycott in Toronto. Govea, who had worked in the fields with her parents as young child, left college to join the UFW in 1966 and stayed with the organization for 15 years. In July 1968, she joined Ganz and Catholic priest Mark Day in Toronto to lead the grape boycott in Canada. So successful was the group in gaining public notice and support that the mayor of Toronto proclaimed November 23, 1968, as "Grape Day" in honor of the boycott. Later, Govea reflected on the challenges facing the NFWOC with so little resources: "When we went out, we had to lose all shame and be willing to ask for everything. And we were asking people to quit their jobs and drop out of school and come work with us full time. We were asking people to give us money; we were asking people to let us live in their home, and sleep on their floor. We were asking people to feed us. We were asking people for leaflets . . . anything you could think of, we were asking for, because we didn't have it, and we needed it in order to do the boycott" (Shaw 2008, 30–31).

The boycott caught the imaginations of all kinds of Americans, including teenagers. In Indianapolis, a 14-year-old named Jeffrey St. Clair, who had read a biography of Chavez, was so energized by news reports of the protests that he decided to launch his own boycott. He gathered five or six of his friends and began to target a grocery store each weekend for non-violent action. "On my first picket, I parked myself in front of a Kroger's on the south side of Indianapolis—the albino suburb of a city that's whiter than Carrera marble. I harangued housewives about the conditions of farm workers on their way in and on the way out. They looked at me as if I was a lunatic, horrified at the prospect that I was one of their neighbor's children. Would one of their own come home one day in the grip of a similar fever?" On one occasion, Jeffrey and his friends became such nuisances that one of the shoppers called the local sheriff who told the boys to leave. Jeffrey refused. He was whisked off to jail. "It was my first arrest," said St. Clair. "There would be others in the months and years ahead. The usual story of an obnoxious child. Thank you, Cesar Chavez for giving me my start in a life of political crime" (St. Clair 2003).

In urban centers across the United States, contingents of farm workers arrived to do battle in the boycott. The groups in each city usually consisted of a few single men; an Anglo support staff recruited from the local communities; and one or two farm worker families, including their children. In Detroit, for example, Hijinio Rangel, a farm worker from Dinuba, California, outside of Fresno, arrived with his wife, Maria, and his eight children.

In early 1968, a church in Visalia, California, organized a debate on the question of the church's relationship to the strike and the national boycott of table grapes. The main speakers were Chavez, Hartmire, and Allan Grant, a prominent Presbyterian layman from Visalia, who was also president of the California Farm Bureau, the main organization of growers. The meeting was stormy, a battle for the allegiance of Presbyterians that would continue in the pages of *Presbyterian Life*, the flagship magazine of what was then known as the United Presbyterian Church.

Two kinds of people objected to the presence of so much religion in the strike, Chavez said: secular union people who didn't want religion to mix with economics, and conservative religious people who didn't want religion "used" in this way. To both views, Chavez simply noted that religion was a part of the Latino people.

The Assassination Tragedies—1968

When Robert Kennedy announced his candidacy for president on March 16, 1968, he knew that the state of California would be critical in his uphill battle for the Democratic nomination. Running on a promise of ending the war in Vietnam and leading a return to the generous impulses of the nation in fighting for equal rights for minorities and help for the poor, Kennedy was fighting against much of the Democratic Party establishment. When President Lyndon Johnson told the nation on the night of March 31 that he would not seek reelection, the campaign for the Democratic presidential nomination soon became a contest between Vice President Hubert Humphrey, supported by most of the Democratic Party regulars; Senator Eugene McCarthy of Minnesota, who had taken up the mantle of an antiwar candidate and had nearly defeated Johnson in the New Hampshire primary in early March; and Kennedy.

Chavez asked Marshall Ganz to be the chief organizer of a UFWOC campaign to elect Robert Kennedy to the presidency. With much political acumen and deft strategies for mobilizing the Latino vote in California, Ganz gathered together a team of organizers that zealously saturated selected

Mexican American communities to register new voters and get them to the polls for the election scheduled for June 6. Chavez himself made numerous public appearances on behalf of Kennedy, often several a day. There were rallies across the Central Valley and in the neighborhoods of East Los Angeles, where the union set up phone banks, pounded on doors handing out leaflets, and hosted house meetings and downtown rallies.

Ganz and his lieutenants were able to recruit many volunteer organizers who, with much drive and commitment, took on the election as a cause closely aligned with *La Causa* itself. On one fateful night, however, the election frenzy among the union faithful came to a sudden pause. On the evening of April 3, 1968, Martin Luther King Jr. gave a dramatic speech in Memphis, Tennessee, on behalf of striking sanitation workers who planned a march the following day. On the morning of April 4, as King prepared to leave the Lorraine Motel to meet with march organizers, he stepped out from his room on the second floor. He had only an instant more to live. When an assassin's rifle bullet ended his life that day in Memphis, King was only 39 years old.

Chavez was stunned and profoundly saddened by King's assassination. The civil rights leader was not only a heroic figure to many Americans; he was also in Chavez's mind a great teacher and role model.

In the wake of King's assassination, the work of Chavez and his union to elect Robert Kennedy continued apace, the volunteers canvassing door to door encouraging residents to vote. They did vote in large numbers. An unusually large outpouring of Mexican American votes was the difference in the election. Kennedy pulled off the victory.

Late that night, at the Ambassador Hotel in Los Angeles, Chavez, Huerta, and other friends of the farm workers union celebrated Kennedy's victory along with thousands of supporters in the hotel ballroom. Huerta was among many of Kennedy's friends and supporters on stage. Chavez waited in a private room of the hotel with a mariachi band set to play in the senator's honor.

After Kennedy completed his victory speech to a tumultuous ovation, he stayed for a while thanking personally many of those who had helped in his campaign, including Huerta. Along with several associates, Kennedy then walked off the stage, heading from the ballroom through the kitchen. They walked into pandemonium. A lone gunman named Sirhan Sirhan fired several shots, hitting Kennedy, who fell gravely wounded, and several others. Kennedy died the following day.

All of it seemed incomprehensible. In the space of two months, Chavez and the farm workers union had lost two towering and inspirational supporters. Devastated by the two assassinations within the space of two months, they would, nevertheless, carry on the fight.

A Republican Administration in Washington

In late 1968, the grinding stress, the years of long hours, and the fast at last took their physical toll. So painful was his back that Chavez was forced into traction and spent several months bedridden much of the time. Instead of spending long hours driving around the state, he began to receive a constant stream of visitors at his bedside.

The tragedy of losing Robert Kennedy was much more than personal to Chavez, Huerta, and other leaders of *La Causa* as well as to the thousands of its members. It was also a terrible political cataclysm. The hopes of the presidency for Kennedy, an ardent supporter of the union and its works, crumbled in the assassination and the subsequent election of Republican Richard Nixon in the November 1968 elections. A Californian with close ties to the growers and their supporters, Nixon would unquestionably lead an administration unfriendly to the growing power and influence of the UFW.

Its opponents savored now the opportunity to use every possible leverage in the administration and its friends in California to put Chavez in his place, to marshal the forces of agribusiness, and wilt the impudence of a union that dared take on their power and threaten their profits.

Nevertheless, the boycott continued. Throughout 1969, shipments of California table grapes were stopped by strikes in Boston, New York, Philadelphia, Chicago, Detroit, Montreal, and Toronto. In some British ports, dockworkers refused to unload grapes.

In New York, Huerta was like a mobilizing machine, sweeping through the offices and meeting halls of political activists and union leaders, Latino associations, religious groups, peace organizations, and consumer organizations. She took special pride in training farm workers who had left the fields and traveled all the way to New York to help. For the young women who had made the trip, Huerta was a mentor, guiding them in interpersonal relations both within the group and in public and giving them a firsthand experience in social activism. In return, they gave the union growing strength, solidarity, and a youthful, infectious exuberance.

In the spring of 1969, Chavez received a letter from E. L. Barr Jr., president of the California Grape and Tree Fruit League, an organization of growers locked in battle with the UFW. Barr accused UFW strikers of using violence on the picket lines. Whether Barr was serious in his accusations, or, more likely, attempting to goad Chavez, the letter did touch a nerve in the labor leader who, above all, insisted on nonviolence. Chavez answered Barr first by challenging him to prove his accusations and then with an eloquent statement about the intent of the farm workers' movement: "You must understand—I must make you understand—that our membership and hopes and aspiration of the hundreds of thousands of the poor and dispossessed that have been raised on our account, are above all, human beings, no better no worse than any other cross section of human society; we are not saints because we are poor but by the same measure neither are we immoral. We are men and women who have suffered and endured much and not only because of our abject poverty but because we have been kept poor" (Chavez 2008, 61).

By the summer of 1969, Chavez and his wife and eight children still lived in a small two-bedroom house on $10 a week from the union and on food from the communal kitchen in nearby union headquarters. Increasingly ascetic, Chavez gave up liquor and cigarettes. "I can't think back to a time when we were not on strike," he told a *Time* magazine reporter. "Either the union will be destroyed," he said, "or they will sign a contract. There's no other alternative" ("The Little Strike" 1969, 20).

In September, Chavez, recovered sufficiently from his severe back condition, decided once again to go on the road. He left California on a seven-week tour across the country.

It had been nearly four years since Chavez called the strike against many table grape growers of California, nearly four years since his union began its demands for union recognition and collective bargaining. Success had come in slow but steady gains.

But in 1968 grape sales nationwide were off 12 percent. In June 1969, 10 growers representing about 12 percent of the state's table grape production announced that they would sit down with Chavez to write a contract. The boycott had been decisive. One agribusiness leader admitted: "We are definitely hurting. It is costing us more to produce and sell our grapes than we are getting for them." One farm worker said: "It's so beautiful I can hardly believe it" ("Breakthrough" 1969, 36).

Support from the Black Panthers

In 1969, Chavez and his union gained support from another civil rights group—the Black Panther Party (BPP). In some ways, the alliance of the two groups was unlikely. The BPP was African American, militant, and urban, and the UFW was largely Mexican American, nonviolent, rural, and religious in orientation. But the two organizations also had much in common: the fight for racial and economic justice and for labor solidarity.

Founded in Oakland, California, in October 1966, by Bobby Seale, the son of a carpenter from Texas, and Huey P. Newton, son a Baptist minister from Louisiana, the BPP first organized on behalf of the African American population in Oakland and other cities suffering under harsh police brutality. As the organization grew, so did its aims, confronting issues of employment, poverty, education, and housing. Its political slant was socialist, demanding an end of choking capitalist greed against all minorities. Bobby Seale declared that the struggle of the BPP was against capitalist exploitation of working-class people of all races and ethnic groups.

In early 1969, although the grape boycott had attracted considerable attention nationwide, UFW organizer Fred Ross decided that the union should also conduct a secondary boycott of the Safeway grocery store chain, the largest buyer of California grapes after the U.S. Department of Defense. The Black Panthers signed on, agreeing to take the lead in certain areas, especially in California.

With their black jackets, berets, and dark glasses, the Panthers could be an intimidating sight at picket lines. After seeing the Panthers in action at some Safeway stores in Los Angeles, one UFW member concluded that the Panthers actually acted as a restraint on anyone thinking about harassing farm workers on the lines because they "scared the hell out of them."

When Gilbert Padilla conducted boycott activities in Philadelphia, he asked for the help of the Panthers. "I [sought] them [out] whenever I went somewhere. I looked for them." Another UFW organizer, Eliseo Medina, worked with Fred Hampton and the Panthers in Chicago. When some of the UFW members asked Chavez to square his position on nonviolence and the mutual support between the union and the Black Panthers, a militant group, Chavez said, "We may not agree with the philosophy of the Black Panther Party, but they are our brothers, and non-violence extends to standing up for [whoever] is being persecuted" (Araiza 2009, 200).

Especially in the nationwide grape boycott, BPP chapters in numerous cities offered help to the UFW. They provided housing, walked picket lines, attended rallies, and recruited other supporters.

The interaction between the civil rights organizations and the UFW brought mutual respect and understanding to those who were involved—the crossing of racial lines for a common purpose; the friendships gained as they fought side by side; the feeling that they were all fighting for a common purpose of class solidarity. Richard Ybarra, Chavez's bodyguard and son-in-law, said of his experience in the UFW: "I learned about diversity by working there because it was all about people, not about color. . . . It was never about race or color differences. It was always about similarities." After the alliance between the UFW and the BPP in the struggle against Safeway, the two groups continued to support each other in subsequent campaigns. It was this kind of alliance that made Chavez both thankful and proud (Araiza 2009, 200).

Major Contracts with Growers—1970

The boycott was having a profound economic impact. Union workers in various cities across the country refused to handle table grapes and consumers sympathetic to the cause refused to buy them. The industry lost more than $25 million in sales. Had the Department of Defense not increased its purchases of table grapes from 6.9 million pounds in 1968 to 11 million pounds in 1969, the losses would have been even greater.

By the spring of 1969, the boycott had, in the words of Coachella grower Lionel Steinberg, president of David Freedman & Company, "literally closed Boston, New York, Philadelphia, Chicago, Detroit, Montreal, [and] Toronto completely from handling table grapes" (Maika and Maika 1982, 195).

In early April 1970, Steinberg became the first table grape grower to sign a contract with Chavez and his union. Steinberg dramatically resigned from the California Grape and Tree Fruit League, claiming that the league had falsified statistics to minimize the effectiveness of the union's strike and boycott of the table grape industry. "We cannot continue to try to sweep this problem under the rug," he told fellow growers. He said the labor action had turned the Coachella Valley into "a disaster area" that could wipe out many businesses within a year. Later, Steinberg said, "I had a high regard for Cesar—he was an honest man." Yet, he remained perplexed by his adversary. "He was running the union with priests and nuns and Ivy Leaguers on sabbatical. It was more like a political crusade than a trade union effort" (Oliver 1999, 15).

Later that summer, after a speaking engagement on the night of July 25, 1970, Chavez returned to his home in Delano to find a message from John Giumarra Jr., nephew of the founder of the Giumarra Company, the largest table grape grower in California and one of Chavez's toughest adversaries. The company controlled 11,000 acres and employed more than 2,000 farm workers at harvest. After five years of *La Huelga*, the company was ready to deal with the UFW.

The union responded to the Giumarra call with a demand that the company bring the growers who still were holding out with it to the bargaining

On July 29, 1970, Giumarra Vineyards Corporation, the major table grape grower in California and a major adversary of Chavez, along with other grape growers, signed contracts with the farm workers union. The strike against the grape growers had lasted five years. When John Giumarra Jr., shown above, and the other growers negotiated with Chavez and his colleagues, it represented a milestone victory in the fight for workers rights. (AP/Wide World Photos)

table. Jerry Cohen recalled: "Giumarra was the biggest fish of all, and Cesar and I were both anxious to force the issue and demand that the whole Delano bunch join Giumarra in any talks." As the two drove to the Stardust Motel in Delano for a first meeting at 2:30 in the morning, they figured that if Giumarra had given in so would the rest of the growers. "We told

Giumarra to round up all the Delano growers," Cohen said, "or we would not proceed" (Cohen).

Giumarra agreed to contact the other growers, and they responded. On July 29, after meeting for three days, the union and the 29 growers signed contracts that brought an end to the five-year table grape strike. Richard Chavez recalled: "And there were . . . hundreds, thousands, outside," because the meeting room was filled to capacity. "And you could see the growers coming in here. The way I describe that scene," he continued, "is like when you're taking lambs to the slaughter. They know they are going to be slaughtered! And it was a really *great* moment. I mean . . . knowing that it was over. . . . Knowing that we had *successfully* beaten them, that we had successfully defeated them with the boycott, was a great feeling. They knew it, we knew it, and everybody knew it. So it was a great feeling" (National Historic Landmark Nomination).

After the contracts were completed, the younger Giumarra said, "We are happy that peace will come to this valley. It has been a mutual victory. With the power of the union, the power of the people and the ability of the men in this valley to grow the finest crops in the world, we can get these products into the marketplace where they can bring a higher return to the farmers, so that they can sit down at some future time and negotiate to give a higher return to the workers." Giumarra's uncle said simply, "I enjoyed the fight while it lasted." An elated Chavez, wearing an embroidered Filipino shirt that he donned only on special occasions, remarked, "He was so relieved it was all over, and so were we" ("The Black Eagle Wins" 1970, 14).

Almost an entire industry was now under union contract. For the first time, more than 70,000 farm workers had gained legal protection of their basic rights to fair wages and benefits, fair hiring systems, job security measures, and safe working environments. The contract called for a wage of $1.80 plus 20 cents for each box picked. Before the strike, the workers made approximately $1.10 an hour. In addition, growers would begin to contribute to a health plan and the agreement included stringent safety requirements on the use of pesticides.

For the workers this was not merely a victory for wages and better working conditions; for them, the battle was for dignity and for affirmation. On this day, as they jubilantly sang the songs of *La Causa*, as they sang "*Nosotros venceremos*," the civil rights song of "We Shall Overcome," as they shouted the slogans of "*Viva La Huelga*," they were asserting newly won respect.

They celebrated in Delano. It had been five years since the infant union had dared take on the grape growers. This was a day for which the union leaders had labored for so long, a day for the campesinos, the field workers, many with their backs pained and bent by years in the fields, their hands roughed and skin weathered like leather. Today, as they met in Delano, many of their eyes filled as Chavez, along with the growers, signed the contract that gave their union formal representation.

Challenging the Lettuce Growers

As jubilant farm workers celebrated their new labor contracts in the summer of 1970, Chavez faced another major challenge. In California's Salinas Valley, lettuce growers were attempting to avoid the same fate that befell the grape growers. A narrow, fertile pocket of about 100 miles, the Salinas Valley produced a major portion of the nation's vegetables—lettuce, broccoli, artichokes, and other produce.

And now, almost every lettuce grower in the area, witnessing the growing power of Chavez's union, began signing union contracts with the Teamsters Union, agreements far more favorable to the growers than any contracts they could possibly work out with Chavez's farm workers' union. Once again the Teamsters were attempting to add to their already considerable power by destroying Chavez's union.

In 1967, representatives of the UFWOC and the Teamsters had signed an agreement, renewed at the beginning of the lettuce strike, laying out the jurisdictional limits for each union. It recognized the right of the UFWOC to organize farm workers; it recognized the Teamsters as the rightful union for the truck drivers, canneries, packing sheds, and other parts of the agricultural industry. In once again attempting to sign up farm workers, the Teamsters were violating the terms of the pact. Chavez was furious at the blatant violation of the agreement.

As organizer Marshall Ganz said later, "Victory brings new challenges and new opportunities, which themselves become challenges. As UFWOC focused on launching its lettuce boycott, farm workers across the country began to call on the union to expand into Oregon, Washington, Idaho, Kansas, Wisconsin, Ohio, Arizona, New Mexico, Colorado, Texas, and Florida" (Ganz 2009, 230).

The Republican establishment in Sacramento regarded Chavez and his union, with its ties to Democratic politicians and the civil rights movement, as a noxious force in the state that had to be repelled politically and legally. Governor Ronald Reagan, contemptuous generally of labor unions and labor leaders, was especially cold toward Chavez, a man who threatened the state's agribusiness establishment that was so closely tied to the

Republican Party. Reagan and his allies mocked the farm workers' grape strike. The governor, for example, often popped a grape into his mouth before photographers and offered grapes to reporters and visitors to the governor's mansion.

In the summer of 1970, 6,000 Salinas Valley Teamster drivers and packing workers struck California lettuce growers. The strike had a serious impact , preventing much of the nation's summer lettuce crop from reaching consumers. The price of iceberg lettuce tripled. When the strike ended, the contract included a special agreement by the growers to give the Teamsters, not the UFWOC, access to farms and the right to organize farm workers. Through a strike within the lettuce industry but not including farm workers, the Teamsters had essentially forced the growers into making a deal that cut out the UFWOC.

Although he had not planned to take on the lettuce growers so quickly after the grape boycott, Chavez responded forcefully to the collusion between the Teamsters and the companies.

While declaring "all-out war," on the Teamsters, Chavez told a reporter that he regretted the continuing jurisdictional conflicts because it diverted him and the union from constructive aims: medical clinics, research programs on the effects of pesticide exposure, and an experimental educational program for rural minority-group children. "All these dreams," he said sadly, "will have to wait for a while" ("The Black Eagle Wins" 1970, 14).

Chavez and his lieutenants were outraged. Chavez went on a hunger strike to protest the Teamsters' actions. Although a state district court imposed a temporary injunction to stop UFWOC members from walking off the job, it was clear that the union had no intention of backing off this new challenge from the Teamsters. And so, once again, the UFWOC and the Teamsters held secret talks to avert another strike. Although a temporary agreement seemed to settle the dispute temporarily, by August 12 the two sides were again warring.

Some 6,000 UFWOC workers struck the Salinas Valley growers on August 23 in what was the largest farm worker strike in U.S. history. On August 24, 1970, Chavez called for a strike against the lettuce ranches in Salinas and Santa Maria Valley. Within three days, an estimated 10,000 workers had walked out of the fields. The fight was on. From Monterey County to Santa Cruz, the strikers waved flags, sang, and handed out literature. Growers quickly hired additional armed guards who were not reluctant to flash guns before the eyes of the picketers. Jerry Cohen, general counsel for the UFWOC, said of the scene: "It looked like a revolution, and some of these right-wing growers thought it was" (Ferriss and Sandoval 1997, 170).

As more workers walked off the job in the succeeding weeks, shipments of fresh lettuce nationwide almost ceased, causing the price of lettuce to double almost overnight. With lettuce growers suffering grievous financial losses, a state district court enjoined Chavez and his union from picketing. The union refused to obey the court order. Instead, in late September 1970, the UFW asked consumers nationwide to boycott all lettuce that had not been picked by members of the UFWOC.

Sporadic violence erupted in the lettuce fields. In late July, U.S. Treasury agents notified the UFWOC that they had learned of a so-called bounty of $25,000 that had been placed on the head of Chavez. Sketchy details identified the suspected trigger man as a hired gun wanted in another ambush slaying. They described the man as missing part of his right ear and sporting a "Born to Lose" tattoo on his right calf.

On September 5, 1970, gunfire broke out near the pickets, as goons wielding baseball bats hit some of the strikers and belted their cars, flattening their tires, and breaking windshields. A rancher threatened to blow the guts out of the protestors as he shot a rifle in the air. There were cascades of rocks aimed at the strikers. On November 4, a UFWOC regional office was bombed. A few weeks later, federal investigators indicted six Teamster men of violating gun-control laws by bringing in firearms and explosives to use against the UFWOC. They were later sent to San Quentin Prison.

On December 4, 1970, federal marshals arrested and jailed Chavez after the union, disregarding an injunction, aimed its verbal assaults and boycott against major lettuce grower Lester "Bud" Antle. At the Monterey County jail in Salinas, Coretta Scott King, widow of Martin Luther King Jr., made a visit to see Chavez. Also, former Olympic gold medal–winning decathlete Rafer Johnson escorted Ethel Kennedy, widow of Robert F. Kennedy, only to be jeered by an antiunion mob on the steps of the jail. However, 2,000 farm workers, carrying the red-and-black flag of the union, and waving banners proclaiming "*La Causa*," cheered Mrs. Kennedy. City police and Monterey County sheriff deputies prevented a riot.

On December 23, Chavez was released by the Supreme Court of California. The next day he called a strike against six additional lettuce growers. The additional pressure worked.

The bitter strike ended on March 26, 1971. Once again, the Teamsters and UFWOC signed a jurisdictional agreement reaffirming the UFW's right to organize field workers.

It had been the largest farm labor strike in California history, and the show of union power had an immediate impact. Within the first week, InterHarvest, the largest lettuce grower, granted a 30 percent wage increase bargained by Huerta. Not only did the increase in wages to $2.10 far exceed anything that the Teamsters had been able to offer farm workers, but Huerta also negotiated an agreement by the company to eliminate the use of DDT and other dangerous pesticides that Chavez and the union had denounced. A week later, Pic N Pac, also granted wage increases.

By the end of 1970, the UFWOC had negotiated some 200 contracts covering nearly 70,000 farm workers. The contracts provided pay raises, the use of union-run hiring halls, the beginning of regulation of pesticide use, the creation of a "Farm workers' Fund" for social services, and the funding of a health and welfare fund that the union named after Robert F. Kennedy.

In 1971, Cesar and his family and most of the union's administrators moved from Delano to Keene, California, located southwest of Bakersfield in the foothills of the Tehachapi Mountains. They opened new headquarters at the site of a former public tuberculosis sanatorium. Chavez called the new headquarters "*La Paz*," a shortened version of "*Nuestra Senora Reina de la Paz*" or "Our Lady, Queen of Peace."

The victories in several strikes and the increased union membership approaching 70,000 required the UFWOC to fulfill its promises, and Chavez had decided that the Delano facility was too small to encompass all of the union's activities. It expanded benefit programs, established medical clinics and retirement communities, trained farm workers to serve as organizers and representatives to administer contracts. By the middle of 1972, some 300 staff in 25 field offices from California to Florida carried on union work.

The staff still worked mostly for a pittance and out of deep commitment to a cause. But the union contracts began to increase workers' wages and thus increased the dues. Also, the union's fundraising generated nearly half a million dollars in 1971, much of it used for social services and clinics.

Through their pivotal contracts, their national boycott, the notoriety of their clashes with hired thugs, the violence on the picket lines, Chavez and his forces had not only mobilized thousands of supporters and millions of Americans who favored his work on behalf of farm laborers; they had also created, as Chavez knew they would, fierce enemies from among antilabor forces, Republican political operatives, and others who felt threatened by the union's successes. It was during these tense years that several plots to assassinate Chavez came to the attention of the FBI and other police authorities. Fortunately, unlike the tragedies of 1968 and the loss of both Robert Kennedy and Martin Luther King Jr., Chavez survived the planned attempts on his life.

By early 1972, the UFWOC controlled assets of nearly $1 million and income from dues totaling nearly $2 million. No longer merely an organizing committee, Chavez and his colleagues had turned the organization into a full-fledged, successfully functioning union providing needed services to its members. Leaders of the national AFL-CIO decided to recognize the farm workers' union, offering it a full charter as the United Farm Workers of America, AFL-CIO (UFW). Chavez and Huerta and all the others who in Delano had set out to establish such a union no longer seemed like dreamers but were at last recognized as successful organizers.

Taking on the Arizona Political Establishment

In 1972, the Arizona state legislature passed and Governor Jack Williams signed a bill highly prejudicial against farm workers. The Arizona law, especially favoring the large lettuce-growing industry in the state, prohibited farm workers from having a union, from engaging in boycotts, and from pressuring any individuals from purchasing agricultural goods.

Shortly after the passage of the legislation, Governor Williams, asked to meet with representatives of the farm workers, said, "As far as I'm concerned these people do not exist" (Levy 2007, 463).

Chavez decided on a spiritual fast. As the fast became national news, the famous visitors began to arrive in Arizona—Joseph Kennedy, son of Robert Kennedy, folksinger Joan Baez, Coretta Scott King, and others. When Arizona politicians mocked Chavez's actions, and when growers charged that it was nothing but a publicity stunt, Chavez, as he had done in 1968, became an increasingly sympathetic figure.

As the days of the fast wore on, Chavez agreed to a campaign suggested by Marshall Ganz, LeRoy Chatfield, and Jim Drake that would, in Chavez's words, "make the governor who signed the bill pay for it" (Shaw 2008, 149–150).

The union would launch a campaign to recall the governor through a massive voter registration drive. In response to some at one of the meetings who said "*No se puede*" ("It cannot be done"), Dolores Huerta insisted that from now on they would never say it could not be done. From now on, they would say "*Sí se puede*" ("Yes we can do it"). "*¡Sí se puede!*" became a battle cry for the Arizona fight and others that followed.

Into Arizona marched many union forces. Volunteers swelled the ranks from Arizona citizens who fanned out across the state encouraging Mexican Americans, Native Americans, and others to register. On makeshift tables and even ironing boards, volunteers set up in areas heavily trafficked, especially shopping areas. In only four months, 100,000 new voters had put their names on recall petitions, and, most important, registered to vote.

Although the Republican attorney general eventually blocked the recall election through legal maneuvering, the UFW had changed the electoral demographics of Arizona. Its brief overwhelmingly successful registration drive paved the way in succeeding elections for Mexican Americans and Native Americans to win several seats in the Arizona state legislature; others won local council and school board races; and a few became judges. When Raul Castro became the first Mexican American governor of Arizona in 1974, his margin of victory was 4,100. The UFW drive had made a powerful impact.

Politics in California—1972

In 1972, California's growers, aligned with the state Republican Party, attempted to put the UFW out of business. As Republicans have done with many other issues over the years in California, they set out to weaken farm workers' rights with a ballot initiative. Since the formation of the UFW, many had questioned whether the organization was essentially a labor union or a social movement. Now, with this challenge, the question was whether the UFW could quickly become a potent political force.

The so-called Agricultural Labor Relations Initiative, known as Proposition 22, was an attempt to curtail workers' rights to organize and bargain collectively. Under Proposition 22, "secondary boycotts" such as the ones the UFW conducted against Safeway grocery stores during the grape boycott would be illegal, as would "publicity directed against any trademark, trade name of generic (species) nature of agricultural product." Growers could be granted injunctions automatically when a strike or boycott was made against California's agricultural products. The initiative would also place severe restrictions on who could participate in elections for union representation. If it passed Proposition 22 would have likely eliminated up to 75 percent of Mexican American farm workers from participation in union elections.

LeRoy Chatfield took the assignment from Chavez to manage a grassroots political campaign in the state to defeat the growers' initiative. For a time, labor activists who were working on the lettuce boycott now traveled across California handing out literature and bumper stickers, lining up potential voters, especially in Latino communities, and standing on corners holding large signs that read "Justice for Farm Workers, No on 22." They set up a tent city in Lincoln Park in East Los Angeles to house hundreds of farm workers who left their work in the fields temporarily to work on the campaign.

The campaign organizers carefully divided the city into grids to take advantage of the various demographic conditions. They were on the job from dawn to dusk coordinating transportation, setting up phone banks, shuttling volunteers as they knocked on door after door.

The UFW was not alone in its massive drive to stop Proposition 22. The state Democratic Party, the AFL-CIO, and various charitable and religious organizations gave time and money. Although growers had deep pockets to run many advertisements on radio and television in support of the measure, the results on election night became a testament to the commitment and dedication of thousands of individuals who, most for the first time in their lives, immersed themselves in the most direct kind of political contact possible. From those thousands of men and women whose hands they shook, whose voices were on the phones, and who honked from their cars when passing the campaigners, and who held signs on the street corners thundered a resounding vote of support. The tally on election night was 58 percent no and 42 percent yes.

The Prop 22 election marked a significant turning point in Latino voter participation in California and a model of grassroots organizing that would spawn increasing numbers of electoral successes in coming years.

The UFW would increasingly target races in California and in other states to influence elections. The host of community organizers among the top echelon of UFW leaders—Chavez, Huerta, and their associates—became, in time, adroit and crafty political organizers. Huerta said later, "You've got to participate on the political level—supporting progressive candidates and helping them get elected. The corporate world does the same thing with money. Since working people don't have money, you've got to get out there and organize and help people get elected. You then have to keep that relationship going with that legislator" (Aledo and Alvarado 2006, 13).

Continuing to Battle the Teamsters

Despite its victories and its recognition as a fully chartered union under the AFL-CIO, the UFW leaders realized that consolidating the union's gains and growing its power were major challenges. The Teamsters, for example, remained eager to oust the farm workers from the Chavez union. They had the support of growers, California politicians, and, of course, the White House. The Teamsters had been the only major union to support Richard Nixon his 1968 campaign for president. In 1972, Charles Colson, one of

Nixon's advisors, sent a memo to several federal departments emphasizing the administration's desire that the Teamsters prevail in their struggle with Chavez. "We will be criticized if this thing gets out of hand and there is violence," he wrote. "But we must stick to our position. The Teamsters Union is now organizing in the area and will probably sign up most of the grape growers this coming spring and they will need our support against the UFW" (Levy 2007, 473).

Indeed, in early 1973 the farm workers' three-year contracts were up for renegotiation. Once again, the Teamsters loomed as a major threat. Despite the earlier jurisdictional agreements between the UFW and the Teamsters that farm workers would be under the province of the UFW, the Teamsters again reneged.

On April 14, 1973, more than 30 three-year contracts that Chavez had signed with growers in the Coachella Valley expired. Only two growers decided to renew those contracts. Thirty others signed with the Teamsters. A bitter Chavez charged that the agreements "weren't contracts, they were marriage licenses. Tomorrow you will see the growers and the Teamsters skipping hand in hand into the fields on their honeymoon" ("Again, *la Huelga*" 1973, 85).

The move triggered a series of strikes by Chavez and his union that started in Coachella and moved into the San Joaquin Valley. Supported by millions of dollars in aid from the AFL-CIO, approximately 10,000 farm workers walked out of the fields. Some began singing the well-known civil rights movement anthem, "We Shall Overcome."

Again, the strikers faced tough strong-arm tactics. Many were arrested or beaten. It was not the attackers, however, that went to jail. Throughout the summer local judges, with close personal and political ties to the growers, issued injunctions limiting legitimate strike activity. More than 3,500 farm workers were jailed in 1973. On April 20, 1973, for example, 135 picketers were arrested for violating a court injunction and sent to jail. One of those arrested was Linda Chavez, Cesar's daughter.

In late June 1973, two cars drove next to a trailer in which Francisco Campos lived with his wife and young daughter. Goons burned down the trailer. Fortunately the family survived with their lives. Campos who had joined the UFW a few months earlier told investigators that the Teamsters had warned him weeks earlier that they were going to burn down his home if he did not back off his strike activities. They stuck to their word. He stuck to his commitment to *La Causa*. It was a mission, he said, that he would never abandon.

In July 1973, Gallo Brothers, the nation's largest winery, struck a blow against the NFW. The company signed a four-year contract with the Teamsters. In announcing the agreement, the company declared that the workers voted 150 to 1 in favor of the Teamsters; what the company did not tell the press was that nearly all of the regular workers were on strike when the vote was taken. Those workers supported the NFW.

And so the labor battle raged. Other wineries refused to negotiate with the NFW. The local police, especially in Kern and Tulare counties, turned especially aggressive against the strikers. These were echoes from the Deep South and the civil rights movement—beatings with billy clubs, vicious dogs with long leashes, mace, metal pipes, baseball bats, tire irons, deputies in riot gear creating their own riots, police and strikebreaker goons getting in the faces of the protestors and yelling racial and ethnic insults. Police helicopters swept low attempting to scatter picketers with the dirt raised by the swirling blades. In Arvin, California, a farm worker named Juan de la Cruz, was shot down and killed. And, as in the civil rights movement, the protestors filled the jails to the point that jails choked to the breaking point. One of those arrested was Dorothy Day, former editor of the *Catholic Worker*, now 76 years old. On July 21, the Kern County sheriff released more than 100 strikers because the jail had no place for them.

In Fresno, the courts, in four months, issued 58 injunctions against the strikers and arrested more than 3,500 protestors. Nearly 2,000 went to jail, including 70 priests and nuns. At the Giumarra Vineyards in Lamont, protestors surrounded by Kern County deputies and strikebreaker thugs hired by the company kneeled down to pray. Undeterred, the police and goons charged the kneeling group, beat them with clubs, and sprayed mace. Chavez compared the treatment of the union members and farm workers to that of the protestors in the civil rights campaign in Selma, Alabama.

On August 13, 1973, Fresno authorities decided to release all of the strikers. The bureaucratic nightmare facing the courts of Fresno would have been daunting to say the least. One of those freed was Father Eugene Boyle of San Francisco who had been in jail for more than two weeks. At a meeting on the lawn in front of the courthouse, Father Boyle told hundreds of farm workers, "This is the greatest number of religious persons ever jailed in the United States. I hope it says something about our deep and profound belief in your cause. We know you will overcome" (Levy 2007, 505).

The fierce, heated battle with the growers and Teamsters continued in the late summer of 1973. But with union funds depleted from the strike,

Chavez decided once again to shift tactics. Five hundred farm workers left in caravans of cars headed to destinations in every part of the country. They were on the move to increase the intensity of the boycott.

In a letter distributed in cities across the United States, Chavez pleaded for consumers to back the union in this critical time. "You are the crucial element they cannot control . . . please boycott *all* grapes and Gallo wines and don't buy or eat iceberg (head) lettuce unless you are sure it bears our label. . . . Please join with us in our struggle for self-determination and dignity" (Chavez 1974).

The boycott letter and the work of his lieutenants in the field to influence the public were only partially successful. Chavez faced formidable and determined enemies and a growing belief among even some of his closest supporters that the union could not ultimately prevail in a protracted war with the growers.

Conrado Rodriguez, one of the NFW members who traveled from California to Washington, D.C., to participate in the boycott, told a reporter about one of the special difficulties facing many field workers who had suddenly found themselves in the middle of a major labor movement. "When I came to boycott," he said, "I speak only about 10 percent. Now, I speak about 50 percent. . . . It's difficult to understand when people ask questions. I never had an education. I had to work in the fields . . . in the fields it is not necessary to speak English. . . . In this kind of cause, sometimes people don't understand what you want. . . . I have to learn the words. Boycott grapes. Boycott lettuce" (Rose 1990, 286).

As the union gained new supporters such Conrado Rodriguez, the spirits of long-time Chavez allies who had been with him since the beginning remained high. For example, Gilbert Padilla, Chavez's valued friend from their days in the CSO, traveled to Washington, D.C., to become director of the boycott in the nation's capital. Padilla enlisted the help various union groups as well as clergy and students to set up picket lines, especially at Safeway stores. He gave speeches at AFL-CIO conventions in neighboring states such as Maryland, Virginia, and the Carolinas. The steel union was especially receptive to the boycott, contributing both manpower and donations.

As the growers began to feel the impact of the boycott, Chavez sought to deepen its impact by expanding its influence to Europe. In the fall of 1974, he planned a trip to Europe to visit various leaders in the European labor movement. Financed by gifts from the World Council of Churches, Dorothy Day, and several European labor unions, Chavez, Helen, and others left the United States on September 16.

In talks with various union heads in London, Oslo, Stockholm, and other European cities, Chavez was welcomed warmly and given assurances that their organizations would assist in the boycott. While in Europe he spoke with various kinds of groups, from construction workers to carpenters. He spoke about organizing and the value of unions and the power of boycotts.

The highlight of the trip for Chavez and the focus of the international press on the trip was Chavez's visit to the Vatican to meet with Pope Paul VI. In words that had deep personal vindication to Chavez who had infused the farm worker movement with religious teaching and fervor, Pope Paul VI said on September 25, 1974: "We wish to tell you of the real joy that is ours to be informed of the fidelity of the people of your culture and origin, our beloved sons and daughters, to the Church of Christ and to know of their generous endeavor to foster adherence to their glorious Catholic spirit. We know, in particular, of your sustained effort to apply the principles of Christian social teaching. . . . We pray that this laudable spirit of cooperation will continue and that, through the all-powerful assistance of the Lord, harmony and understanding will be promoted with liberty and justice for all" (Statement by Pope Paul VI 1974).

On the Political Campaign Trail Again: Fighting for Democrat Jerry Brown—1974

After eight years of dealing with the intractable opposition of Governor Ronald Reagan, Chavez and his union looked forward to the election of 1974. Here was an opportunity to help elect a man and a party to the executive mansion in Sacramento that could help the union legislatively in a major way.

The Democratic candidate was Jerry Brown, son of former governor Pat Brown. With an unusual educational background, including Jesuit studies as well as a Yale Law School degree, Brown had been elected California's secretary of state in 1970. After winning the Democratic primary, Brown faced off against Houston Flournoy, the California state controller.

In 1974, Brown visited *La Paz* to seek Chavez's endorsement for his gubernatorial campaign. "The place was totally off the beaten path," Brown remembered later, "yet there were hundreds of people around—mostly young and with infectious vitality and enthusiasm. It was clear that the United Farm Workers was a movement. Nuns were typing in the outer office, herb tea was served along with vegetarian food in the common dining room, and young volunteers went about their work with a sense of mission. Frankly, I was drawn to it. The critics kept repeating that Chavez had to form a real union that knew how to get along with management and service collective bargaining contracts. True enough, but from my point of view, the UFW was on the forefront of working for genuine social change—not merely its illusion—and that required precisely the dedication and sacrifice which Chavez inspired" (Brown 1993, 2).

Brown and Chavez already shared much mutual respect. Brown was supportive of *La Causa* and other progressive causes and saw the UFW as a strong ally. Indeed, Brown hired LeRoy Chatfield, who had led the UFW's political blitz against Proposition 22, as a top campaign aide.

Chavez and his lieutenants were ready to mobilize forces to help Brown; nevertheless, they wanted specific assurances that, if elected governor, he would support legislation favorable to California's farm workers, a law that would protect the rights of those working in the harvest fields freely to exercise collective bargaining and other activities enjoyed by other labor unions to protect their workers.

So determined was Chavez to secure Brown's assurances of supporting legislation in return for the union's active political participation that several farm workers and college students carrying the union's Aztec eagle flag appeared at Brown's campaign headquarters. UFW counsel Jerry Cohen had told the delegation not to leave Brown's door until the prospective governor gave them his word that he would push for such legislation. Brown agreed and announced support of such a bill.

With the help of the union's vigorous work on the campaign trail, Brown triumphed in the November election. For the first time in the history of his union, Cesar Chavez now had a friend in the governor's mansion.

LeRoy Chatfield, with no prior experience in political organizing, had now successfully run UFW's two massive grassroots campaigns. In reaching out to individuals who had never previously voted, mobilizing phone banks, pursuing door-to-door canvassing, gaining access to the press, and dissecting the voting blocs of the state district by district, Chatfield and his colleagues had created a model for the union and for other labor and Latino political organizers. Chavez and his union had now become a dynamic political force in state politics.

Chavez, the Farm Workers, and the Chicano Movement

The turbulent decade of the 1960s, rocked by assassinations, the civil rights movement and its violent clashes, and the ever-deepening divide over the war in Vietnam, also saw the rise of a movement to enhance social and political justice for Mexican Americans. The word *Chicano*, once a slur endured by Latino minorities, now became a word of ethnic pride and potential.

In New Mexico in 1966 Reies Lopez Tijerina founded the *Alianza Federal de Pueblos Libres* ("Federal Alliance of Land Grants"), a group dedicated to an improbable fight to reclaim Spanish and Mexican land grants held by Mexicans and Indians before the U.S.-Mexican War. In his quest to claim a part of a national forest reserve for Mexican American inheritance, he invaded and occupied a courthouse and inflicted a gunshot wound on a deputy sheriff, an action that led to his incarceration. His movement, quixotic and hopeless, nevertheless gained much notice and helped galvanize Mexicans and Mexican Americans across the Southwest.

In Denver, Colorado, in 1965, Rodolfo (Corky) Gonzales, an ex-prizefighter, wrote an epic poem called "I am Joaquin/*Yo Soy Joaquin*," in which he eloquently spoke about the historical struggles faced by Mexican Americans in the United States. In the mid-1960s he founded an urban civil rights and cultural movement called the Crusade for Justice. In 1968, Gonzales led a Chicano contingent to the Poor People's March on Washington, D.C., and issued a "Plan of the Barrio," which demanded better housing, education, and restitution of pueblo lands. Gonzales was also an organizer of the Annual Chicano Youth Liberation Conference, which brought together large numbers of Chicano youth from throughout the United States and provided them with opportunities to express their views on self-determination. The first conference in March 1969 produced a document, "*El Plan Espiritual de Aztlan* ('The Spiritual Plan of Aztlan')," which developed the concept of ethnic nationalism and self-determination in the struggle for Chicano liberation.

In East Los Angeles, David Sanchez and other Chicanos founded the Young Citizens for Community Action (YCCA). As they began donning brown berets, the organization's members became popularly known by their hats. The Brown Berets, established as a group whose main function was to address social problems such as police brutality and the lack of social activities among Latinos, quickly attained a militant aura, some of them carrying machetes and talking tough about Anglos. Mostly the group came to prevent, not instigate, eruptions of violence.

In 1968 hundreds of Chicano students from several high schools in East Los Angeles, including Garfield, began a political campaign protesting poor-quality education, overcrowded conditions, and racist curriculums. In early March, they walked out of their classes. They called the protests "blowouts."

In the late 1960s, a group of students in Texas formed the Mexican American Youth Organization (MAYO) that began using the term *Raza Unida* as a slogan and a description of their goals to develop grassroots activism, promote pride in being Chicano, attack racism in the schools and in local and state government, and develop a political agenda. In 1970, MAYO members in Crystal City, Texas, established a political party and named it *El Partido de la Raza Unida*, which changed to *Raza Unida* Party when they filed for official recognition at the state level. The party eventually spread to chapters in cities across the country.

Throughout the 1960s and early 1970s, the Chicano movement increased ethnic pride, labor activism, and sought to remedy, through social and political action, the educational and community needs of Latinos. The movement produced a new generation of activists and leaders who brought to national attention a variety of issues vital to the Mexican American community. One of their heroes was Cesar Chavez. His movement of social justice for farm workers, steeped in Mexican American culture, speaking to the rights of ethnic minorities, and demonstrating the power of community and political organization, stood as a towering symbol to the Chicano movement.

Nevertheless, as Chavez often pointed out, his labor union and his crusade in behalf of farm workers was not, as such, a Chicano movement. From the beginning his work included Filipinos, blacks, and other minorities, laborers who suffered under oppression and in whose behalf Chavez sought to mobilize their strength, energy, and, most important, their power to change the conditions under which they were forced to work.

But in fighting for the farm workers, Chavez also believed that he was fighting a battle on behalf of the entire Mexican American community, one emerging from a stereotype of the lounging peasant under a sombrero. "What Cesar wanted to reform was the way he was treated as a man," said his brother Richard. "We always talked about change, but how could we go about it?" ("The Little Strike" 1969, 20).

The Death of El Cortito

To the farm worker in the field, one of the great enemies was a simple tool that growers provided to the workers. It was a short-handled hoe called *el cortito* ("the short one"). Lettuce growers, maintaining that the implement was the fastest and most efficient, insisted that the workers use it. Get rid of the short-handled hoe, the growers argued, and the thinning and weeding would be mishandled, the growers would suffer crop losses, and many of them would go bankrupt. Even when the UFW provided testimony from numerous workers and physicians that the tool caused ruptured spinal disks, arthritis, and other serious back injuries, the lettuce growers would not allow other equipment.

Farm worker Roberto Acuna remembered the simple, short tool. "The hardest work would be thinning and hoeing with a short-handled hoe," he said. "The fields would be about a half a mile long. You would be bending and stooping all day. Sometimes I wouldn't have dinner or anything. I'd just go home and fall asleep and wake up just in time to go out to the fields again. There were times when I felt I couldn't take it anymore. It was 105 in the shade and I'd see endless rows of lettuce and I felt my back hurting. I felt the frustration of not being able to get out of the fields" (Terkel 1974, 34–37).

A farm worker picking melons in California's Imperial Valley. Such stoop labor, made worse by the insistence of the growers that workers use such tools as the short-handled hoe, caused severe back problems for large numbers. One of the principal goals of the farm workers movement was to force growers to improve working conditions in the fields. (Library of Congress)

Cesar Chavez had often been forced to use the tool in his early days in the lettuce fields and sugar-beet fields along the Sacramento River—along the rows after rows in the searing heat, alone with the hoe and the bag, for a grinding succession of hours and days hunched in an unforgiving shape. Some laborers called it "the devil's instrument." Like most farm workers, Chavez suffered debilitating back pain throughout his life, largely because of the twisted posture that the tool demanded. In those early days in the lettuce fields and in weeding sugar-beet fields along the Sacramento River, Chavez learned to despise the short-handled hoe as an extension of servitude of Mexican American workers in the fields by their employers. If the short-handled hoe was "the devil's instrument," Chavez concluded, the growers were doing the devil's bidding.

On January 1, 1975, after intense lobbying by the UFW through attorney "Mo" Jourdane and the support of California governor Jerry Brown, the short-handled hoe was finally outlawed. Challenged in the courts, the California Supreme Court took up *Sebastion Carmona et al. vs. Division of Industrial Safety*, and upheld the ban on the short-handled hoe. As Jourdane said of the victory, never again would new generations of farm workers face "a flat-out symbol of oppression—a way to keep control of workers and make them live humbled, stooped-over lives" ("Latino Attorney Honored" 2001).

Thus, the victory was not only a giant step forward in protecting the health and well-being of farm workers; it was also profoundly symbolic. The Mexican Americans who worked the fields would from this day forward stand taller.

References

"Again, *la Huelga*." 1973. *Time*, May 7, 85.

Aledo, Milagros, and Maria Alvarado. 2006. "Dolores Huerta at Seventy-Five: Still Empowering Communities; Interview with Co-Founder of United Farm Workers of America." *Harvard Journal of Hispanic Policy* (Annual): 13.

Araiza, Lauren. 2009. "'In Common Struggle against a Common Oppression': The United Farm Workers and the Black Panther Party, 1968–1973." *Journal of African American History* (Spring): 200.

Bardacke, Frank. 1993. "Cesar's Ghost: Decline and Fall of the U.F.W." *The Nation*, July 26, 130–136.

"The Black Eagle Wins." 1970. *Time*, August 10, 14.

"Breakthrough for *La Huelga*." 1969. *Time*, July 27, 36.

Brown, Edmund G. 1993. "Chavez Based His Life on Sharing and Frugality." *San Francisco Examiner*, April 25, 2.

Chavez, Cesar. 1974. "A Letter from Cesar Chavez." *New York Review of Books*, October 31. http://www.nybooks.com/articles/9359.

Chavez, Cesar. 2008. *An Organizer's Tale.* Edited by Ilan Stavans. New York: Penguin Classics, 227. http://www.farmworkermovement.org/essays/essays/Gringo justice.pdf.

Cohen, Jerry. "Gringo Justice: The United Farm Workers Union, 1967–1981," 8–9. The Papers of Jerry Cohen, Amherst College Library, 58. https://www.amherst. edu/media/view/85629/original/Gringojustice.pdf.

Daniel, Cletus E. 1987. "Cesar Chavez and the Unionization of California Farm Workers." In *Labor Leaders in America,* edited by Melvin Dubofsky and Warren Van Tine. Urbana: University of Illinois Press.

"Farm Union Pins Its Hopes on Victory in Coast Grape Strike." 1967. *New York Times,* October 2, 43.

Federal Bureau of Investigation. File on Cesar Chavez and the United Farm Workers, Part 5A. www.fbi.gov/foia/electronic reading room/cesar chavez and united farm workers.

Ferriss, Susan, and Ricardo Sandoval. 1997. *The Fight in the Fields: Cesar Chavez and the Farm Workers Movement.* New York: Harcourt Brace.

Ganz, Marshall. 2009. *Why David Sometimes Wins: Leadership, Organization, and Strategy in the California Farm Worker Movement.* New York: Oxford University Press.

Goepel, Wendy. "The Story of Wendy Goepel Brooks, Cesar Chavez and La Huelga." www.farmworkermovement.us/essays/.../007%20Brooks_Wendy.pdf.

Gordon, Jennifer. 2005. "Law, Lawyers, and Labor: The United Farm Workers Legal Strategy in the 1960s and 1970s and Role of Law in Union Organizing Today." *Pennsylvania Journal of Labor & Employment Law.* http://www.law.upenn. edu/journals/jbl/articles/volume8/issue1/Gordon8U.Pa.J.Lab.&Emp.L.1 (2005). pdf.

Huerta, Dolores. 2009. "We've Got the Power." *The Progressive,* July, 36.

John F. Kennedy Presidential Library, National Archives and Records Administration. 1968. Robert F. Kennedy Statement on Cesar Chavez, March 10. http://www. archives.gov/research/arc/.Bottom of Form.

"Latino Attorney Honored by Farm Workers' Rights Group." 2001. November 21. http://laprensasandiego.org/achieve/november21/lawyer.htm.

Levy, Jacques E. 2007. *Cesar Chavez: Autobiography of* La Causa. Minneapolis: University of Minnesota Press.

"The Little Strike That Grew to *La Causa.*" 1969. *Time,* July 4, 20.

Maika, Linda C., and Theo J. Maika. 1982. *Farm Workers, Agribusiness, and the State.* Philadelphia: Temple University Press.

Matthiessen, Peter. 1969. Sal Si Puedes: *Cesar Chavez and the New American Revolution.* New York: Random House.

National Historic Landmark Nomination: Forty Acres, National Park Service. http:// www.nps.gov/nhl/designations/samples/CA/FortyAcres.pdf.

Oliver, Myrna. 1999. "Lionel Steinberg; Grower Signed 1st Pact with Chavez's Union." *Los Angeles Times,* March 10, 15.

Robert F. Kennedy Conference. 2000. November 18. John F. Kennedy Library and Museum, Douglas Brinkley presentation. www.jfklibrary.org/~/Robert%F%20 Kennedy%20Conference.pdf.

Rodriquez, Richard. 2010. "Saint Cesar of Delano." *Wilson Quarterly* (Winter): 6–20.

Rose, Margaret. 1990. "From the Fields to the Picket Line: *Huelga* Women and the Boycott, 1965–1975." *Labor History* (Summer): 284–285.

Shaw, Randy. 2008. *Cesar Chavez, the UFW, and the Struggle for Justice in the 21st Century.* Berkeley: University of California Press.

St. Clair, Jeffrey. 2003. "Render unto Cesar: Songs and Dances from the Fields of Pain." *Dissident Voice,* April 12. http://dissidentvoice.org/Articles4/StClair_Chavez.htm.

"Statement by Pope Paul VI at Private Audience for Cesar Chavez and Party." 1974. September 25. http://chavez.cde.ca.gov/ModelCurriculum/Teachers/Lessons/Resources/Documents/PCCCP2_Box9_21_Statement_by_Pope_Paul_VI.pdf.

Terkel, Studs. 1974. *Working.* New York: Avon Books.

United Farm Workers. 2005. "Veterans of Historic Delano Grape Strike Mark 40th Anniversary with Two-Day Reunion in Delano and *La Paz.*" *El Malcriado,* Special Edition, September 17–18. http://www.ufw.org/_page.php?menu=research&inc=history/05.html.

Veterans of Hope Project. Interview with Dolores Huerta. http://www.veteransofhope.org/show.php?vid=51&tid=42&sid=69.

SEVEN

Wielding Political Power: The Agricultural Labor Relations Act of 1975

In early 1975 Chavez was now ready once again to take to the road to demonstrate the need for reform, ready to push strongly for state legislation to grant farm workers legal rights they heretofore lacked, ready to put pressure on Governor Jerry Brown to back up his campaign promise of supporting a farm worker bill.

The tactic would be the so-called March to Modesto. On February 22, 1975, several hundred members of the UFW began a 110-mile march from San Francisco to Modesto, headquarters of the E&J Gallo Winery. Other contingents of the march headed out from Stockton and Fresno. Gallo would thus be approached from the north, south, and west, in a kind of siege on the winemaker. Although just a few hundred marchers left San Francisco and the other locations, more than 15,000 people had joined them by the time they reached Modesto on March 1.

They stretched over a mile long, with farm workers singing labor songs, waving the union flag, engaging in conversations with onlookers along the route, chanting slogans—"Chavez si, Teamsters no; Gallo wine has got to go!" An ebullient Chavez met the marchers in Modesto and declared to the boisterous crowd that Gallo must now realize that the union was not going away.

After this show of strength, Chavez met with Brown. Now was the time, Chavez asserted, that farm workers legislation become a reality and not merely a campaign promise. After a succession of meetings, proposals and counterproposals, Brown, his assistants, and union representatives, especially Jerry Cohen, shaped the outlines of a bill that would represent a significant step in establishing bargaining rights for farm workers in California.

Picketers rally against Gallo wine. The E&J Gallo Winery, founded in Modesto, California, in 1943, was an intransigent foe of Chavez and his union. The UFW would continue its battles with Gallo well into the 21st century. (Wayne State University/ Walter P. Reuther Library)

After the bill was crafted by Brown's office, especially by California secretary of agriculture Rose Bird, Brown spoke with an array of interested parties—bishops and religious groups that supported Chavez, supermarket executives, and union officials. He sent out thousands of letters to enlist the broadest base of support. Later, Brown said, "I saw my role as a catalyst. I wanted that bill, and I brought all the forces together and constantly mixed them and made them interact in a way that made things possibly more propitious for solution" (Levy 2007, 531).

Legislators reached broad agreement on a bill on May 7, just 68 days after the Modesto march. The California State Senate passed the bill on May 26, the California State Assembly passed the bill two days later, and Brown signed the legislation into law on June 4, 1975. The act went into effect on August 28, 1975. Chavez was joyous.

For farm workers the passage of California's Agricultural Labor Relations Act was a legislative triumph of profound consequences, not necessarily for the economic gains it immediately afforded the workers, but the power it confirmed on them. With a preamble that declared the support of justice for all agricultural workers, the 1975 law represented the first bill of rights for farm workers in the continental United States, protecting the right of farm workers to unionize and boycott, and guaranteeing secret ballots in farm workers' union elections. It guaranteed farm worker unions a seven-day turnaround for secret ballot elections, important for a highly mobile workforce, and gave workers much stronger remedies for employer violations.

UFW counsel Jerry Cohen said later: "I was able to craft and then negotiate the details of the law with Governor Jerry Brown because of the pressures generated by ten years of organizational strife. Thousands of farm workers took responsibility for bettering their lives by striking, picketing, boycotting, and engaging in civil disobedience to fill rural California jails. When they struck, picketed, boycotted, and went to jail, they dealt me a strong hand which I simply played out. The coalition of forces which came together to support the law was extraordinary: growers sick of strikes, stores tired of boycott lines, and county officials who no longer wanted their jails filled with farm workers" (Cohen).

Under the provisions of the ALRA, a union was required to prove that it represented a majority of the workers. With the passage of the act, the UFW and the Teamsters would go head to head in elections at various California companies that hired farm workers. With this unprecedented opportunity to demonstrate that the majority of workers in these companies preferred Chavez's union, his lieutenants went to political war with fierce determination. A force of more than 200 volunteers fanned across harvest fields throughout agricultural areas all over the state cajoling, persuading workers to sign ballots on behalf of the UFW. When the individual elections at the companies ended, the UFW had prevailed in 214 companies, the Teamsters in 115.

On March 10, 1977, the Teamsters and the UFW reached a five-year jurisdictional agreement granting Chavez's union exclusive rights to represent the field workers covered by the Agricultural Labor Relations Act. The UFW agreed that the Teamsters would have labor jurisdiction in industries surrounding agricultural production, such as canneries, packing sheds, and frozen food operations.

After weeks of secret negotiations among union leaders, Chavez met with Teamsters president Frank Fitzsimmons near San Francisco to sign the agreement. Asked why the Teamsters had finally agreed to the jurisdictional divide with the UFW, Fitzsimmons said, "We now get in a position where we are not accused . . . . We are not the people suppressing the farm workers." Asked whether the peace that just broke out between the two unions would endure, Chavez emphasized that it was a written agreement negotiated with the top leadership. "Besides," he said, "It's ten years later, and we're tired of fighting each other" ("Cesar's Triumph" 1977, 70–71).

Thus, in the spring of 1977, Chavez enjoyed victory. Nevertheless, he knew, as well as anyone, that the union must press ahead with as much fire and ingenuity as it could muster. Enemies of the union lurked, and political fortunes were always suspect. But this was clearly a giant victory for Chavez. *Newsweek* ran a story entitled "Cesar's Triumph."

References

"Cesar's Triumph." 1977. *Newsweek*, March 21, 70–71.

Cohen, Jerry. "Gringo Justice: The United Farm Workers Union, 1967–1981," 8–9. The Papers of Jerry Cohen, Amherst College Library, 58. https://www.amherst.edu/media/view/85629/original/Gringojustice.pdf.

Levy, Jacques E. 2007. *Cesar Chavez: Autobiography of* La Causa. Minneapolis: University of Minnesota Press.

EIGHT

Cracks in the Foundation

With the creation of a farm workers' union, subsequent victories in several strike actions, the launching of formidable national boycotts, and the enormous legislative victory in 1975 of the passage of California's Agricultural Labor Relations Act, Cesar Chavez and his union had already achieved what most observers felt years earlier would be impossible. From a position near total anonymity and literally no financial assets, he, Dolores Huerta, and a few others had changed the face of farm labor for Mexican Americans in the California harvest fields. It is not surprising that a number of writers cited the biblical clash of David and Goliath in characterizing the farm labor movement. And yes, as Marshall Ganz, one of the union's central figures, titled a book in 2009, *David Sometimes Wins*.

By January 1978, the UFW had brought 25,000 new workers under contract. The benefits for farm workers were impressive: wages rose significantly, and many received health and pension benefits for the first time in their lives. At its height two years later, the UFW had more than 50,000 members under contract and as many as 50,000 more "affiliated" farm workers. In addition, because of the jurisdictional pact negotiated by Jerry Cohen and the UFW legal team in early March 1977, the Teamsters were no longer threatening to strike new farm worker deals with the growers. Cohen said, "I remember feeling that nothing could stop us. We had generated enough power to win contracts and the law, beating a strong coalition of forces: agribusiness, a multibillion dollar industry; the Teamsters; various recalcitrant small-minded local officials; and powerful enemies in high places" (Cohen).

But in the late 1970s, at a time of the great ascendancy of the UFW, internal pressures and tensions began to crack its foundation. Chavez seemed preoccupied with consolidating the gains the union had already achieved at the expense of aggressively continuing to recruit new members. He channeled much of the union's energy toward leveraging its political clout and maneuvering the political system to the union's advantage. He also began to focus more intently on making the organization something much more than a labor union.

LeRoy Chatfield, one of the clergymen who early on joined Chavez's efforts to organize farm workers wrote, "Cesar Chavez was committed to building something more than a union mostly concerned with wages and working conditions, he planned to empower communities of poor people—in this case, farm workers—by involving them in economic self-help programs and teaching them how to work cooperatively together for the benefit of the entire community. Even then, he was astraddle the philosophical divide: 'are we a union? or, are we a movement?' that would simmer on the back burner until the late 70's when the issue boiled over one last time and created a divide that could not be bridged" (Chatfield).

When such union leaders as Eliseo Medina, Marshall Ganz, and Jerry Cohen began to express views on possible union strategy and direction that diverged from those of Chavez, the union leader reacted defensively, exerting even more strongly his control over almost all organizational activity. Some of his lieutenants began, among themselves, to criticize his iron-fisted administration and dominance of union policy.

The first serious fracture erupted over a request by Jerry Cohen and his legal team for a slight increase in the low salaries each received from the union. Each of the lawyers could have commanded far greater salaries from other employers. But to Chavez, the request for additional salary seemed a failed test of purity. Although Chavez and Cohen continued to work together for a time under strained relations, within a few years the entire legal team would depart—individuals who had steered the union through rough waters and had, in most cases, prevailed in the courts. Their departure would prove to be a staggering loss.

Personal disagreements became increasingly combustible between Chavez and other of his lieutenants. Always with an aesthetic bent, Chavez suddenly became infatuated with a strange drug rehabilitation organization called Synanon and its leader Charles Dederich and demanded that his lieutenants engage in some of the practices of the cultlike group in order to receive purification. Whether from growing fatigue or depression, Chavez thus became increasingly detached from some of his closest associates.

Thus, the UFW in the late 1970s began to lose talented people, either by their own decision to leave or pushed out by Chavez himself. Philip Vera Cruz, onetime vice president of the union, said that the one thing the union would never tolerate was for people to criticize Cesar. "Cesar was seen as so important, so indispensable, that he became idolized and even viewed by some followers as omnipotent," Cruz said. "If a union leader is built up as a symbol and he talks like he was God, then there is no way you can have true democracy in the union because the members are just generally deprived of their right to reason for themselves" (Shaw 2008, 253).

In 1977, when Chavez, against the wishes of many of his friends, decided to meet with leaders of the authoritarian Marcos regime in the Philippines, Philip Vera Cruz, a Filipino and longtime opponent of the regime, became so outraged that he also left the union.

In the summer of 1978, after being elevated to second vice president, Eliseo Medina planned an ambitious organizing drive. But Medina, along with others, became gradually disillusioned with the direction from the top, which seemed scattered, suspicious, and lacking clear direction. Convinced that the union had abandoned most of its organizational zeal and was moving in the wrong direction, Medina left Chavez in late 1978. He would move on to a highly successful career with the Service Employees International Union, rising to the position of executive vice president. Through the force of a dynamic personality and fierce determination, Medina had, according to Dolores Huerta, become an heir apparent to Chavez. "He would have been president if he'd stayed," said Huerta. "We were so close," Medina recalled. "And then it began to fall apart. . . . At the time we were having our greatest success, Cesar got sidetracked. Cesar was more interested in leading a social movement than a union per se" (Pawel 2006, A1).

Marshall Ganz, the superb organizer who worked closely with Chavez for nearly two decades, saw the transformation of the UFW in organizational terms. "Despite frequent claims by critics that Chavez had more interest in leading a movement than in building a union," Ganz wrote, "he did not ignore the formidable administrative challenges the UFW faced." Chavez did face those challenging times with vigor and energy, and, indeed, many of the union's greatest accomplishments came when Ronald Reagan was governor of California and Richard Nixon was president. But the organizing efforts so critical in these times faded in the late 1970s. Chavez and his allies, Ganz wrote, "did not create an organizational infrastructure to meet these challenges. Instead, in the name of preserving the movement, Chavez consolidated his internal control so he could respond to these challenges on his own terms. Chavez's later moves stifled creative internal deliberation as he began to replace experienced UFW leaders with a new, younger cadre, for whom loyalty was the essential qualification" (Ganz 2009, 242).

Other internal disagreements battered the union. Officials in the UFW local field offices were not elected by the workers under contract in those areas, as they were in most other unions. Instead, they were appointed by the UFW executive board under the direct control of Chavez. New agreements negotiated with companies now provided for company-paid union representatives. These paid union reps seemed to Chavez a threat to his leadership. He even began to suspect that some of these union reps were planning to organize a separate union. From the beginning, Chavez knew there would be internal struggles—personal quarrels, differences in favored strategies, and the move by many confidants to other places and other jobs. But Chavez now seemed totally unwilling to sacrifice any of his personal control over union affairs.

Within the next few years, some of the top organizing leaders in the union left to find other avenues to fight for social justice. Gilbert Padilla had worked with both Chavez and Huerta before the advent of the union. His old friend's curious behavior and accusatory ranting puzzled and worried Padilla. He began to question Chavez's emotional state and was particularly angered when Chavez decided to abandon plans for a clinic in the city of Parlier, instead turning the site over to a builder as an investment opportunity for the union. "I knew Cesar was the man, el jefe," he said later, "but I didn't think the movement belonged to him. I thought it belonged to the workers." Padilla left the union (Pawel 2006, A1).

Aristeo Zambrano moved to Salinas in 1974 and got a job cutting broccoli at a UFW-organized company—Associated Produce. Elected to a UFW committee in 1976, he became a paid representative, lost favor with Chavez, and was fired. As he looked back, Zambrano said that Chavez had tried to make every decision in the union. "If a car in Salinas needed a new tire, we had to check with Cesar in La Paz. He controlled every detail of union business. And nobody was allowed to say Chavez made a mistake, even when he had." Zambrano recalled a closed meeting during a local strike in 1979 when Chavez announced that he had decided to call off the strike and to send the picket captains and strike coordinators to work on the ongoing boycott. "We thought the strike should be extended, not called off," Zambrano said. "Well, he couldn't call off the strike without our support, and we did continue to fight and we won. Which made us stronger. That meeting, and its aftermath, was a political challenge to Cesar. It meant that the situation in the union had changed. He was going to have to deal with us—with the direct representatives of the workers—and, in some way or other, share power with us." To this direct challenge to his authority, Chavez reacted harshly. Zambrano and others who defied his authority were banished from the union (Bardacke 1993).

In succeeding years, a number of the most valuable and productive members of the UFW departed amidst growing tensions, accusations, and misunderstandings. They included Marshall Ganz, Chris Hartmire, Jim Drake, Eliseo Medina, Jessica Govea, and LeRoy Chatfield. The organizational chaos and disruption ensuring from the loss of such key union figures left the UFW severely wounded.

The Lettuce Strike of 1979

Despite the internal turmoil within his ranks, Chavez, in January 1979, decided to launch a strike against 11 lettuce growers in the Imperial and Salinas valleys. At the onset of the strike, the UFW workers, acting with much precision and enthusiasm, seemed much different from the earlier days of union strikes when everyone, from management on down, was inexperienced, lurching ahead with little preparation. Now, field workers up and down the valleys, disciplined and prepared, went about the business of picketing and fending off grower intimidation with much grit and determination.

But on February 10, 1979, the lettuce strike turned deadly. Shortly before noon on day 22 of the strike, 27-year-old UFW member Rufino Contreras and a half dozen fellow strikers attempted to speak with a crew of scab laborers in a field owned by Mario Saikhon. Three armed foreman suddenly appeared and opened fire. As the strikers scattered back toward the public road, one was lying face down in the mud. It was Contreras. When Rufino's father and other strikers attempted to reenter the field to help Contreras, the foreman again opened fire. The confrontation lasted for more than an hour before the sheriff arrived and called for an ambulance. Contreras died at the hospital.

The three foremen were quickly released on bond. Soon, the local judge refused to try the men because he said there was no way to prove which of the three had fired the killing shot.

Rufino's brother, Jose, recalled that on Friday, February 9, "Rufino had just received the papers that his wife was eligible for the union's medical insurance and he was showing them to his friends. Like everybody, he was a good union member. He was proud of it and that day he was very happy" ("Major Themes in the Farmworkers Struggle").

On Wednesday, February 14, the Contreras family, joined by 9,000 farm workers and others including Governor Jerry Brown, attended the funeral. Chavez called February 10, 1979, "a day of infamy for farm workers. It was a day without hope. It was a day without joy. The sun didn't shine. The birds didn't sing. The rain didn't fall. Why was this such a day of evil?

Because on this day greed and injustice struck down our brother, Rufino Contreras. What is the worth of a man? What is the worth of a farm worker? Rufino and his father and his brother together gave the company 20 years of their labor. They were faithful workers who helped build up the wealth of their boss, helped build up the wealth of his ranch. What was their reward for their service and their sacrifice? When they petitioned for a more just share of what they themselves produce, when they spoke out against the injustice they endured, the company answered them with bullets. The company sent hired guns to quiet Rufino Contreras" ("Major Themes in the Farmworkers Struggle").

Chavez took his message and his anger on the road. Less than two months after the killing, Chavez said to a crowd at Harvard University's School of Government, "We asked for a little more money and the employers responded with bullets. The hunting season is on every time we hit the picket line. . . . It is unfortunate that the men, women, and children who plant and harvest the greatest quantity of food ever in this country don't have enough for themselves" (Forst 1979).

The violence continued. When police lobbed tear-gas canisters into bands of strikers on a number of occasions, the strikers responded by lobbing the canisters back at the police. They were, of course, dragged off to the police station. Numerous fights broke out. Chavez continually pointed out to newspaper reporters and anyone else who would listen that all the violence was almost always triggered by those opposed to the strike.

In late summer of 1979, Chavez escalated his protests. For 12 days, two separate groups of farm workers near San Francisco began a march to Salinas. As in the now-famous march to Sacramento that had been so effective for the union years earlier, the marchers gained numbers as they sang, chanted slogans, and passed by the summer harvest fields. Many farm workers simply threw down their tools and joined up. By the time the marchers reached Salinas, the group numbered more than 25,000 individuals. Chavez, who fasted for part of the journey, looked wan and tired. Yet, when the marchers reached Salinas, they filled the center of town and celebrated.

Losing Ground in Sacramento

In November 1982, Republican George Deukmejian, who received nearly $1 million in campaign contributions from growers, became governor of California. Chavez and other UFW leaders realized that, once again, major challenges and fights loomed. The growers helped elect Deukmejian; he did not disappoint them.

Soon, he packed the Agricultural Labor Relations Board with representatives who supported the interests of the growers and who had little use for the farm labor election law. Members of the board who had taken positions sympathetic to Chavez soon found themselves transferred to other agencies or out of California state government altogether. Under the new leadership of the board, enforcement of election law became mired in delay and inaction. Growers soon realized that if they simply ignored the farm workers law, they would not be prosecuted. Even on some of the farms that had held elections and had chosen the UFW as their union, the process came to a grinding halt with the Republicans in control in Sacramento. The board itself took a 27 percent cut in the state budget with little complaint from its members.

The growers felt freed from what they regarded as union and state government strangulation. For example, they began more openly to shuttle nonunion labor from Mexico into the harvest fields.

In the winter months in California, with the harvests shifting south, migrant workers would gather as early as 1:00 A.M. in Calexico, across the border from their homes in Mexicali, and wait in lines, sometimes for hours, along the main street until they were picked up by contractors hired by the companies. Trucked to the fields, the workers would spend long days and then be hauled back to Calexico in the late afternoons. Chris Schneider, one of the UFW's lawyers, told of the ways in which various companies operated in violation of the 1975 act: "We've got compelling proof that a lot of these companies, like Sun Harvest and Growers Exchange and Bruce Church, are just changing their names, firing union workers, lowering wages and continuing operations with labor contractors who hire workers from the shape-up at 4 A.M. along the main street in Calexico, and then truck them to the fields at rock-bottom wages." Gradually, the UFW would over the next several years lose most of its contracts with growers (Street 1985, 330).

As the political landscape withered under the new administration, Chavez and his union fought against potentially demoralizing circumstances. And on September 21, 1983, they again faced tragedy. At Sikkema Dairy near Fresno, a young farm worker named Rene Lopez was shot to death by company thugs harassing UFW representatives. Twenty-one years old, bilingual, a recent graduate of Carruthers High School in Fresno, Lopez had been asked by coworkers at the diary to be their spokesman in asking for an increase in the paltry wages being paid by the company.

When company owner Fred Sikkema threatened to fire some of the workers and to force the remaining ones to do additional labor with no additional pay, Lopez approached the UFW for advice. Soon, the workers went on strike, and, at the same time, gathered to decide whether to join the UFW. On the day of the election, shortly after he has cast his own ballot to join the UFW, a company enforcer enticed Lopez to walk toward his car and then shot him point black in the face. The gunman was sentenced to seven years in prison, but the district attorney refused to file charges against Fred Sikkema for hiring the killer.

At Lopez's funeral in Fresno, UFW workers from around California gathered to pay tribute. One small wreath said "*Querido Novio*" ("Beloved Sweetheart"). Lopez was to have been married on the weekend he was murdered.

Chavez said at his funeral, "Rene was young, but he had already felt the call to social justice. His mother, Dolores, said that he came home one day with the stub of his union authorization card, showed it to her, and said, 'Here is my first union card, now I am important, now I am a man.' . . . But death comes to all of us and we do not get to choose the time or the circumstances of our dying. The hardest thing of all is to die rightly. Rene Lopez died rightly; he is a martyr for justice" ("Renee Lopez").

Against the ravishing political tide in Sacramento and the renewed power of the growers to ignore his union, Chavez again sought to regain the initiative. "We thought we could redress our grievances through the board," Chavez said, "but that is not to be. That is definitely not to be. We have to change our tactics now" (Street 1985, 330).

In a number of public speeches, Chavez lashed out at Republicans, both in the California state house and in the White House. In a speech in September 1984, he accused the GOP of being enemies of the poor and the workers, giving wealthy Americans outrageous tax cuts while at the same time driving down the wages of the middle and lower classes. This was class warfare at its most degrading. Of President Reagan himself, Chavez, in a bitter quip, characterized him as a man with an extraordinary sense of religion and politics. In Reagan's eyes, Chavez said, there is a special place for both government and God. Reagan's administration gives to the rich; his God is there for the rest of Americans.

On Sunday, February 10, 1985, six years to the day of UFW striker Rufino Contreras's murder in the lettuce fields, Chavez led 3,000 workers on a six-mile memorial march from the town of Heber to Calexico. At a rally in Calexico, he told the marchers that Deukmejian was conspiring with growers to undermine the farm labor law and charged that, since he had taken office, 4,000 farm workers had been fired and had lost $80 million in wages. He called on the workers to protest in Calexico by engaging in a one-day sick-out in honor of Contreras and what he had died trying to achieve.

Realizing that seeking redress of grievances through the farm labor board under Republican control was futile, Chavez made plans to boycott certain broccoli and lettuce growers. As one UFW member told a reporter: "We really have no other alternative. It's clear that the law isn't working. That means you're going to see a lot of marches, more boycotts and economic action at the workplace. It's the only thing a lot of these growers understand" (Street 1985, 330).

Looking down the road two or three decades, Chavez was still optimistic. The new boycotts and marches, he said, would drive home to Americans the continuing need to reform the harvest fields of California and the farm labor areas in the rest of the United States. And it would be the Latino community in California that would turn the page on state and national politics.

Crusading against Pesticide Poisoning

Chavez decided to increase the pressures on the growers in another controversial area—the use of pesticides. As part of the grape boycott, he would launch a campaign called "Wrath of Grapes"—a wordplay takeoff on John Steinbeck's famous novel about the tribulation of farm workers in California and also the title for a short documentary film the UFW produced claiming evidence of birth defects and high cancer rates of farm workers caused by the use of pesticides in the southern San Joaquin Valley.

The pesticides, Chavez claimed, mostly applied on crops from airplanes, often drifted far afield, landing on living areas of farm workers and their families. Even when the poisons accurately hit their targets, the workers had to labor amidst the chemicals on and around the plants they picked. Chavez and the union began to show studies suggesting that children were especially vulnerable to the pesticides, with illnesses as varied as cancer and liver disease.

One farm worker later remembered often being sprayed by airplanes. "You came out of there looking like Santa Claus," he said, "you were so full of white powder." The white powder was DDT (Rodriguez 2010).

The UFW emphasized in its new information campaign that thousands of acres of California soil had been irrevocably contaminated by the prodigious use of the chemicals. Continuous use of the pesticides in such quantities, the UFW charged, would ultimately produce an ecological disaster.

A mother holds her baby born with a birth defect likely caused by pesticide use, circa 1990s. The UFW's second grape boycott focused on the use of pesticides, claiming evidence of high cancer rates and birth defects caused by the extensive use of pesticides, especially in the San Joaquin Valley. Chavez called his new campaign the "Wrath of Grapes," a wordplay on John Steinbeck's famous novel about the plight of California farm workers. (Wayne State University/Walter P. Reuther Library)

The UFW focused on five pesticides that had been listed as possibly hazardous by the Environmental Protection Agency. As the charges and countercharges over the pesticide issue mounted, both sides armed themselves with studies and scientists producing a flurry of conflicting evidence. Chavez himself began to arrange speaking engagements around the country to press the issue.

"A powerful self-serving alliance between the California governor and the 14 billion dollar agricultural industry," Chavez charged, "has resulted in a systematic and reckless poisoning of not only California farm workers but of grape consumers throughout our nation and Canada." Referring to the deliberate scuttling of the provisions of the 1975 Agricultural Labor Relations Act, Chavez said, "Blatant violations of California labor laws are constantly ignored. And worst of all, the indiscriminate and even illegal use of dangerous pesticides has radically increased in the last decade causing illness, permanent disability and even death. We must not allow the Governor of California and the selfish interests of California grape growers to threaten lives throughout North America" ("Cesar Chavez's Wrath of Grapes Speech" 1986).

The Longest Fast

In the summer of 1988 Chavez began another fast. Now 61 years old, he sought to draw attention to the toxic chemicals that threatened farm workers in the field. He called it "The Fast for Life."

This time, Chavez decided to involve in his fast his supporters and those who agreed with his stance. Picket lines formed in various cities composed of volunteers, some of whom agreed to join Chavez in his water-only fast. In New York, Boston, Detroit, Philadelphia, San Francisco, and Los Angeles, demonstrators formed picket lines, handed out literature, and carried signs that read "Don't Buy Poison Grapes."

Comedian Dick Gregory visited Chavez in Delano as did Kathleen Kennedy Townsend and other Kennedy family members. In New York local community and labor activists joined in holding demonstrations that persuaded a number of grocery stores to remove grapes from their shelves.

The fast and its demonstrations across the country were reminiscent of the early days of Chavez's national protest movement, a harkening back, a revival—fists in the air with shouts of "*La Huelga*"; celebrities such as Martin Sheen, Edward James Olmos, Lou Diamond Phillips, and Ethel Kennedy on television and radio announcing their support of Chavez and his cause.

After 36 days, a weary and malnourished Chavez gave in to the entreaties of his family and doctors and ended the fast. On August 21, 1988, more than 6,000 people gathered to celebrate, including Chavez's 96-year-old

Poster supporting lettuce boycott, 1978. The UFW's national boycotts of grapes, lettuce, and other products used artistic weapons to much effect. With the inspiring union symbol of the Aztec eagle highlighted in the background, this depiction of farm workers in the field attracted wide attention. (Library of Congress)

mother, Juana. At his right at the ceremony sat Ethel Kennedy and at his left civil rights leader Jesse Jackson.

He had lost 33 pounds from his 165-lb. frame. Through an hour-long Mass he frequently wiped tears from his face, and, finally, ate a piece of bread handed to him by Ethel Kennedy. "Today is a special day because we bring Cesar Chavez back to the world of the living," Kerry Kennedy, 28, told the spectators. Her father, Robert F. Kennedy, had been with Chavez when he broke his first fast in 1968. Jackson said, "The children of this valley have a right to breathe free. This is an appeal of mercy. Stop the grapes and save the children!" (Plummer 1988, 52).

A few weeks after Chavez ended his fast, Dolores Huerta endured a different kind of physical suffering in the fight against pesticides. While picketing against the Republican Party's refusal to act against pesticide poisoning of farm workers, Huerta was clubbed by a police officer. Rushed to the hospital, the 58-year-old UFW veteran suffered serious injury that included several broken ribs and a ruptured spleen that had to be removed. The attack by the police, captured on film by local television cameras, led to a number of lawsuits that forced the San Francisco Police Department to change some of its practices regarding crowd control. Huerta received a large court judgment against the police and donated the money to the union.

For Huerta it was a vivid reminder of the violence that she and thousands of other protestors had faced for many years. Some had lost their lives. She had nearly lost hers.

Full Circle

Chavez continued to campaign against pesticides into the 1990s. He fought in the courts, as growers tried to use such legal loopholes as switching ownership rights to void previous contracts with the union. He went from town to town trying to convince consumers not to eat grapes until grapes were pesticide-free.

In 1992, Chavez and his son-in-law, UFW vice president, Arturo Rodriguez, orchestrated walkouts in vineyards in the San Joaquin and Coachella valleys. They succeeded in winning pay hikes. Most important, the victories demonstrated to younger activists that nonviolent protest was still a potent force. Not only in California, but in cities in the Midwest young activists took on such industrial giants as Campbell Soup, and young labor leaders took their place in Hawaii, Oregon, Pennsylvania, New Jersey, and other states.

In April 1993, Chavez traveled back to the tiny southwest Arizona town of San Luis, near Yuma, where the Chavez family, a half century earlier, had been forced out of their small farm and had begun their lives as migrant farm workers. He was there to help UFW attorneys defend the union against a lawsuit brought by Bruce Church Inc., a giant Salinas, California–based lettuce and vegetable producer.

In the days before his court appearance, Chavez, already exhausted, decided to begin a short fast in order, he told his friends, to regain moral strength. After the fast and after testifying for two days on the witness stand, Chavez was driven around Yuma by a longtime friend, David Martinez. They passed the playground where Cesar and his brother Richard had played stickball. When he retired for the evening, he took with him a book about Native American art and went to sleep. On April 23, 1993, he died during the early morning hours. He was only 30 miles from the spot where the Immaculate Conception Church once stood, where he had been baptized. At age 66, he died young. His father lived to 101; his mother to 99.

On April 29, 1993, at the UFW headquarters in Delano, more than 40,000 mourners honored Chavez. There were scores of famous entertainers and individuals of high standing. But mostly there were farm workers.

Many holding their children's hands, they lined up and filed slowly beside the plain pine box built by his brother Richard. Mostly they were Latinos, fathers and mothers who said that they wanted to be able to share with their children in celebrating the life of a man of greatness, a man of their own.

References

Bardacke, Frank. 1993. "Cesar's Ghost: Decline and Fall of the U.F.W." *The Nation*, July 26, 130–136.

"Cesar Chavez's Wrath of Grapes Speech." 1986. Milestone Documents. http://www.milestonedocuments.com/documents/full-text/cesar-chavezs-wrath-of-grapes-speech/.

Chatfield, LeRoy. "Forty Acres Delano: United Farm Workers." Farmworker Movement Documentation Project. http:/farmworkermovement.com/category/commentary/forty-acres-delano-united-farm-workers/.

Cohen, Jerry. "Gringo Justice: The United Farm Workers Union, 1967–1981," 8–9. The Papers of Jerry Cohen, Amherst College Library, 58. https://www.amherst.edu/media/view/85629/original/Gringojustice.pdf.

Forst, Edward. 1979. "Chavez Speaks on Lettuce Workers Strike." *Harvard Crimson*, April 6. http://www.thecrimson.com/article/1979/4/6/chavez-speaks-on-lettuce-workers-.

Ganz, Marshall. 2009. *Why David Sometimes Wins: Leadership, Organization, and Strategy in the California Farm Worker Movement*. New York: Oxford University Press.

"Major Themes in the Farmworkers Struggle; Si Se Puede!" Cesar E. Chavez and His Legacy Exhibit, Rufino Contreras (1951–1979). http://clnet.ucla.edu/research/chavez/themes/ufw/rufino.htm.

Pawel, Miriam. 2006. "UFW: A Broken Contract." *Los Angeles Times*, January 8, A1.

Plummer, William. 1988. "Cesar Chavez Breaks His Longest Fast as His Followers Pray for an End to the Grapes of Wrath." *People Weekly*, September 5, 62.

"Rene Lopez." http://clnet.ucla.edu/research/chavez/themes/ufw/rene.htm.

Rodriguez, Joe. 2010. Exhibit in San Jose Triggers Memories of Farm Labor for Old Braceros." San Jose *Mercury News*, April 1. http://www.mercurynews.com/joe-rodriguez/ci_14803741?nclick_check=1.

Shaw, Randy. 2008. *Cesar Chavez, the UFW, and the Struggle for Justice in the 21st Century*. Berkeley: University of California Press.

Street, Richard Steven. 1985. "It's Boycott Time in California." *The Nation*, March 23, 330.

NINE

The Continuing Fight

In the rise of the farm worker movement, Cesar Chavez, Dolores Huerta, and the other leaders melded strong passion, commitment, and belief from various elements: religious heritage anchored in Christian social justice practiced by individuals and groups from all faiths; militant, nonviolent social protest principles exemplified in the American civil rights movement and in the teachings of Indian leader Mahatma Gandhi; and the community organizing skills developed by Saul Alinsky, Fred Ross, and other leaders of community organizations fighting for equal rights and justice for the workers and others left on the outside of the American dream.

The mantle of leadership of the UFW now fell to Arturo Rodriguez, the husband of Linda Chavez, Cesar's daughter. First active with the UFW in 1969 at the University of Michigan where, as a student, he helped organize support for union boycotts, Rodriguez became a field organizer in California and a member of the UFW executive board.

By the time he assumed leadership of the union, its membership rolls had severely declined. Rodriguez vowed to launch increased efforts to move the union back to basics, back to recruiting and organizing farm workers to the union, especially those new to the harvest fields. Early on, he aimed his guns at the California strawberry industry, vowing to organize the 20,000 to 25,000 pickers employed for six months or more picking berries at about five cents a pint. Thus, the slogan was a "Five cents for fairness" campaign, promising workers it would seek to double their wages, and, at the same time, assuring the public that the cost of strawberries would rise only a nickel in the supermarket. Huerta charged that strawberry workers made an average of $8,000 a year with no health insurance or other benefits. Such conditions, she intimated, amounted to something close to slave labor.

In late March 1996, the UFW organized marches in New York City, San Antonio, San Francisco, Los Angeles, and Chicago to demand rights for California strawberry workers. In the front line of the marchers in New York and

San Francisco were familiar faces from the early days of the farm worker movement, such as Jerry Brown and Richard Chavez, brother of Cesar.

When the UFW targeted the largest employer of strawberry pickers, a subsidiary of Monsanto, the company took the challenge by selling its strawberry farms to investors, who renamed them Coastal Berry. Even though AFL-CIO president John Sweeney hailed the UFW's strawberry campaign, it took several years before the union won the right to represent 1,500 Coastal Berry workers. The vast strawberry industry remained largely non-union.

Nevertheless, the UFW won other important victories, including contract signings by growers in a variety of crops in California, Washington state, Florida, and elsewhere, and several pieces of legislation strengthening farm workers' legal rights and health and safety protections. Since 1999, the UFW helped win a number of new laws and regulations aiding farm workers including seatbelts in farm labor vehicles, fresh protections for workers cheated by farm labor contractors, an historic binding mediation law, and new pesticide protections.

In 2007, the United Farm Workers signed its first contract with Salinas-based D'Arrigo Bros., California's third-largest vegetable company. The agreement covered 1,800 farm workers in the Salinas and Imperial valleys.

Success or Failure?

In 2005, the magazine *Economist* ran an article describing the wretched conditions endured by farm workers in the Giumarra's family vineyards in California's San Joaquin Valley. Mostly illegal immigrants from Mexico, they labored for a wage of $7 an hour and 30 cents for each box. Many worked for 10-hour shifts. Often the workers collapsed in the stifling heat that exceeded 100 degrees; some were occasionally found dead. At the urging of the UFW, Republican Governor Arnold Schwarzenegger issued an emergency regulation to help prevent further heat deaths of farm workers and all outdoor employees.

Here in the San Joaquin Valley, site of one of the most significant victories of the UFW—the 1970 representation agreement signed by John Giumarra and the union—the news reported from the fields seemed tragic for those who had struggled so hard for farm worker rights. Here in Giumarra's fields, it was as if the great movement launched by Cesar Chavez had never occurred.

Indeed, more than a quarter century after the enactment of the most proworker and prounion labor relations law in the United States in 1975, the Agricultural Labor Relations Act, fewer workers were under union contract in California agriculture than before the law was enacted.

The dissension in the ranks of the leaders of the union had unquestionably been a root cause of the decline of the union in the fields as well as Chavez's reluctance to delegate authority. So had his peculiar attraction to the Synanon cult and his insistence that UFW leaders participate in its authoritarian and divisive practices. In addition, the union's organizing efforts drifted as its leaders turned much of their attention to a variety of political causes and fundraising activities.

And the immigration issue became an increasingly corrosive influence on union power. In the last years of Chavez's life and beyond, illegal immigration by Mexicans to the United States increased dramatically. For members of the UFW and union organizers, the appearance of hundreds of thousands of new arrivals anxious to work for wages less than those earned by union members became a profound threat. During his own leadership of the union, Chavez, although sympathetic to those crossing the border, insisted that the union must support efforts to close the influx of new workers. The continuing arrival of newcomers who were increasingly used as scab labor threatened the very existence of the union. Indeed, in the early 1990s newspapers again began documenting the poor conditions for farm workers in series entitled "Fields of Pain" and the "New Harvest of Shame."

At the beginning of the new century, the UFW began to change its position on immigration, becoming a leading voice inside the AFL-CIO in favor of ending employer sanctions and legalizing unauthorized foreigners. Labor organizer Bert Corona, who supported Chavez and the UFW during the 1970s and 1980s said: "I did have an important difference with Cesar. This involved his, and the union's position, on the need to apprehend and deport undocumented Mexican immigrants who were being used as scabs by the growers. . . . [I] believed that organizing undocumented farm workers was auxiliary to the union's efforts to organize the fields. We supported an open immigration policy, as far as Mexico was concerned." In 2000, the UFW adopted Corona's basic position. When the AFL-CIO's Executive Council called for the legalization of unauthorized foreigners, UFW President Rodriguez concurred (Martin).

But even as the fields continued to be filled by undocumented workers and the rolls of UFW members paled by comparison to the dues-paying membership of the union in its heyday, the influence of the movement begun by Chavez, Huerta, and others had produced profound changes.

In 2006, looking back over the accomplishments of the UFW and her own organizing activities, Dolores Huerta said, "It is extremely rewarding to see all that we have accomplished and the millions of people we have helped. Also, in regards to my work with the Farm Workers Union, knowing that we have secured laws requiring toilets in the field, drinking water, rest periods and unemployment insurance is a great feeling. People that work under farm worker contracts now have medical plans that cover their entire families. When you stop to think that some family somewhere was able to get an operation and that somebody's life has been saved as a result of the work that we do, then you realize just how heavy these accomplishments are. So it's really quite wonderful to reflect on that" (Aledo and Alvarado 2006, 13).

And, as many of the older farm workers testified, there were the emotional and psychological triumphs of challenging head on an established order with little more weaponry than grit and commitment. These were triumphs of spirit and endurance difficult to measure but impossible to underestimate.

Enduring Influences

In January 2009, Julie Chavez Rodriguez, granddaughter of Cesar Chavez, delivered the opening lecture for the 23rd Annual Martin Luther King Jr. Symposium at the University of Michigan. As a child she sometimes walked beside her grandfather at UFW rallies. Years later, she became director of the Cesar E. Chavez Foundation and participated in numerous initiatives to press for social justice and to carry "the torch of fairness of equality." "Both Dr. King and my grandfather were radical in their beliefs about justice and about organizing," she said. "They had faith in the community to do what's right, even when no one was looking. And they knew violence couldn't be part of the solution." The lesson, she said, is "not to be afraid. Stand up and fight for what you believe in" (Bogater 2009).

One of the most enduring legacies from the battles in the fields of the 1960s and 1970s is the abiding influence that Chavez and other UFW leaders had on a successive generation of organizers.

When Eliseo Medina, a 21-year-old farm worker, arrived in Chicago in 1967 he carried with him $20 and a bag of UFW buttons. His mission: to persuade supermarkets to stop selling grapes. Wide-eyed at the traffic and the big-city atmosphere, relatively unschooled in the labor union tactics, the youngster from California's Central Valley shook off his fears and plunged into the work with raw enthusiasm for the cause. He became the central figure in the UFW's boycott effort in Chicago. Although he left the UFW in 1978, he never stopped his zealous organizing efforts. In 2006, he was executive vice president of the Service Employees International Union (SEIU) overseeing locals across the country that organized janitors and health care workers.

Fred Ross Jr., the son of the organizer who had such a critical influence on Cesar Chavez, also joined the SEIU. Ross helped train a new generation of organizers, "some of whom have been the sons and daughters of former UFW organizers. It has been a special joy to see them continue the legacy," Ross said, "as they now operate on the frontlines in Texas, Florida, and Orange County, California" (Levy 2007, xviii).

Joan Brown Campbell, general secretary of the National Council of Churches, said, "Many people in the U.S. churches got their first experiences of what it means to be in a struggle for justice alongside other people through their participation as volunteers in the farm workers movement and related boycotts" ("Champion of Farm Workers Dies" 1993).

Pat Henning, chief of staff of the California Assembly's Labor Committee, who for several days fasted with Chavez in 1988, agreed. "There's a whole

UFW activist Eliseo Medina leads a picket line in 1972 outside the Talisman Sugarcane Company in Florida. One of the legacies of the early farm workers fights is the abiding influence Cesar Chavez and other UFW leaders had on a successive generation of community organizers and political and labor organizations. Eliseo Medina became a high-ranking executive with the Service Employees International Union (SEIU). (AP/Wide World Photos)

generation of Catholic activists in social justice from the 60s that owe their origins of who they are today to Cesar Chavez and the UFW," Henning said. Chavez was "the only one" who was "able to unify the social justice issue with a cultural and religious emphasis. No other organizer was quite able to do that" (Jones 1993, 5).

Antonio Villaraigosa, born in East Los Angeles in 1953, to a Mexican immigrant father and a California-born mother of Mexican descent, volunteered in Chavez's grape boycott when he was 15 years old. While pursuing a BA degree in history from UCLA and a law degree from People's College of Law, he continued to support the movement and later became a union organizer for the United Teachers of Los Angeles. In 1994, Villaraigosa was elected to the California State Assembly, thus launching a political career that would ultimately lead to his victory in a race to become the 41st mayor of the City of Los Angeles.

Many other veterans of the UFW have passed on the techniques and continue the struggle for social justice for the less politically and socially powerful. From staring down shotguns of California growers to setting up community meetings, Jim Drake was a consummate organizer. Drake, who followed Chris Hartmire to the union from the California Migrant Ministry, worked with Chavez for 16 years. After leaving the UFW in 1978, he organized woodcutters in Mississippi, helping unite independent contractors into the Mississippi Pulpwood Cutters Association, a group that set up purchasing cooperatives and a credit union. In 1983, he signed on with the Industrial Areas Foundation, an international federation of broad-based community organizations, that led him to a group called Valley Interfaith in the Texas Rio Grande Valley, where he worked to provide adequate water and sewage facilities. Later, he organized churches in New York City's South Bronx area in a campaign to build 800 units of affordable housing and to open a model public high school.

Ed Begley Jr., son of Hollywood actor Ed Begley, became interested in the grape and lettuce boycotts. In 1985, he recognized Chavez in a coffee shop and approached him. After they talked, Begley asked Chavez if he could help. In 1987, Begley began to work with the UFW on the pesticide issue, donating money and helping to organize the liberal Hollywood political community behind the cause. In 1990, he met Chavez at an environmental film festival in Colorado. "He invited me to take a walk with him," Begley says. "We went to a church. He lit a candle. And we talked about the sanctity of life and the creation. He talked about how environmentalists must not only have respect for nature, but also for the workforce that puts food on the table and how they should be protected from hazardous chemicals. The next time I saw him I was carrying his casket down the streets of Delano" (St. Clair 2003).

In early 1967, Chavez traveled to New York to make several appearances. During that trip, he met with a writer for *New Yorker* magazine. With the tumultuous cultural movements of the 1960s in full force, where did Chavez's movement fit? "I do know," he said, "there's a tremendous change going on in this country. There are things happening in America, such as anti-war rallies and civil-rights demonstrations, that no one has ever seen before. There are very few countries in which such things *could* happen, but they *can* happen here, and that's what gives our system its strength" (Chavez 2008).

Chavez's movement, with its energy and appeal to the religious and cultural heritage of Mexican Americans, sparked among workers in the harvest fields an idea that life could improve, that the system holding down the workers was not too intractable and too powerful that it could not be changed. Through sheer determination and will, Chavez and his lieutenants had lashed out at the stereotypes and the defeatism and convinced large numbers of people that they could fight back and improve their lives.

In a celebrated speech at the Commonwealth Club in San Francisco in 1984, Chavez declared, "The UFW survival, its existence—were not in doubt in my mind when the time began to come . . . after the union became visible, when Chicanos started entering college in greater numbers, when Hispanics began running for public office in greater numbers, when our people started asserting their rights on a broad range of issues and in many communities across this land. The union survival, its very existence, sent out a signal to all Hispanics that we were fighting for our dignity. That we were challenging and overcoming injustice, that we were empowering the least educated among us, the poorest among us. The message was clear. If it could happen in the fields, it could happen anywhere: in the cities, in the courts, in the city councils, in the state legislatures. I didn't really appreciate it at the time, but the coming of our union signaled the start of great changes among Hispanics that are only now beginning to be seen" ("Cesar Chavez Speech at Commonwealth Club" 1984).

The UFW developed a model for Latino political involvement for grass-roots campaigns into the 21st century. The house meetings, voter registration and petition drives, door-to-door outreach, and the imaginative public events that caught the attention of the media and the public helped transform the political environment of California and other states with growing Latino constituencies.

Chavez and the UFW laid the groundwork for California's increase in Latino voting. Other UFW veterans such as Marshall Ganz later refined and expanded the UFW model in a series of 1980s political campaigns. The grassroots mobilization and voter outreach model spread throughout California through numerous labor and political organizations and fueled the transformation of California politics. In Colorado, New Mexico, and other states where greater Latino influence began to boost the fortunes of progressive candidates, the UFW organization techniques have proven critical.

On March 31, 2010, President Barack Obama, in declaring that date "Cesar Chavez Day," said, "Since our Nation's earliest days of independence, we have struggled to perfect the ideals of equal justice and opportunity enshrined in our founding documents. As Cesar suggests, justice may be true to our nature, but as history teaches us, it will not prevail unless we defend its cause. Few Americans have led this charge so tirelessly, and for so many, as Cesar Chavez. To this day, his rallying cry—'*Sí, se puede,*' or 'Yes, we can,'—inspires hope and a spirit of possibility in people around the world. His movement strengthened our country, and his vision lives on in the organizers and social entrepreneurs who still empower their neighbors to improve their communities" (White House).

President Obama knew well the slogan "Yes, we can." In 2008, he used the words in his campaign for president.

What the UFW accomplished, and how the union accomplished it, will never be forgotten—not by the workers themselves nor by the thousands of social activists who have been inspired and energized by the farm workers' struggle.

And the struggle continues. Despite the efforts of Chavez, Huerta, and many others, most farm workers are still mired in poverty. But because of the union and the movement they inspired, the workers have genuine hope for themselves and their families. Chavez said that history would be on the side of the workers, especially the Mexican Americans who were taking their proper place in American society, despite the formidable opposition they faced. The reactionaries saw the future, Chavez said, and they were afraid. Hispanics and their children were on the rise, would in the near future constitute a formidable political force in California and other states, would drive Republicans from the California state legislature, would send Latinos to the United States Congress, and would wield ever-increasing social and economic power.

In those towns such as Salinas, Delano, Fresno, Bakersfield, and Modesto, those towns that had been the battlegrounds of the farm workers, it would be the children and grandchildren of those workers who would be in the majority, not the children and grandchildren of the growers. And from the lessons learned in the farm workers' fights, they could seize the power. There will be, Chavez said, triumph in the end. His vision still seems prescient.

References

Aledo, Milagros, and Maria Alvarado. 2006. "Dolores Huerta at Seventy-Five: Still Empowering Communities; Interview with Co-Founder of United Farm Workers of America." *Harvard Journal of Hispanic Policy* (Annual): 13.

Bogater, Jillian. 2009. "King, Chavez Shared Social Justice Spirit on Road to Change." MLK Symposium, University of Michigan. *The University Record Online*, January 22. http://www.ur.umich.edu/0809/Jan19_09/20.php.

Cesar Chavez Speech at Commonwealth Club. 1984. "What the Future Holds for Farm Workers and Hispanics." San Francisco, November 9. http://www.commonwealthclub.org/archive/20thcentury/84-11chavez-speech.html.

"Champion of Farm Workers Dies." 1993. *The Christian Century*, May 12, 513.

Chavez, Cesar. 2008. *An Organizer's Tale*. Edited by Ilan Stavans. New York: Penguin Classics, 227. http://www.farmworkermovement.org/essays/essays/Gringo justice.pdf.

Jones, Arthur. 1993. "Millions Reaped What Cesar Chavez Sowed." *National Catholic Reporter*, May 7, 5.

Levy, Jacques E. 2007. *Cesar Chavez: Autobiography of* La Causa. Minneapolis: University of Minnesota Press.

Martin, Philip. "Promise Unfulfilled: Why Didn't Collective Bargaining Transform California's Farm Labor Market?" Center for Immigration Studies. http://www.cis.org/Unionization-CaliforniaFarmLabor.

St. Clair, Jeffrey. 2003. "Render unto Cesar: Songs and Dances from the Fields of Pain." *Dissident Voice*, April 12. http://dissidentvoice.org/Articles4/StClair_Chavez.htm.

White House. http://www.whitehouse.gov/the-press-office/presidential-proclamation-cesar-chavez-day.

Biographies of Key Figures

Fred Ross

One of the nation's preeminent community organizers, Fred Ross graduated from the University of Southern California, intending to become a schoolteacher. Unable to find work during the Depression, he managed to get a position with the state relief administration doing social work and then found a job with the Farm Security Administration (FSA). Placed in charge of a migrant labor camp in the Coachella Valley of California, Ross soon became deeply involved with the challenges facing farm workers and other migrants and began to seek ways to encourage those workers to fight for their rights.

For a time, Ross worked with the renowned grassroots community organizer Saul Alinsky in community efforts with Mexican Americans in Los Angeles. In 1947, with the help of Edward Roybal, later an influential congressman from California, Ross created the Community Service Organization (CSO), a group that sought to organize Latino communities in citizenship drives, voter registration, and electoral campaigns. After working in Los Angeles for six years, he moved on to San Jose, the largest Latino center outside of Los Angeles.

It was Ross who gave both Cesar Chavez and Dolores Huerta valuable training in organizing that they would put to use in founding the United Farm Workers.

Ross continued to be an advisor and confidant to Chavez, Huerta, and other leaders of the UFW for the remainder of his life.

Ross's son, Fred Ross Jr., followed in his father's footsteps by becoming a community organizer. He and his father helped found Neighbor to Neighbor, an organization that provided a vital training ground for young activists to become organizers.

Dolores Huerta

Born in New Mexico in 1930, Dolores Huerta spent her early years in Stockton, California. Following her graduation from high school, she earned a teaching certificate from Delta Community College and took a job at an elementary school attended mostly by children of migrant laborers.

Disillusioned and angry about the poverty she saw among the children, she decided she could make a greater contribution in social work. In 1955, she met Fred Ross, who persuaded her to join the CSO, the grassroots organization dedicated to ending segregation and racism against Mexican Americans in California and providing a variety of services including low-cost medical care and job referral. She agreed to help Ross organize a Stockton chapter of the CSO. Attractive, dynamic, she took on the work of the CSO with a passion Ross had seldom observed.

While working for the CSO, Huerta met Cesar Chavez who had formed his own CSO branch in San Jose, California. In 1962, they left the CSO to form a union of farm workers. At the time, Huerta was in the middle of her second divorce, had seven children, and no financial assets. Yet, she forged ahead, convinced that she and Chavez could make an important difference.

On Sunday, September 30, 1962, in an abandoned movie theater in Fresno, California, approximately 200 workers gathered to show their solidarity to a new union. Calling the new organization the National Farm Workers Association, they adopted a union motto: "*¡Viva la causa!*" or "Long Live the Cause!" By 1964, they had signed up more than 1,000 families. Soon, the NFWA was even able to create its own credit union and provide services such as immigration counseling and voter registration.

From the union's first major strike against grape growers in 1965 through the labor and political battles in succeeding years, Huerta marked out for herself a dominant role, displaying extraordinary leadership skills, negotiating prowess, and uncanny political instincts.

In the 1980s, for example, Huerta participated in numerous political campaigns, spoke on behalf of the UFW, testified at the state and federal levels on the dangers of pesticides, advocated for amnesty for undocumented workers, and supported the strawberry workers' strike in California.

After Chavez's death in 1993, Huerta continued the UFW's work in the political arena and at the collective bargaining table. In 1999 she assumed the title of vice president emeritus of the UFW.

Well into the 21st century, Huerta remained an active crusader for the rights of farm workers, feminist causes, and progressive political ideals.

She also launched the Dolores Huerta Foundation, having the mission: "To inspire and motivate people to organize sustainable communities to attain social justice."

Eliseo Medina

The son of a bracero who worked in the California fields under the guest worker program, Eliseo Medina moved to Delano, California, at age 10 after spending almost two years in Tijuana waiting for permission to cross the border because his mother insisted on obtaining legal entry.

In 1965, as a 19-year-old grape picker, Medina joined the historic grape strike in Delano and became one of Cesar Chavez's most influential lieutenants. A year after he first joined the union, Medina appeared on the cover of its newspaper, *El Malcriado*, as one of the UFW's "Young Tigers."

For 13 years, he participated in most of the major organizing battles fought by the union and rose to the rank of second national vice president. Many considered Medina to be a logical successor to Chavez as head of the UFW. Nevertheless, in the summer of 1978, Medina left the UFW over disputes about the direction in which the union was headed.

After organizing university workers in California and public employees in Texas, Medina joined the Service Employees International Union (SEIU) where he rose to executive vice president, the first Mexican American to reach such a high position in the organization. He worked closely on immigration initiatives, helped to strengthen ties between the Catholic Church and the labor movement, and concentrated on issues such as worker rights and access to health care.

Jerry Cohen

Born in Chicago, Cohen graduated from Amherst College in 1963. He then earned a law degree from the University of California, Berkeley before beginning his formal legal career. During his university years, he was active in the free speech movement and anti-Vietnam War protests.

In 1967 his work at the California Rural Legal Assistance Office attracted the attention of Cesar Chavez. Cohen became Chavez's personal attorney and general counsel of the UFW, directing the UFW legal department for the next 14 years.

Cohen and his excellent team of underpaid lawyers won numerous suits directed by and against the union including fights against using trespass laws to thwart union organizing. He negotiated an influential jurisdictional accord with the Teamsters that ended years of struggle between the two unions. He negotiated important contracts with growers. He also worked closely with Governor Jerry Brown in creating the landmark California Agricultural Labor Relations Act of 1975.

He resigned from the UFW in November 1980. Cohen continued to advise and serve as legal counsel to a number of organizations and causes, especially Neighbor to Neighbor, founded by Fred Ross Jr., a group that organized key constituencies to pressure members of Congress on progressive legislation. The group used the house meeting tactic developed by Ross's father that proved so successful during the years in which Cohen was general counsel of the UFW.

Jim Drake

Ohio-born in 1937, Jim Drake spent most of his first 10 years in Oklahoma and then moved to California, where his father taught school and his mother managed the school cafeteria. He graduated from Occidental College, where he majored in philosophy, and then Union Theological Seminary. Just as he was about to accept a position as a pastor, he was offered a job by Chris Hartmire, a minister and director of the California Migrant Ministry, a group that worked closely with Cesar Chavez's union of farm workers. Drake took on major responsibilities for the UFW in California, Texas, and Arizona, even as he remained on the ministry's payroll.

In 1965, as grape pickers in Delano, California, struck a vineyard owned by Schenley Distillers, Drake helped the UFW organize a national boycott of the company's liquor. The company settled in March 1966. Drake went on to be one of the union's lead organizers.

In 1978, he left the farm worker ministry and the union to organize woodcutters in Mississippi. In Texas, he formed the Valley Interfaith Organization, which persuaded the state to provide water and plumbing in the shantytowns known as "colonias."

In 1987, Drake organized South Bronx Churches, a coalition of more than 40 churches that joined forces to build 800 housing units and persuade the city to build a new high school, the Bronx Leadership Academy. In 1994, he helped form the Greater Boston Interfaith Organization—a regional coalition of 100 religious and community organizations.

Gilbert Padilla

Born in 1927 in a labor camp near Los Banos, California, Gilbert Padilla, a child of migrant farm workers, traveled with his family throughout California, picking cotton, tomatoes, and fruit. He later served in the U.S. Army, earning many commendations.

In 1956 Padilla met Cesar Chavez, then an organizer for the CSO. For the next eight years Chavez and Padilla worked together in the CSO, conducting citizenship classes and voter registration drives, and engaging in many activities to gain rights for farm workers and others in need. When Chavez left the CSO to begin organizing a farm workers' union, Padilla joined him.

For 18 years, Padilla helped build the United Farm Workers Union, serving as secretary-treasurer from 1973 until 1980. He led union membership drives in California and Texas and participated in boycotts in Philadelphia and Washington, D.C.

Padilla left the UFW in 1980 for a variety of jobs in political and social work. For a time he was president of the Fresno Civil Service Commission. In 2005 he joined other CSO veterans in a project to document and pass on the lessons that empowered the organization's community organizing efforts.

Marshall Ganz

Marshall Ganz spent his early years in Bakersfield, California, with his father, a rabbi, and his mother, a teacher. He entered Harvard but left a year before completing his studies to travel to the South and join the civil rights movement, becoming a field secretary with the Student Nonviolent Coordinating Committee (SNCC). In the fall of 1965, he joined Cesar Chavez and became, in his 16 years with the UFW, director of organizing and a member of the national executive board. It was Ganz, more than any other UFW leader, who developed the political tactics that gained increasing voter participation by Mexican Americans in California.

He left the UFW in 1981 and formed an institute to recruit, train, and develop organizers. Over the years, he worked with mayoral, congressional, senate, and presidential campaigns, including that of Barack Obama, developing new techniques for mobilizing citizen participation and strategies for grassroots campaigns.

In 1991 he returned to Harvard, completed his undergraduate work in American history and government, and graduated magna cum laude in June 1992. He continued his studies at the Kennedy School of Government, where he earned an MPA in June 1993 and began to teach organizing. He joined the faculty in 2000 upon completing his PhD in sociology at Harvard.

He taught community organizing and trained individuals involved in community-based organizations, advocacy groups, and unions. In 2009, Oxford University Press published Ganz's book, *Why David Sometimes Wins: Leadership, Organization, and Strategy in the California Farm Worker Movement.* Ganz dedicated the book as follows: "To the organizers who, with helpful heart, critical eye, and skillful hand, bring us together to change ourselves, our communities, and our world."

Luis Valdez

When Luis Valdez, one of 10 children of a farm worker in Delano, California, was a young boy, a schoolteacher showed him the art of puppetry. While in high school, he appeared on local television showing off his skills. After graduating from high school, Valdez worked his way through San Jose State University, earning a BA in English. It was there that he produced his first play.

After working for the San Francisco Mime Troupe for a year, he decided to join Cesar Chavez in 1965 and to direct his artistic talents on behalf of striking farm workers. He founded *El Teatro Campesino* ("The Farmworkers' Theater") that began performing theatrical sketches at union meetings and along picket lines.

Although the headquarters of the UFWOC had no staging facilities and although most of the cast members had no previous experience on stage, Valdez was able to create a form of artistic expression that provided not only entertainment to the members of the union but also fired up their enthusiasm for the cause.

Chavez also turned to Valdez to write the "Plan of Delano," a statement of purpose for the protestors in their picketing and marches.

By 1967 Valdez and *El Teatro Campesino* had left the vineyards and was producing plays in San Francisco and elsewhere. In 1968, *El Teatro* won an Obie (a distinguished off-Broadway award) for "demonstrating the politics of survival."

The theatrical movement launched by Valdez on behalf of farm workers evolved into *teatro chicano*, an agitprop theater that blended traditional stage styles with Mexican humor, character types, folklore, and popular culture into one-act plays called *actos*. Following Valdez's lead, Mexican American theatrical groups sprang up across the country, producing plays on issues facing Latinos, from the drive for bilingual education and the struggles for unionization to drug addiction and the Vietnam War.

His unique artistic expression combined with his goal of social change brought Valdez to the forefront of Chicano theater. In producing *Zoot Suit* in 1978, Valdez became the first Chicano director to have a play produced on Broadway.

In 1987, he directed the hit film *La Bamba*, chronicling the life of Hispanic rock star Richie Valens. He created several performances for the Public Broadcasting Service (PBS) and later taught at California State University, Monterey Bay. *El Teatro Campesino* launched its 2010 season in California still under the direction of Luis Valdez.

Jessica Govea

By the age of four, Jessica Govea worked alongside her parents in the cotton fields of Kern County, California. When her father, Juan Govea, a Mexican-born railroad worker, became involved with the CSO in the mid-1950s, she helped distribute flyers for the organization. She was nine years old. While in her teens she became president of Junior CSO and led a petition drive to build a park following the traffic death of a neighborhood child. Jessica Govea was thus an activist from her earliest years.

In 1966, at age 19, she began full-time work with the UFW organizing committee and worked closely with Chavez and other UFW union leaders over a 16-year period. In 1968, she helped lead grape boycotts in Toronto and Montreal. Govea became a national director of organizing for the UFW, and, in 1977, was elected to the union's national executive board.

Heading up a number of the union's voter registration drives, she was particularly successful in helping the union in its support of Jerry Brown's successful run for governor of California and in Robert Kennedy's primary campaign for president. She also worked passionately to spread information about the dangerous use of pesticides.

After leaving the UFW in 1981, she worked with the national leadership of the coffee-processing workers' union in El Salvador to develop and implement a plan to rebuild the union after the war in that country.

She was a faculty member in the Labor Studies and Employment Relations Department at Rutgers University. Later she directed the Labor In-House Programs for Cornell's Industrial and Labor Relations School in New York City.

She died in January 2005, of breast cancer, at age 58. A spirited public speaker, she was also a gifted singer. Jerry Cohen, the UFW counsel, wrote that those who heard her sing such songs as "Cu-cu-ru-cu-cu Paloma" never forgot her voice.

Arturo Rodriguez

Arturo Rodriguez first became active in the UFW grape boycott in 1969 as a student at the University of Michigan, where he received a master's degree in social work. Born in Texas in 1949, he had, before his student days at Michigan, received a Catholic school education in San Antonio's La Salle High School, and later at St. Mary's University where he earned a BA degree.

Rodriguez first met Cesar Chavez in 1973 and his daughter Linda Chavez a year later. He married Linda in 1974 at *La Paz*, the UFW's headquarters. The two worked together on the boycott in Detroit in 1975.

Actively involved in many organizing activities, Rodriguez was elected to the UFW National Executive Board in 1981. After the death of Chavez in April 1993, Rodriguez became UFW president.

On the first anniversary of the Chavez's passing in April 1994, Rodriguez led a 343-mile Delano-to-Sacramento march or pilgrimage retracing the steps of an historic trek by Chavez in 1966. Some 20,000 supporters greeted the marchers at the steps of the state Capitol in Sacramento.

Under Rodriguez's direction, the UFW began an effort to reinvigorate its organizing efforts. The union did succeed in reaching agreements with the nation's five largest vegetable growers, and with prominent wineries and dairies. The union achieved a major victory in reaching agreement with vegetable grower D'Arrigo Brothers, one of the most intransigent companies toward the union for more than 30 years. Farm workers under UFW contracts have a host of benefits not available to the majority of farm workers in California and the rest of the country.

Under Rodriguez's direction, the UFW was influential in persuading California governor Arnold Schwarzenegger to issue the first state regulation to help prevent farm and other outdoor workers from dying or becoming ill because of extreme heat. Rodriguez and the union remained active in numerous political arenas and in working with various social help organizations on behalf of farm workers and others.

Under Rodriguez, the union made increased use of Radio Campesina, a chain of stations based in California geared toward news and music of interest to Mexican Americans.

Primary Documents

The Plan of Delano, 1965

During the Delano grape strike and the march to Sacramento in the spring of 1966, Luis Valdez often read aloud a document called "The Plan of Delano." Cesar Chavez had turned to Valdez with his unique artistic ability to help pen a statement declaring the reasons for the farm worker movement. Valdez remembered from his reading of history the famous "Plan of Ayala," a document written by Emiliano Zapata and his supporters in 1911 during the Mexican Revolution. Calling for land reform and freedom, it became the rallying cry for the Zapatismo movement. Zapata himself was from a small southern Mexican state and was rebelling against the members of the wealthy class who had stolen land with impunity. The Plan of Ayala was designed to make clear to peasant groups the injustices of the Mexican government under the regime of Porfirio Diaz and called for radical land reform. The assassination of Zapata in April 1919 ended the hopes of his followers for his ascension as leader of Mexico, but the plan remained an iconic symbol of the aspirations of the poor and dispossessed. The Plan of Delano echoed those sentiments more than four decades later.

PLAN for the liberation of the Farm Workers associated with the Delano Grape Strike in the State of California, seeking social justice in farm labor with those reforms that they believe necessary for their well-being as workers in the United States.

We, the undersigned, gathered in Pilgrimage to the capital of the State in Sacramento in penance for all the failings of Farm Workers as free and sovereign men, do solemnly declare before the civilized world which judges our actions, and before the nation to which we belong, the propositions we have formulated to end the injustice that oppresses us.

We are conscious of the historical significance of our Pilgrimage. It is clearly evident that our path travels through a valley well known to all

Mexican farm workers. We know all of these towns of Delano, Madera, Fresno, Modesto, Stockton, and Sacramento, because along this very same road, in this very same valley, the Mexican race has sacrificed itself for the last hundred years. Our sweat and our blood have fallen on this land to make other men rich. The pilgrimage is a witness to the suffering we have seen for generations.

The penance we accept symbolizes the suffering we shall have in order to bring justice to these same towns, to this same valley. The pilgrimage we make symbolizes the long historical road we have traveled in this valley alone, and the long road we have yet to travel, with much penance, in order to bring about the revolution we need, and for which we present the propositions in the following PLAN:

1. This is the beginning of a social movement in fact and not in pronouncements. We seek our basic, God-given rights as human beings. Because we have suffered—and are not afraid to suffer—in order to survive, we are ready to give up everything, even our lives, in our fight for social justice. We shall do it without violence because that is our destiny. To the ranchers, and to all those who [oppose us], we say, in the words of Benito Juarez, "EL RESPETO AL DE-RECHO AJENO ES LA PAZ."

2. We seek the support of all political groups and protection of the government, which is also our government, in our struggle. For too many years we have been treated like the lowest of the low. Our wages and working conditions have been determined from above, because irresponsible legislators who could have helped us, have supported the rancher's argument that the plight of the Farm Worker was a "special case." They saw the obvious effects of an unjust system, starvation wages, contractors, day hauls, forced migration, sickness, illiteracy, camps and sub-human living conditions, and acted as if they were irremediable causes. The farm worker has been abandoned to his own fate—without representation, without power—subject to mercy and caprice of the rancher. We are tired of words, of betrayals, of indifference. To the politicians we say that the years are gone when the farm worker said nothing and did nothing to help himself. From this movement shall spring leaders who shall understand us, lead us, be faithful to us, and we shall elect them to represent us. WE SHALL BE HEARD.

3. We seek, and have, the support of the Church in what we do. At the head of the pilgrimage we carry LA VIRGEN DE LA GUADALUPE

because she is ours, all ours, Patroness of the Mexican people. We also carry the Sacred Cross and the Star of David because we are not sectarians, and because we ask the help and prayers of all religions. All men are brothers, sons of the same God; that is why we say to all of good will, in the words of Pope Leo XIII, "Everyone's first duty is protect the workers from the greed of speculators who use human beings as instruments to provide themselves with money. It is neither just nor human to oppress men with excessive work to the point where their minds become enfeebled and their bodies worn out." GOD SHALL NOT ABANDON US.

4. We are suffering. We have suffered, and we are not afraid to suffer in order to win our cause. We have suffered unnumbered ills and crimes in the name of the Law of the Land. Our men, women, and children have suffered not only the basic brutality of stoop labor, and the most obvious injustices of the system; they have also suffered the desperation of knowing that the system caters to the greed of callous men and not to our needs. Now we will suffer for the purpose of ending the poverty, the misery, and the injustice, with the hope that our children will not be exploited as we have been. They have imposed hunger on us, and now we hunger for justice. We draw our strength from the very despair in which we have been forced to live. WE SHALL ENDURE.

5. We shall unite. We have learned the meaning of UNITY. We know why these are just that—united. The strength of the poor is also in union. We know that the poverty of the Mexican or Filipino worker in California is the same as that of all farm workers across the country, the Negroes and poor whites, the Puerto Ricans, Japanese, and Arabians; in short, all of the races that comprise the oppressed minorities of the United States. The majority of the people on our Pilgrimage are of Mexican decent, but the triumph of our race depends on a national association of all farm workers. The ranchers want to keep us divided in order to keep us weak. Many of us have signed individual "work contracts" with the ranchers or contractors, contracts in which they had all power. These contracts were farces, one more cynical joke at our impotence. That is why we must get together and bargain collectively. We must use the only strength that we have, the force of our numbers. The ranchers are few; we are many. UNITED WE SHALL STAND.

6. We shall Strike. We shall pursue the REVOLUTION we have proposed. We are sons of the Mexican Revolution, a revolution of the

poor seeking, bread and justice. Our revolution will not be armed, but we want the existing social order to dissolve, we want a new social order. We are poor, we are humble, and our only [choice] is to Strike in those [ranches] where we are not treated with the respect we deserve as working men, where our rights as free and sovereign men are not recognized. We do not want the paternalism of the rancher; we do not want the contractor; we do not want charity at the price of our dignity. We want to be equal with all the working men in the nation; we want just wages, better working conditions, a decent future for our children. To those who oppose us, be they ranchers, police, politicians, or speculators, we say that we are going to continue fighting until we die, or we win. WE SHALL OVERCOME.

Across the San Joaquin Valley, across California, across the entire Southwest of the United States, wherever there are Mexican people, wherever there are farm workers, our movement is spreading like flames across a dry plain. Our PILGRIMAGE is the MATCH that will light our cause for all farm workers to see what is happening here, so that they may do as we have done. The time has come for the liberation of the poor farm worker.

History is on our side.

MAY THE STRIKE GO ON! VIVA LA CAUSA!

Source: UFW and Wayne State Archives, http://www.aztlan.net/plandela.htm.

Informant Interview to FBI on Cesar Chavez, September 23, 1966

From Cesar Chavez's earliest days as a community organizer and his efforts to launch a labor union for farm workers, his growing number of enemies, including the growers and agribusiness interests, Republican politicians, and local police, began to question his patriotism. Was he a communist or a socialist? Did he consort with enemies of the state? Was he a so-called fellow traveler, enabling those who attacked America to gain a greater foothold? The Federal Bureau of Investigation spared no effort to find out the true intentions of this upstart social worker and progressive who challenged American business interests. Throughout his career, agents staked out rallies, protest marches, and strike sites. They interviewed hundreds of individuals who came in contact with Chavez. Essentially they found nothing incriminating. Instead, they found much praise and admiration for his idealism, energy, and talent. The follow-ing report is typical.

Interview, September 23, 1966

[DELETED] advised . . . that he had known CESAR ESTRADA CHAVEZ since 1952. He said he first met [DELETED] said that CHAVEZ began with the CSO in 1952 as a volunteer organizer and that he became a paid employee with the CSO in the same capacity in 1953. [DELETED] said that almost immediately CHAVEZ became the leader of the San Jose Chapter of the CSO and that inasmuch as the IAF founded and sponsored CSO chapters, it would be proper for him to state that CHAVEZ was an organizer for IAF from 1953 to 1958. He said that from September 1958 until 1961, CHAVEZ was National Director of CSO and accordingly, was paid by CSO. [DELETED] said that since 1961 or early 1962, CHAVEZ has been Director of the National Farm Workers Association (NFWA), now the UFWOC-AFL-CIO. [DELETED] said that CHAVEZ in working for CSO and IAF performed his services in various areas of California.

[DELETED] considers CHAVEZ to be a very close associate [DELETED]. He related that when he first met CHAVEZ he realized that CHAVEZ was "a man among men, thoroughly loyal and dedicated to the goal of better-ing the lot of the Mexican people." [DELETED] said CHAVEZ is extremely intelligent and a very hard worker. He said CHAVEZ is a "self-starter" and that he required very little supervision. [DELETED] said that CHAVEZ de-veloped into the best organizer that he has ever known and that it became apparent during their association that this would be CHAVEZ'S destiny. [DELETED] characterized CHAVEZ as "the greatest Mexican leader today and he is one of the greatest leaders in America today." [DELETED] said CHAVEZ is a man of profound judgment, that his decisions are almost al-ways correct, and that he is not the type to make snap judgments. He said that CHAVEZ is extremely well read and is able to draw on a wealth of past experience, even though he has had little formal education. He said that CHAVEZ is self-taught, that he has the uncanny ability to work well with people, and that he is trusted, admired, and well liked by almost everyone with whom he comes in contact. He said that CHAVEZ'S personal life is im-peccable and that he has absolutely no question of the loyalty of CHAVEZ to the United States. . . .

Source: Federal Bureau of Investigation, File on Cesar Chavez and United Farm Workers, Part 6B, 32–34, http://foia.fbi.gov/foiaindex/chavez.htm.

Statement of Senator Robert F. Kennedy, Delano, California, March 10, 1968

To most Mexican Americans, Robert F. Kennedy became an enduring heroic figure. More than any other Anglo, many believed, Kennedy represented a political figure of power who understood their frustrations and challenges and was determined to combat the injustices they faced. The lives of Chavez and Kennedy, each of whom had great admiration for the other, intersected in vital but tragic ways in 1968. As Chavez decided to break his fast for nonviolence on March 10, 1968, Kennedy flew to California to be at his side. According to Peter Edelman, a Kennedy aide and speechwriter, it was on that flight that Kennedy revealed to him that he had decided to run for the presidency and would announce it the following week. Kennedy's remarks at the end of the fast reveal the profound respect he felt for Chavez and his movement. Kennedy would go on to run for the presidency. Chavez and his union would fight vigorously for his victory in the California primary. In the early morning of June 5, 1968, his assassination shattered the dreams of millions.

This is a historic occasion. We have come here out of respect for one of the heroic figures of our time—Cesar Chavez. But I come here to congratulate all of you, you who are locked with Cesar in the struggle for justice for the farm worker, and the struggle for justice for the Spanish-speaking American. I was here two years ago, almost to the day. Two years ago your union had not yet won a major victory. Now, elections have been held on ranch after ranch and the workers have spoken. They have spoken, and they have said, "We want a union."

You are the first—not the first farm workers to organize—but the first to fight and triumph over all the odds without proper protection from Federal law.

You have won historic victories.

Others, inspired by your example, have come to offer help—and they have helped. But the victories are yours and yours alone. You have won them with your courage and perseverance. You stood for the right—and would not be moved.

And you will not be moved again.

The world must know, from this time forward, that the migrant farm worker, the Mexican-American, is coming into his own rights. You are winning a special kind of citizenship: no one is doing it for you—you are winning it yourselves—and therefore no one can ever take it away.

And when your children and grandchildren take their place in America—going to high school, and college, and taking good jobs at good pay—when you look at them, you will say, "I did this. I was there, at the point of difficulty and danger." And though you may be old and bent from many years of labor, no man will stand taller than you when you say, "I marched with Cesar."

But the struggle is far from over. And now, as you are at midpoint in your most difficult organizing effort, there are suddenly those who question the principle that underlies everything you have done so far—the principle of non-violence. There are those who think violence is some shortcut to victory.

Let me say that violence is no answer. And those who organized the steel plants and the auto plants and the coal mines a generation ago learned from bitter experience that that was so. For where there is violence and death and confusion and injury, the only ones who benefit are those who oppose your right to organize. Where there is violence, our nation loses. Violence destroys far more than it can ever create. It tears at the fabric of our society. And let no one say that violence is the courageous route. It takes far greater commitment, far more courage to say, "we will do what must be done through an organization of the people, through patient, careful building of a democratic organization." That road requires far greater militancy. But along that road lies success. Along that road lies the building of institutions and cooperative businesses, of clinics, and schools and homes. So we come here, you and I, in a great pilgrimage to demonstrate our commitment to non-violence, to democracy itself. Just a few miles from here is the tower of the Voice of America—broadcasting across vast oceans and whole continents, the greatness of America. And we say together, we will build, we will organize, we will make America fulfill its promises and we will make our voices heard. We will make America a better place for all Americans.

But if you come here today from such great distances and at such great sacrifice to demonstrate your commitment to nonviolence, we in Government must match your commitment. That is our responsibility.

We must have a Federal law which give farm workers the right to engage in collective bargaining—and have it this year.

We must have more adequate regulation of green-card workers, to prevent their use as strikebreakers—and we must have that this year.

We must have equal protection of the laws. Those are the words of the Fourteenth Amendment to the Constitution of the United States. The California Labor Code, the Federal Immigration Laws, the Federal Labor

Department Regulations—these are laws which are supposed to protect you. They must be enforced. From now on.

So I come here today to honor a great man, Cesar Chavez. I come here today to honor you for the long and patient commitment you have made to this great struggle for justice. And I come here to say that we will fight together to achieve for you the aspirations of every American—decent wages, decent housing, decent schooling, a chance for yourselves and your children. You stand for justice and I am proud to stand with you.

Viva La Causa.

Source: John F. Kennedy Presidential Library, National Archives and Records Administration, http://www.archives.gov/research/arc/.

Cesar Chavez's "Letter from Delano," 1969

In 1969, E. L. Barr Jr., president of the California Grape and Tree Fruit League, accused Cesar Chavez and the UFW of resorting to violence in the grape boycott. The accusation was a challenge to everything for which Chavez had stood in his social movement and labor organizing work for farm workers—a nonviolent campaign based on the principles of Mohandas Gandhi and those demonstrated by Martin Luther King Jr. in his struggle in the black civil rights movement. It is true that in some instances, especially involving his cousin Manuel Chavez, there had been reported physical assaults by union members in resisting the importation of scab labor from Mexico to break up strikes. But the incidents were few compared to the incessant violent tactics used against members by goon squads hired by growers. And Chavez, on more than one occasion, responded to reports of violence by union members by denouncing such actions and even engaging in fasts to "purify" the cause. He aggressively challenged Barr's assertions.

Dear Mr. Barr:

I am sad to hear about your accusations in the press that our union movement and table grape boycott have been successful because we have used violence and terror tactics. If what you say is true, I have been a failure and should withdraw from the struggle; but you are left with the awesome moral responsibility, before God and man, to come forward with whatever information you have so that corrective action can begin at once. If for any reason you fail to come forth to substantiate your charges, then you must be held responsible for committing violence against us, albeit violence of the tongue. I am convinced that you as a human being did not mean what you said but rather acted hastily under pressure from the public relations firm that has been hired to try to counteract the tremendous moral force of our movement. How many times we ourselves have felt the need to lash out in anger and bitterness.

Today on Good Friday 1969 we remember the life and the sacrifice of Martin Luther King, Jr. who gave himself totally to the nonviolent struggle for peace and justice. In his "Letter from Birmingham Jail" Dr. King describes better than I could our hopes for the strike and boycott: "Injustice must be exposed, with all the tension its exposure creates, to the light of human conscience and the air of national opinion before it can be cured." For our part I admit that we have seized upon every tactic and strategy consistent with the morality of our cause to expose that injustice and thus to heighten the sensitivity of the American conscience so that farmworkers will have without bloodshed their own union and the dignity of bargaining with their agribusiness employers. By lying about the nature of our movement, Mr. Barr, you are working against nonviolent social change. Unwittingly perhaps, you may unleash that other force which our union by discipline and deed, censure and education has sought to avoid, that panacean shortcut: that senseless violence which honors no color, class or neighborhood.

You must understand—I must make you understand—that our membership and the hopes and aspirations of the hundreds of thousands of the poor and dispossessed that have been raised on our account are, above all, human beings, no better and no worse than any other cross-section of human society; we are not saints because we are poor, but by the same measure neither are we immoral. We are men and women who have suffered and endured much, and not only because of our abject poverty but because we have been kept poor. The colors of our skins, the languages of our cultural and native origins, the lack of formal education, the exclusion from the democratic process, the numbers of our slain in recent wars—all these burdens generation after generation have sought to demoralize us, to break our human spirit. But God knows that we are not beasts of burden, agricultural implements or rented slaves; we are men. And mark this well, Mr. Barr, we are men locked in a death struggle against man's inhumanity to man in the industry that you represent. And this struggle itself gives meaning to our life and ennobles our dying.

As your industry has experienced, our strikers here in Delano and those who represent us throughout the world are well trained for this struggle. They have been under the gun, they have been kicked and beaten and herded by dogs, they have been cursed and ridiculed, they have been stripped and chained and jailed, they have been sprayed with the poisons used in the vineyards; but they have been taught not to lie down and die nor to flee in shame, but to resist with every ounce of human endurance and spirit. To resist not with retaliation in kind but to overcome with love and compassion, with ingenuity and creativity, with hard work and longer hours, with stamina and patient tenacity, with truth and public appeal, with friends and allies, with mobility and discipline, with politics and law, and with prayer and fasting. They were not trained in a month or even a year; after all, this new harvest season will mark our fourth full year of strike and even now we continue to plan and prepare for the years to come. Time accomplishes for the poor what money does for the rich.

This is not to pretend that we have everywhere been successful enough or that we have not made mistakes. And while we do not belittle or underestimate our adversaries—for they are the rich and the powerful and they possess the land—we are not afraid nor do we cringe from the confrontation. We welcome it! We have planned for it. We know that our cause is just, that history is a story of social revolution, and that the poor shall inherit the land.

Once again, I appeal to you as the representative of your industry and as a man. I ask you to recognize and bargain with our union before the economic pressure of the boycott and strike takes an irrevocable toll; but if not, I ask you to at least sit down with us to discuss the safeguards necessary to keep our historical struggle free of violence. I make this appeal because as one of the leaders of our nonviolent movement, I know and accept my responsibility for preventing, if possible, the destruction of human life and property. For these reasons and knowing of Gandhi's admonition that fasting is the last resort in place of the sword, during a most critical time in our movement last February 1968 I undertook a 25-day fast. I repeat to you the principle enunciated to the membership at the start of the fast: if to build our union required the deliberate taking of life, either the life of a grower or his child, or the life of a farm worker or his child, then I choose not to see the union built.

Mr. Barr, let me be painfully honest with you. You must understand these things. We advocate militant nonviolence as our means for social revolution and to achieve justice for our people, but we are not blind or deaf to the desperate and moody winds of human frustration, impatience and rage that blow among us.

Gandhi himself admitted that if his only choice were cowardice or violence, he would choose violence. Men are not angels, and time and tide wait for no man. Precisely because of these powerful human emotions, we have tried to involve masses of people in their own struggle. Participation and self-determination remain the best experience of freedom, and free men instinctively prefer democratic change and even protect the rights guaranteed to seek it. Only the enslaved in despair have need of violent overthrow.

This letter does not express all that is in my heart, Mr. Barr. But if it says nothing else it says that we do not hate you or rejoice to see your industry destroyed; we hate the agribusiness system that seeks to keep us enslaved, and we shall overcome and change it not by retaliation or bloodshed but by a determined nonviolent struggle carried on by those masses of farm workers who intend to be free and human.

Sincerely yours,

Cesar E. Chavez

United Farm Workers Organizing Committee, A.F.L.-C.I.O.

Delano, California.

Source: Cesar Chavez, "Letter from Delano," in Peter B. Levy, ed., *100 Key Documents in American Democracy* (Westport, CT: Greenwood, 1994), 442–445.

Extract from Statement of Dolores Huerta before Senate Subcommittee on Migratory Labor, July 15, 1969

In the summer of 1969, the U.S. Senate Subcommittee on Migratory Labor, chaired by Senator Walter Mondale (D-MN), held hearings to study the problems surrounding a sizable percentage of the American labor force that was relatively unprotected by federal law—migratory workers. Mondale declared that the hearings were designed to elicit information on the extent of the powerlessness of migrant workers to influence their own lives. From witness after witness, that powerlessness became clear—how they were deprived of political and economic power, deprived of cultural identity and pride, and denied the rights that most Americans casually took for granted. Mondale and others on the subcommittee later remarked about the power of the testimony they heard, about the unschooled eloquence of men and women who had spent years of grinding work in the fields or who had worked as community organizers trying to help those who had so little. Dolores Huerta's testimony in July 1969 was especially revealing.

Mrs. Huerta. Mr. Chairman, and members of the committee, we are again glad to be here and present our long, sad story of trying to organize the farmworkers.

We have had tremendous difficulties in trying to organize farmworkers. I don't think, first of all, that we have to belabor the reason why farmworkers need a union. The horrible state in which farmworkers find themselves, faced with such extreme poverty and discrimination, has taught us that the only way we can change our situation is by organization of a union.

I don't believe that it can be done any other way. Certainly, we can't depend on Government to do it, nor can we expect them to take the responsibility. On the other hand, our problem is the government's responsibility, I think, when they try to keep the farmworkers from being organized or actually take action that makes it difficult for farmworkers to organize. . . .

As you know, UFWOC has undertaken an international boycott of all California-Arizona table grapes in order to gain union recognition for striking farmworkers. We did not take up the burden of the boycott willingly. It is expensive. It is a hardship on the farmworkers' families who have left the small valley towns to travel across the country to boycott grapes.

But, because of the table grape growers' refusal to bargain with their workers, the boycott is our major weapon and I might say a nonviolent weapon, and our last line of defense against the growers who use foreign labor to break our strikes.

It is only through the pressure of the boycott that UFWOC has won contracts with major California wine grape growers. At this point, the major obstacles to our efforts to organize farmworkers are obstacles to our boycott.

Our boycott has been met with well-organized and well-financed opposition by the growers and their sympathizers. Most recently, several major California grape growers joined with other agribusiness interests and members of the John Birch Society to form an employer-dominated "union," the Agricultural Workers Freedom To Work Association (AWFWA), for the sole purpose of destroying UFWOC. AWFWA's activities have been described in a sworn statement to the U.S. Government, which I would like permission to place in the record at the close of my remarks.

In spite of this type of antiunion activity, our boycott of California-Arizona table grapes has been successful. It is being successful for the simple reason that millions of Americans are supporting the grape workers strike by not buying table grapes.

After 6 weeks of the 1969–70 table grape harvest, California table grape shipments to 36 major cities are down 20 percent from last year, according to U.S. Department of Agriculture reports. The price per lug for

Thompson seedless grapes is at least $1 less than it was at this time of last year's harvest. And I might add that that has dropped even more since this statement was written.

It is because of the successful boycott that, on Friday, June 13, 1969, 10 major California growers offered to meet with ITFWOC under the auspices of the Federal Mediation Service. UFWOC representatives and ranch committee members met with the growers for 2 weeks. Progress is being made in these negotiations, which are presently recessed over the issue of pesticides.

However, the U.S. Department of Defense table grape purchases have been very detrimental to our effort.

Now that the boycott has brought us so close to a negotiated settlement of this 3-year-old dispute, we learn that the U.S. Department of Defense (DOD) has doubled its purchases of table grapes. We appear to be witnessing an all-out effort by the military to bail out the growers and break our boycott. Let me review the facts behind this imposing Federal obstacle to farmworker organizing. . . .

The DOD argues in its fact sheet that "The total Defense Supply Agency purchases of table grapes represent less than 1 percent of U.S. table grape production." Data from the California Co-op and Livestock Reporting Service indicate, however, that "table" grapes may be utilized in three different ways: fresh for table use; crushed for wine; or dried as raisins. I refer to table I that is attached to this statement. Looking at table II, it is clear that DOD purchases of table grapes for fresh use represents nearly 2.5 percent of all U.S. fresh table grape production.

Table grape prices, like those of other fruits and vegetables, are extremely susceptible to minor fluctuations in supply. DOD purchases of some table grapes are probably shoring up the price of all table grapes and, at a critical point in the UFWOC boycott, are permitting many growers to stand firm in their refusal to negotiate with their workers.

It is obvious that the DOD is taking sides with the growers in this dispute. The DOD fact sheet states that "The basic policy of the DOD with regard to awarding defense contracts to contractors involved in labor disputes is to refrain from taking a position on the merits of any labor dispute. This policy is based on the premise that it is essential to DOD procurement need to maintain a sound working relationship with both labor and management." Nevertheless, many unions in the United States are decrying this fantastic increase in DOD table grape purchases. . . .

DOD table grape purchases are a national outrage. The history of our struggle against agribusiness is punctuated by the continued violations of health and safety codes by growers, including many table grape growers. Much of this documentation has already been submitted to the Senate Subcommittee on Migratory Labor. Such violations are so well documented that Superior Judge Irving Perluss, of California, recently ruled that a jobless worker was within his rights when he refused to accept farm labor work offered him through the California Department of Employment on grounds that most of such jobs are in violation of State health and sanitation codes. . . .

If the Federal Government and the DOD is not concerned about the welfare of farmworkers, they must be concerned with protecting our servicemen from contamination and disease carried by grapes picked in fields without toilets or washstands.

Recent laboratory tests have found DDT residues on California grapes. Economic poisons have killed and injured farmworkers. Will they also prove dangerous to U.S. military personnel?

Focusing on other forms of crime in the fields, we would finally ask if the DOD buys table grapes from the numerous growers who daily violate State and Federal minimum wage and child labor laws, who employ illegal foreign labor, and who do not deduct social security payments from farmworkers' wages? . . .

[I]t is clear that DOD is buying adulterated food. For instance, one of the growers the Department of Defense lists as their No. 1 customer is the Giumarra Corp. The Giumarra Corp. was convicted of several counts of violation of law in Kern County. The violations were for not having toilets in the field, and working minors without due regard to the law.

What was the sentence when the Giumarra Corp. was guilty of violating these laws? For 23 counts of violations, they were fined $1,150, but this fine was suspended.

Of course, the Government subsidy that they later on received in that year, $274,000, not only paid for the fine, but offset any losses they may have suffered from the boycott.

The same grower, the Giumarra Corp., used DDT, Parathion, and so forth. All of these are known to have bad effects on the workers, and in accumulation, on the consumer that eats the grapes.

The same grower, the Giumarra Corp., which had 32 occupational injuries reported in 1 year, the majority of which were caused by pesticides in its fields.

Jack Pandol, another grower whom the Department of Defense purchases from, reported seven occupational injuries from pesticides. Another had even more. He had 48 injuries in 1967.

Let me add one other thing as long as we are talking about health. The health care of farmworkers is almost nonexistent, and the rate of tuberculosis is 200 percent above the national average. When you consider that many of the people now picking the grapes are being brought in from Mexico, that they are people without any type of legal residence papers, and therefore, have not been processed through the health regulations that usually apply to immigrants coming into this country, you can imagine what the contamination possibilities are, when the people are coming from a country with lower health standards than the United States.

There is one other thing I want to point out. When people pick table grapes, one of the things they are ordered to do is to be careful not to take off any of the "bloom." The bloom is all the dust, and filth on the grapes. If you wipe it off so the grapes are shiny then the grape will rot much faster. For the same reason, grapes are not washed by the picker or packer, and any of those pesticides or other things that may be on the grapes come straight to the consumer, and grapes are also very difficult to wash. Those grapes are picked and packed right in the field; they don't go through any other kind of processing. They are taken off the vines, put in a box, lidded, taken into the cold storage, and shipped to the customers, and that is the way they come directly to the customers.

The Department of Defense increasing purchases of table grapes is nothing short of a national outrage. It is an outrage to the millions of American taxpayers who are supporting the farmworkers' struggle for justice by boycotting table grapes. How can any American believe that the U.S. Government is sincere in its efforts to eradicate poverty when the military uses its immense purchasing power to subvert the farmworkers' nonviolent struggle for a decent, living wage and a better future?

Many farmworkers are members of minority groups. They are Filipino and Mexican and black Americans. These same minority people are on the frontlines of battle in Vietnam. It is a cruel and ironic slap in the face to these men who have left the fields to fulfill their military obligation to find increasing amounts of boycotted grapes in their mess kits. . . .

The people in the union have to take a tremendous amount of harassment, such as the materials of State Senator Hugh Burns' Committee on Un-American Activities in California. The man who made up that committee report was sitting in his home in Three Rivers. He never once went to Delano. Yet, he wrote a report which has been used all over the country in which he tried to redbait the members of the union.

Among other mistruths, he says 3 years of Cesar Chavez' life are missing, and suggests he was getting some kind of subversive training.

Those are the 3 years he spent in the U.S. Navy. That should be put in the record.

Gunmen have gone to our offices, taken canceled checks, membership files, and some of these membership files have been used in blacklisting for jobs.

Our insurance has been canceled for our cars and we would like to have the committee investigate this. We would like to have the committee investigate the Aetna Insurance Co. and ask them why it is they canceled our insurance. Our record has been good.

At one point, the Texaco Co. refused to sell gas to our gas station. There are many types of harassment which can be used against an organization. Our telephone lines are tapped. Many times, when we are in an extremely important conversation, you don't complete the call, because something interferes with the wires. This happens all the time. . . .

Source: U.S. Senate, 91st Congress, 1st Session, Hearings before the Subcommittee on Migratory Labor of the Committee on Labor and Public Welfare, Part 3-A, Migrant and Seasonal Farmworker Powerlessness, July 15, 1969, 551–562, http://www.archive.org/details/migrantseasonalf03unit.

Extract from Remarks of Cesar Chavez before U.S. House of Representatives Education and Labor Committee, October 1, 1969

The issue of illegal immigration was a perplexing problem for Cesar Chavez throughout his career. Although sincerely sympathetic to the plight of Mexicans who crossed the border seeking work, he knew that their exploitation by growers had a deleterious effect on his hopes of creating a successful union of farm workers. Especially during strikes by Chavez's union, the growers used illegal immigrants as scab labor, willing to work for far less than what the union was demanding for its own workers. UFW members often picketed the offices of the Immigration and Naturalization Service demanding that the U.S. government do more to stem the tide of border crossings. In 1969, Chavez testified before the U.S. House of Representatives Education and Labor Committee. His remarks that day on the issue of illegal immigration were similar to those he would make 10 years later at a congressional hearing.

. . . If we do nothing else today, we would like to make it very clear that in rural America today, when farm workers declare a strike, it is not only a strike that happens, but it is a whole revolution in that community. It becomes a civil liberties issue, it becomes a race issue, and it becomes a desperate struggle just to keep the movement going against such tremendous odds.

We have experienced things that we never dreamed we would be confronted with when we began the strike. These small communities are so well knit and the grower influence is so predominant that when we struck in Delano, we not only had the growers against us, but we had the other public bodies like the city council, the board of supervisors, the high school and elementary school districts, passing resolutions and propaganda against the strike and against the union. There was no voice whatsoever from the other side wanting to mediate or offering their services or their influence to find a solution to the problem. The community wanted to destroy us as soon as possible.

We want you to know that in America today, a vast majority of farm workers are poor, and the vast majority are from minority groups. We are brown and black. Also it is good to understand that a lot of the work force are recent immigrants, not only from Mexico, but from Asia, from Portugal, from Arabia, from other parts of the world where people are constantly being brought into work in agriculture.

We also want you to know that the employers have used—and I should say very well—the tactic of setting one racial group against the other. This has been a long-standing trick of theirs to break the unions.

Even today in negotiations we find that it takes a lot of time to get the employers to understand that the people should live together and that there should be no separation of workers in camps by racial groups. Today the employers that we're striking have a Filipino Camp, a Mexican Camp, a Negro Camp, and an Arab Camp in some cases.

We want you to know how hard it is for us to get justice because of the concentration of power in the hands of employers. The local authorities come into play immediately to try to destroy the efforts of organizing. At the beginning of the strike, there were mass arrests by the Delano Police Department and by the County Sheriff's Department. We found that the best counteraction was to let the public know what was happening in the valley.

We see the indifference of the local courts. We see how employers can come in and can get injunctions at will, and we see how the injunctions break our strikes. We have some very sad memories of these experiences.

We see that bringing the employers to court when they have broken the law is almost impossible.

The indifference of the federal agencies in regard to enforcement of those few regulations that apply to farm workers is also very bad. We have cases with the Federal Food and Drug Administration going back two years. The celebrated case of the label switching is an example. We were boycotting the Giumarra Company and Giumarra was able to use over 100 different labels from other employers for his grapes. We had the proof in several cities. We could not get the FDA to take any actions against the growers for lying to the public about the source of their products.

As to the pesticides and their hazard to the workers, we can't do anything with the FDA. Instead of trying to intervene and to do something about the outrageous problem which has became a literal 'walking death' for farm workers, the FDA is trying to hide it.

We have had for the last four years a most difficult problem with the Justice Department. A year ago we assigned many of our organizers to do nothing but to check on the law violators coming from Mexico to break our strikes. We gave the Immigration and Naturalization Services and the Border Patrol stacks and stacks of information. They did not pull workers out of struck fields. Today there are thousands of workers being imported in the strike scene. In fact I would say the green carders and illegal entries make up ninety percent of the work force at the strike ranches. This is why we are forced to boycott. We have no enforcement by the Border Patrol. We have been told that it is impossible, there are too many violators, they do not have enough personnel.

I would like to remind the Congressmen present that in the last week and a half we have seen how effective the Border Patrol can be when they want to stop marijuana from being imported into the country. It seems to me it would be a lot less difficult to stop human beings coming across than to stop the weed coming across. It can be done. . . .

Source: Transcript of Public Hearing with Cesar Chavez, Director United Farm Workers Organizing Committee, AFL-CIO and Members of His Staff Held by Members of the U.S. House of Representatives in the Hearing Room of the Education and Labor Committee, October 1, 1969, http://farmworkermovement.org/media/oral_history/Cesar%20Chavez%20Asks_001.pdf.

Extract from Diary of Dorothy Day's Participation in Farmworker Protests, 1973

Born in New York in 1897, social activist and journalist Dorothy Day spent most of her childhood in Chicago and attended the University of

Illinois in Urbana for two years. In 1916 she returned to New York. Influenced by the writings of such authors as Leo Tolstoy and Upton Sinclair, she gained a deep concern for the sufferings of the poor and converted to Catholicism. In 1933, along with Catholic social activist Peter Maurin, Day began the Catholic Worker Movement, which not only published an influential newspaper but founded a number of hospitality houses across the country to serve the homeless, an extension of the work that Jane Addams did at Hull House in Chicago. She worked tirelessly for women's rights, birth control, and workers' rights. She was also an ardent pacifist. In 1973 she participated in a UFW strike in California. Her diary is a revealing glimpse into the pressures faced by those on the picket line.

July 30. We left Kennedy Airport at noon for San Francisco, Eileen Egan and I. She was attending, as I too was supposed to, the 50th Anniversary of the War Resister's International. Joan Baez had invited me to be at her Institute for the Study of Non-violence for the week with some members of Cesar Chavez' United Farm Workers' Union. When we arrived in time for the Institute's Monday night pot luck supper in Palo Alto, plans had changed because of the mass arrests of farm workers who were defying an injunction against mass picketing in Kern County. There was now a strike in the vineyards as well as in lettuce fields because the growers would not renew their contracts with the farm workers and were making new contracts with the Teamsters. The strike was widespread and mass arrests were continuing. Cesar Chavez' union of Farm Workers has everything that belongs to a new social order, so my path was clear. I had come to picket where an injunction was prohibiting picketing, and I would spend my weeks in California in jail, not at conferences.

This first evening was beautiful. Joan Baez sang all evening in the patio of one of the houses belonging to a group interested in land trusts, nonviolence, and the farm strike.

Joan lives up in the hills somewhere near, has a "Christ room" where an old ex-prisoner stays. Lee Swenson, who works with the Institute, drove us to one of the houses where we slept well. We had arrived in California at 2:30 P.M. California time, 5:30 N.Y. time and by N.Y. time were probably in bed well after midnight. It was a long day.

July 31. A very hot drive down the valley to Delano today, arriving as strike meeting ended. Today many Jesuits were arrested. Also sisters who had been attending a conference in San Francisco. Mass in the evening at Bakersfield, ended a tremendous demonstration, flag-carrying

Mexicans—singing, chanting, marching—and when the Mass began there were so many people that it was impossible to kneel, but there was utter silence.

August 1. Up at 2 A.M., picketed all day, covering many vineyards. Impressive lines of police, all armed—clubs and guns. We talked to them, pleaded with them to lay down their guns and clubs. One was black. His mouth twitched as he indicated that, No, he did not enjoy being there. Two other police came and walked away with him. I told the other police I would come back next day and read the Sermon on the Mount to them. I was glad I had my folding chair-cane so I could rest occasionally during picketing, and sit there before the police to talk to them. I had seen a man that morning sitting at the entrance to workers' shacks with a rifle across his knees. (Within two weeks, Juan de la Cruz was shot in the chest by such a rifle.)

August 2. Slept at Sanger with nurses from one of the farm workers' clinics. Up at 4 A.M., was at the park at Parlier before dawn. Cesar came and spoke to us about the injunction and arrests (wonder when he sleeps) and we set out in cars to picket the area where big and small growers had united to get the injunction. When three white police buses arrived some time later we were warned by the police thru the bull horns that we were to disperse, and when we refused, were ushered into the buses and brought to this "industrial farm" (which they do not like us to call a jail or prison though we are under lock and key and our barracks surrounded by riot fencing topped with barbed wire). Here we are, 99 women strikers including 30 sisters, 50 men strikers including two priests. This is a 640-acre farm and can accommodate 300. Now greatly overcrowded. Fr. John Coffield and Bill Butler were my first visitors. Fr. Coffield is an old and dear friend in the Los Angeles diocese who has always rejoiced in tribulation, his own and that of others. Bill is with the Los Angeles House of Hospitality, the Ammon Hennacy House. Eileen is staying with Helen Perry, where I too stayed before arrest. Helen is with the Grail. Had her with us in N.Y. and with Eileen in Vietnam.

August 3. Maria Hernandez got ill in the night. Taken to Fresno Hospital, cardiograph taken and she was put in the Fresno jail. (She was returned to us still ill August 7. She worries about her children.) Lidia Salazar has 3 at home, 11, 8 and 2. Her husband works at a trailer camp. The 11-year old girl takes care of the house and children. I met them, as I'm meeting many families, at visiting hours. Kathleen and Pat Jordan, on a vacation West, visited today. Another Mexican mother in our barracks has ten children and there certainly was a crowd visiting her. Such happy, beautiful families—it reminded me of a tribute paid to the early Christians when they were imprisoned and the hordes of their fellow Christians visited them and impressed their guards.

I must copy down the charges made against me. (We were listed in groups of ten): "The said defendants, on or about August 2, were persons remaining present at the place of a riot, rout, and unlawful assembly, who did willfully and unlawfully fail, refuse and neglect after the same had been lawfully warned to disperse."

Some other women listed in the criminal complaint in my group of ten were Demetria Landavazo De Leon, Maria de Jesus Ochoa, Efigenia Garcia de Rojas, Esperanza Alanis De Perales, etc. How I wish I could list them all!

The second charge made against us was "refusal to disperse and being assembled with two or more persons for the purpose of disturbing the peace and committing an unlawful act."

Other visitors during our imprisonment, or "detainment," were Eugene Nelson, I.W.W. editor of The Industrial Worker who was refused admission because he came between visiting hours. Glenda, a "small grower's" wife (they have 40 acres) who said small people were being crushed between the big growers and corporations. Another 20-acre grower said he was just beginning to make it when the strike came. Their visits hurt of course, but they had no sympathy for the strikers, and strong racist feelings.

During crucial meetings between Cesar Chavez and Teamsters the sisters all signed up for a night of prayer, taking two-hour shifts all through the night, and the Mexican women all knelt along the tables in the center and prayed the rosary together. Barracks A, B, and E were alive with prayer.

Tonight, a young Mexican legal assistant of the Union attempting to talk to us was brutally and contemptuously ordered out. He looked like an El Greco painting. There were only three incidents I could have complained of—one other rudeness, and the attempt to search the bodies of the prisoners for food smuggled in.

Two of the youngest pickets perpetrated a bit of mischief when a woman guard attempted to search a striker. They dumped a paper bag of small frogs at the feet of the guard. They were getting even, they said, because she called them "dirty Mexicans." Today I had interesting conversations with Jo von Gottfried, a teacher of rhetoric in Berkeley, a great lover of St. Thomas and St. Augustine. I tried to understand what "rhetoric" really means and she explained, but I cannot now remember.

August 8. Today Joan Baez, her mother and Daniel Ellsberg visited us. She sang to us and the other prisoners in the yard. There was a most poignant prison song. Her voice, her complete control of it, is remarkable. It tore at your heart. A dramatic song. She was singing when other prisoners were being brought to the dining room, and she turned her back to us and sang to all of them directly, as they stopped their line to listen.

Daniel Ellsberg said Cesar Chavez, the thought of him, had given him courage during his two-year ordeal in the courts.

August 9. I'm all mixed up in my dates. Dr. Evan Thomas came today, 91 and tall, lean, strong looking. God bless him. And Father Don Hessler whom we've known since he was a seminarian at Maryknoll. He suffered years of imprisonment under the Japanese in WW II. After years in Yucatan and Mexico, he now is working in San Antonio with Bishop Flores. He brought with him 4 sisters who belong to Las Hermanas, the national organization of Spanish-speaking sisters. Gerry Sherry of the *San Francisco Moniter* came for an interview. The Catholic Worker has known him many years, in Atlanta, Fresno and San Francisco.

August 11. Good talks with Sister Felicia and with Sister Timothy of Barracks B who are good spokeswomen for our groups. Two blacks representing Newsweek called. They were interested in "the religious slant" of the strike. Greg Howard, photographer, was from Princeton, Thurman White from Stanford.

August 12. Union lawyers visiting us say we'll be free tomorrow. A peaceful Sunday. Mass in the evening. Today the Mexican girls were singing and clapping and teaching the sisters some Mexican dancing. They reminded me of St. Teresa of Avila with her castanets at recreation.

All our praying seemed to bring about some results. Mr. Fitzsimmons, president of Teamsters, canceled or disavowed the contracts signed by another Teamster leader in Delano. He demoted or took some action on the leader who signed them. We really know little. We do know the power of prayer, however.

August 13. We packed our bags last night and a first bus load, me too, left our farm labor camp this morning, reached the jail and were turned back! Then we spent hours in the "rec" hall where a team of "public defenders" whom we were supposed to have seen Sunday, sat around (perhaps I saw one working) while Sister Felicia interviewed all the women in our barracks for the rest of the day and filled out forms which the judge required.

In the evening we finally all were again loaded in vans and brought to Fresno where we, with a great crowd in the park in front of the courthouse, celebrated Mass.

Jan, Chris and Joan were waiting to greet me from the St. Martin de Porres House which is in San Francisco. Cesar Chavez welcomed us all and Helen Chavez and three of her daughters, young and beautiful all of them, were there. A meeting of strikers is scheduled for Friday, so I have time to visit the San Francisco House for two days. (As I am copying these notes from my diary here in the Los Angeles' Ammon Hennacy House some one comes in bringing a newspaper, the Times, carrying gigantic headlines, Teamsters Give Up.)

Strike Continues

It is August 21 as I write and my entry in my diary of August 12 is this same news the L.A. Times presents on August 21, the feast of Pope Pius X. The fact remains that there is still no contract signed by grape growers and Cesar Chavez' union. There have been instead two deaths since, that of Naji Daifullah, an Arab striker from Yemen, Arabia, and of Juan de la Cruz of Delano. We attended the funeral service of Naji at Forty Acres. A mile-long parade of marchers walked the 4 miles in a broiling sun from Delano with black flags, black arm bands and ribbons, and stood through the long service in the broiling sun where psalms from the office of the dead were heard clearly over loud speakers and the words from the book of Wisdom: "In the sight of the unwise they seemed to die but they are at peace." There were Moslem chants, a liturgy with which I am unfamiliar—but it was Arab music. (500 Arabs recently came here from Yemen, Arabia—this land of opportunity—and one has met with death at the hands of a deputy wielding a heavy flashlight which fractured his skull.)

The Mass for Juan de la Cruz was offered by Bishop Arzube of Los Angeles, Spanish-speaking, from Ecuador. Two men have shed their blood, there are no contracts signed as yet, there has been a three-day fast requested by Cesar Chavez, and a renewed zeal in boycotting lettuce and grapes. There is no money left in the treasury of the union, especially after death benefits have been paid to the families of the dead strikers. One of the Mexican girls in jail told me proudly that their $3.50 dues (comparing them with the Teamsters dues of $7.50) paid benefits for lives born and lives lost. And there were all the clinics operating at Calexico, Delano, Sanger and other places. The Farm Workers' Union is a community to be proud of, and would that all our unions might become a "community of communities" such as Martin Buber wrote of in his Paths in Utopia.

(Sister Katherine, who was a fellow prisoner in Barracks B, is working five days a week—and what long hours!—here at the Ammon Hennacy House, and the soup kitchen and clothing room in Skid Row, and she is so like the sisters who have come to help us in her peace and joy and diligence that I feel marvelously at home. She has typed out this column for me.)

Prayer

I must mention a prayer I wrote in the front of my New Testament, and hope our readers, while they read, say this for the strikers:

Dear Pope John—please, yourself a campesino, watch over the United Farm Workers. Raise up more and more leader-servants throughout the country to stand with Cesar Chavez in this non-violent struggle with Mammon, in all the rural districts of North, and South, in the cotton fields, beet fields, potato fields, in our orchards and vineyards, our orange groves—wherever men, women and children work on the land. Help make a new order wherein justice flourishes, and, as Peter Maurin, himself a peasant, said so simply, "where it is easier to be good."

Please help, Pope John, these rural workers to repossess the land in co-ops, land trusts, with credit unions, clinics—a proliferation of "the little way" of St. Therese. Help us, Pope John. Amen.

> Show me the suffering of the most miserable;
> So I will know my people's plight.
> Free me to pray for others;
> For you are present in every person.
> Help me take responsibility for my own life;
> So that I can be free at last.
> Grant me courage to serve others;
> For in service there is true life.
> Give me honesty and patience;
> So that the Spirit will be alive among us.
> Let the Spirit flourish and grow;
> So that we will never tire of the struggle.
> Let us remember those who have died for justice;
> For they have given us life.
> Help us love even those who hate us;
> So we can change the world
> Amen

Source: Dorothy Day, "On Pilgrimage—September 1973," *The Catholic Worker*, 1, 2, 6. Dorothy Day Library, http://www.catholicworker.org/dorothyday/.

Cesar Chavez Speech at Commonwealth Club, San Francisco, November 9, 1984

On November 9, 1984, Chavez was in San Francisco to speak at the Commonwealth Club of California, one of the most prestigious public speaking forums in the United States. Chavez delivered scores of public speeches in his career, almost all of them without notes before crowds of supporters. Few of his speeches can be categorized as formal public addresses. The Commonwealth Club speech is one of those and has achieved ranking as a major piece of political and social oratory. At a time when Chavez was in the midst of beginning a vigorous new boycott of grapes over the issue of the dangers of pesticide use, he decided to give to the public an introspective glimpse into his own life, the daily lives of farm workers, and the imperative nature of the UFW's labor organizing and social movement. With the assistance of Marc Grossman, his longtime press secretary and spokesman, Chavez carefully laid out the gross injustices faced by Mexican American workers and their need to achieve power as a means of creating change.

. . . Twenty-one years ago, this last September, on a lonely stretch of railroad track paralleling U.S. Highway 101 near Salinas, 32 Bracero farm workers lost their lives in a tragic accident. The Braceros had been imported from Mexico to work on California farms. They died when their bus, which was converted from a flatbed truck, drove in front of a freight train. Conversion of the bus had not been approved by any government agency. The driver had tunnel vision. Most of the bodies laid unidentified for days. No one, including the grower who employed the workers, even knew their names. Today, thousands of farm workers live under savage conditions, beneath trees and amid garbage and human excrement near tomato fields in San Diego County; tomato fields, which use the most modern farm technology. Vicious rats gnaw at them as they sleep. They walk miles to buy food at inflated prices and they carry in water from irrigation ditches.

Child labor is still common in many farm areas. As much as 30 percent of Northern California's garlic harvesters are underaged children. Kids as young as six years old have voted in states, conducted union elections, since they qualified as workers. Some 800,000 underaged children work with their families harvesting crops across America. Babies born to migrant workers suffer 25 percent higher infant mortality rates than the rest of the population. Malnutrition among migrant workers' children is ten times higher than the national rate. Farm workers' average life expectancy is still 49 years, compared to 73 years for the average American. All my life, I have been driven by one dream, one goal, one vision: to overthrow a farm labor system in this nation that treats farm workers as if they were not important human beings. Farm workers are not agricultural implements; they are not beasts of burden to be used and discarded. That dream was born in my youth, it was nurtured in my early days of organizing. It has flourished. It has been attacked.

I'm not very different from anyone else who has ever tried to accomplish something with his life. My motivation comes from my personal life, from watching what my mother and father went through when I was growing up, from what we experienced as migrant workers in California. That dream, that vision grew from my own experience with racism, with hope, with a desire to be treated fairly, and to see my people treated as human beings and not as chattel. It grew from anger and rage, emotions I felt 40 years ago when people of my color were denied the right to see a movie or eat at a restaurant in many parts of California. It grew from the frustration and humiliation I felt as a boy who couldn't understand how the growers could abuse and exploit farm workers when there were so many of us and so few of them. Later in the 50s, I experienced a different kind of exploitation. In San Jose, in Los Angeles and in other urban communities, we, the Mexican-American people, were dominated by a majority that was Anglo. I began to realize what other minority people had discovered; that the only answer, the only hope was in organizing. More of us had to become citizens, we had to register to vote, and people like me had to develop the skills it would take to organize, to educate, to help empower the Chicano people.

I spent many years before we founded the union learning how to work with people. We experienced some successes in voter registration, in politics, in battling racial discrimination. Successes in an era where Black Americans were just beginning to assert their civil rights and when political awareness among Hispanics was almost non-existent. But deep in my heart, I knew I could never be happy unless I tried organizing the farm workers. I didn't know if I would succeed, but I had to try. All Hispanics, urban and rural, young and old, are connected to the farm workers' experience. We had all lived through the fields, or our parents had. We shared that common humiliation. How could we progress as a people even if we lived in the cities, while the farm workers, men and women of our color, were condemned to a life without pride? How could we progress as a people while the farm workers, who symbolized our history in this land, were denied self-respect? How could our people believe that their children could become lawyers and doctors and judges and business people while this shame, this injustice, was permitted to continue?

Those who attack our union often say it's not really a union. It's something else, a social movement, a civil rights movement, it's something dangerous. They're half right. The United Farm Workers is first and foremost a union, a union like any other, a union that either produces for its members on the bread-and-butter issues or doesn't survive. But the UFW has always been something more than a union, although it's never been dangerous, if you believe in the Bill of Rights. The UFW was the beginning. We attacked that historical source of shame and infamy that our people in this country lived with. We attacked that injustice, not by complaining, not by seeking handouts, not by becoming soldiers in the war on poverty; we organized.

Farm workers acknowledge we had allowed ourselves to become victims in a democratic society, a society where majority rules and collective bargaining are supposed to be more than academic theories and political rhetoric. And by addressing this historical problem, we created confidence and pride and hope in an entire people's ability to create the future. The UFW survival, its existence—were not in doubt in my mind when the time began to come. After the union became visible, when Chicanos started entering college in greater numbers, when Hispanics began running for public office in greater numbers, when our people started asserting their rights on a broad range of issues and in many communities across this land. The union survival, its very existence, sent out a signal to all Hispanics that we were fighting for our dignity. That we were challenging and overcoming injustice, that we were empowering the least educated among us, the poorest among us. The message was clear. If it could happen in the fields, it could happen anywhere: in the cities, in the courts, in the city councils, in the state legislatures. I didn't really appreciate it at the time, but the coming of our union signaled the start of great changes among Hispanics that are only now beginning to be seen.

I've traveled through every part of this nation. I have met and spoken with thousands of Hispanics from every walk of life, from every social and economic class. And one thing I hear most often from Hispanics, regardless of age or position, and from many non-Hispanics as well, is that the farm workers gave them the hope that they could succeed and the inspiration to work for change.

From time to time, you will hear our opponents declare that the union is weak, that the union has no support, that the union has not grown fast enough. Our obituary has been written many times. How ironic it is that the same forces that argue so passionately that the union is not influential are the same forces that continue to fight us so hard.

The union's power in agriculture has nothing to do with the number of farm workers on the union contract. It has nothing to do with the farm workers' ability to contribute to democratic politicians. It doesn't even have much to do with our ability to conduct successful boycotts. The very fact of our existence forces an entire industry, unionized and non-unionized, to spend millions of dollars year after year on increased wages, on improved working conditions and on benefits for workers. If we were so weak and unsuccessful, why do the growers continue to fight us with such passion? Because as long as we continue to exist, farm workers will benefit from our existence, even if they don't work under union contract. It doesn't really matter whether we have 100,000 or 500,000 members. In truth, hundreds of thousands of farm workers in California and in other states are better off today because of our work. And Hispanics across California and the nation who don't work in agriculture are better off today because of what the farm workers taught people about organization, about pride and strength, about seizing control over their own lives.

Tens of thousands of children and grandchildren of farm workers and the children and grandchildren of poor Hispanics are moving out of the fields and out of the barrio and into the professions and into business and into politics, and that movement cannot be reversed. Our union will forever exist as an empowering force among Chicanos in the Southwest. That means our power and our influence will grow and not diminish. Two major trends give us hope and encouragement. First, our union has returned to a tried and tested weapon in the farm workers non-violent arsenal: the boycott. After the Agricultural Labor Relations Act became law in California in 1975, we dismantled our boycott to work with the law. During the early and mid '70s millions of Americans supported our boycott. After 1975, we redirected our efforts from the boycott to organizing and winning elections under the law. That law helped farm workers make progress in overcoming poverty and injustice.

At companies where farm workers are protected by union contracts, we have made progress in overcoming child labor, in overcoming miserable wages and working conditions, in overcoming sexual harassment of women workers, in overcoming discrimination in employment, in overcoming dangerous pesticides, which poison our people and poison the food we all eat. Where we have organized these injustices soon passed in history, but under Republican Governor George Deukmejian, the law that guarantees our right to organize no longer protects farm workers; it doesn't work anymore.

In 1982, corporate growers gave Deukmejian $1 million to run for governor of California. Since he took office, Deukmejian has paid back his debt to the growers with the blood and sweat of California farm workers. Instead of enforcing the law as it was written against those who break it, Deukmejian invites growers who break the law to seek relief from governor's appointees. What does all this mean for farm workers? It means that the right to vote in free elections is a sham. It means the right to talk freely about the union among your fellow workers on the job is a cruel hoax. It means that the right to be free from threats and intimidation by growers is an empty promise. It means that the right to sit down and negotiate with your employer as equals across the bargaining table and not as peons in the fields is a fraud. It means that thousands of farm workers, who are owed millions of dollars in back pay because their employers broke the law, are still waiting for their checks. It means that 36,000 farm workers, who voted to be represented by the United Farm Workers in free elections, are still waiting for contracts from growers who refuse to bargain in good faith. It means that for farm workers child labor will continue. It means that infant mortality will continue. It means that malnutrition among children will continue. It means the short life expectancy and the inhuman living and working conditions will continue.

Are these make-believe threats? Are they exaggerations? Ask the farm workers who are waiting for the money they lost because the growers broke the law. Ask the farm workers who are still waiting for growers to bargain in good faith and sign contracts. Ask the farm workers who have been fired from their job because they spoke out for the union. Ask the farm workers who have been threatened with physical violence because they support the UFW, and ask the family of Rene Lopez, the young farm worker from Fresno who was shot to death last year because he supported the union as he came out of a voting booth. Ask the farm workers who watch their children go hungry in this land of wealth and promise. Ask the farm workers who see their lives eaten away by poverty and suffering.

These tragic events force farm workers to declare a new international boycott of California grapes, except the 3 percent of grapes produced under union contract. That is why we are asking Americans, once again, to join the farm workers by boycotting California grapes. The newest Harris Poll revealed that 17 million Americans boycotted grapes. We are convinced that those people and that goodwill have not disappeared. That segment of the population which makes the boycotts work are the Hispanics, the Blacks, the other minorities, our friends in labor and the church. But it is also an entire generation of young Americans who matured politically and socially in the '60s and the '70s, millions of people for whom boycotting grapes and other products became a socially accepted pattern of behavior. If you were young, Anglo and/or near campers during the late '60s and early '70s, chances are you supported farm workers.

Fifteen years later, the men and women of that generation are alive and well. They are in their mid 30s and 40s. They are pursuing professional

careers, their disposable incomes are relatively high, but they are still in-
clined to respond to an appeal from farm workers. The union's mission
still has meaning for them. Only today, we must translate the importance of
a union for farm workers into the language of the 1980s. Instead of talking
about the right to organize, we must talk about protection against sexual
harassment in the fields. We must speak about the right to quality food and
food that is safe to eat. I can tell you that the new language is working, the
17 million are still there. They are responding not to picket lines and leaf-
leting alone, but to the high-tech boycott of today, a boycott that uses
computers and direct mail and advertising techniques, which has revolu-
tionized business and politics in recent years. We have achieved more
success with a boycott in the first 11 months of 1984 than we achieved in
the last 14 years, since 1970.

The other trend that gives us hope is the monumental growth of Hispanic influence in this country. And what that means: increased population, increased social and economic clout and increased political influence.
South of the Sacramento River, Hispanics now make up more than 25 percent of the population. That figure will top 30 percent by the year 2000.
There are now 1.1 million Spanish-surnamed registered voters in California. In 1975, there were 200 Hispanic elected officials at all levels of government. In 1984, there are over 400 elected judges, city council members,
mayors and legislators. In light of these trends, it's absurd to believe or to
suggest that we are going to go back in time as a union or as a people.

The growers often try to blame the union for their problems, to lay their
sins off on us, sins for which they only have themselves to blame. The
growers only have themselves to blame as they begin to reap the harvest
of decades of environmental damage they have brought upon the land: the
pesticides, the herbicides, the soil fumigants, the fertilizers, the salt depos-
its from thoughtless irrigation, the ravages of years of unrestrained poisoning of our soil and water. Thousands of acres of land in California have
already been irrevocably damaged by this wanton abuse of nature. Thousands more will be lost unless growers understand that dumping more
and more poison from the soil won't solve their problems in the short or in
the long term.

Health authorities in many San Joaquin Valley towns already warn
young children and pregnant mothers not to drink the water, because of
the nitrates from fertilizers which has poisoned the ground water. The
growers have only themselves to blame for an increasing demand by consumers for higher-quality food, food that isn't tainted by toxics, food
that doesn't result from plant mutations or chemicals that produce red

luscious-looking tomatoes that taste like alfalfa. The growers are making the same mistakes American automakers made in the '60s and '70s when they refused to produce more economical cars and opened up the door to increased foreign competition.

Growers only have themselves to blame for increasing attacks on the publicly financed handouts and government welfare: water subsidies, mechanization research, huge subsidies for not growing crops. These special privileges came into being before the Supreme Court's "one person, one vote" decision, at a time when rural lawmakers dominated the legislature and the Congress. Soon, those handouts could be in jeopardy as government searches for more revenue and as urban taxpayers take a closer look at front programs and who they really benefit. The growers only have themselves to blame for the humiliation they have brought upon succeeding waves of immigrant groups that have sweated and sacrificed for a hundred years to make this industry rich.

For generations, they have subjugated entire races of dark-skinned farm workers. These are the sins of growers, not the farm workers. We didn't poison the land, we didn't open the door to imported produce, we didn't covet billions of dollars in government handouts, we didn't abuse and exploit the people who work the land. Today the growers are like a punch-drunk old boxer who doesn't know he's past his prime. The times are changing; the political and social environment has changed. The chickens are coming home to roost, and the time to account for past sins is approaching.

I am told these days farm workers should be discouraged and pessimistic. The Republicans control the governor's office and the White House. There is a conservative trend in the nation. Yet, we are filled with hope and encouragement. We have looked into the future and the future is ours. History and inevitability are on our side. The farm workers and their children and the Hispanics and their children are the future in California, and corporate growers are the past. Those politicians who ally themselves with the corporate growers and against farm workers and the Hispanics are in for a big surprise. They want to make their careers in politics, they want to hold power 20 and 30 years from now. But 20 and 30 years from now, in Modesto, in Salinas, in Fresno, in Bakersfield, in the Imperial Valley and in many of the great cities of California, those communities will be dominated by farm workers and not by growers, by the children and grandchildren of farm workers and not by the children and grandchildren of growers.

These trends are part of the forces of history which cannot be stopped. No person and no organization can resist them for very long; they are inevitable. Once social change begins it cannot be reversed. You cannot uneducate the person who has learned to read. You cannot humiliate the person who feels pride. You cannot oppress the people who are not afraid anymore. Our opponents must understand that it's not just the union we have built—unions like other institutions can come and go—but we're more than institutions. For nearly 20 years, our union has been on the cutting edge of a people's cause, and you cannot do away with an entire people and you cannot stamp out a people's cause. Regardless of what the future holds for the union, regardless of what the future holds for farm workers, our accomplishments cannot be undone. La causa, our cause, doesn't have to be experienced twice. The consciousness and pride that were raised by our union are alive and thriving inside millions of young Hispanics who will never work on a farm.

Like the other immigrant groups, the day will come when we win the economic and political rewards, which are in keeping with our numbers in society. The day will come when the politicians will do the right thing for our people out of political necessity and not out of charity or idealism. That day may not come this year. That day may not come during this decade, but it will come someday. And when that day comes, we shall see the fulfillment of that passage from the Book of Matthew in the New Testament: "The last shall be first, and the first shall be last." And on that day, our nation shall fulfill its creed, and that fulfillment shall enrich us all. Thank you very much.

Source: "What the Future Holds for Farm Workers and Hispanics," http://www. commonwealthclub.org/archive/20thcentury/84-11chavez-speech.html.

Cesar Chavez's Statement at the End of the "Fast for Life," August 21, 1988

In July 1988, at the age of 61, Cesar Chavez began what would be his last and longest public fast. He called it the "Fast for Life," and its purpose was to alert the public about the dangers of pesticides in the fields. For 36 days he refused food and lost 36 pounds, engendering fear among his friends and doctors that this time he may have gone too far, that this time the frail leader might not survive. Finally, on August 21, before a crowd of 8,000 at the Forty Acres compound, he began to eat again. But the fast was not over, he announced in a statement read by his son Fernando. Others would continue in three-day increments. Led by civil rights leader Jesse Jackson and other notables such as Reverend Joseph Lowery, head of the Southern Christian Leadership Conference, and ac-

tors Martin Sheen, Edward Olmos, Danny Glover, and others, the fast did continue. Volunteers across the country, many of them college students, followed the example and also engaged in short fasts. The protest and boycott against those growers who infested the crops with pesticides and the grocery stores that sold them would continue until Chavez's death five years later and beyond.

My heart is too full and my body too weak to read this message. So I have asked my oldest son, Fernando, to read it to you.

I thank God for the love and support of my family as well as for the prayers and hard work of the members and staff of our Union. I am grateful to the many thousands of people who came to be with me and for the millions who have kept me in their prayers and who have taken up our cause in their own communities. They have opened up their hearts, not just to me, but to the farm workers and the families who suffer from the unrestrained poisoning of our soil, our water, our air and our people.

Many generous people have traveled long distances to be here during the fast. It is especially meaningful to me and all farm workers to have Ethel Kennedy and her children here on this day. Twenty years ago Bobby Kennedy stood with us when few had the courage to do so. We will always carry him in our hearts. Today I pass on the fast for life to hundreds of concerned men and women throughout North America and the world who have offered to share the suffering. They will help carry the burden by continuing the fast in front of their local supermarkets.

The fast will go in hundreds of different places and it will multiply among thousands and then millions of caring people until every poisoned grape is off the supermarket shelves. And the fast will endure until the fields are safe for farm workers, the environment is preserved for future generations and our food is once again a source of nourishment and life.

Source: Statement by Cesar Chavez at the end of his 24-day Fast for Life, http://chavez.cde.ca.gov/ . . . /EXR1_Cesar_E_Chavez_Statements_on_Fasts.pdf.

Extract from Interview with Guadalupe Gamboa, April 9, 2003

The son of Mexican American parents in Texas, Guadalupe Gamboa moved with his family in the late 1940s to the Yakima Valley in central Washington. Living mostly in labor camps, the family, along with Guadalupe, worked the fields. He graduated from high school, and, unlike most of his farm worker friends, was able to go to college. At Yakima Valley Community College, he learned about the newly formed UFW. It was there that he met Tomás Villanueva, who would join him in the work of building a farm workers' movement in Washington State.

. . . I grew up my early years going from labor camp to labor camp. We would work in Washington cutting asparagus and then go and eventually we bought our own truck. [Then we would] get [in] our truck and drive down to Oregon to Willamette Valley and pick beans and then drive down to California and pick cotton with the big companies in California during the winter and then come back in the spring and follow the same routine. So as a child I grew up going from school to school, and the first grade I think I started while I was here in Washington in the spring and I flunked the first grade 'cause I didn't know any English, and there were no programs or anything to make up for the fact that you couldn't understand what they were saying.

So anyway, like myself and our family, there were thousands of Mexican-American migrants from Texas in the early years, just working basically in the row crops, the asparagus, mainly with small growers or big packing houses, like Green Giant and Del Monte, or working in the sugar beets. At that time you had a lot of sugar beets; you had a big sugar processing plant run by U & I—Utah and Idaho Sugar Company in Toppenish. And then there was also a lot of mint, spearmint [and] peppermint that was grown and then distilled for the juices, where the oil was used to flavor candies. And then there was also hops that's used to flavor beer—[in the] hop yards. They were also picking potatoes and working in the carrots, so there were different jobs that people could do, but they pretty much all involved stooping over—very hard physical labor. There were a lot of orchards at that time, but interestingly enough, the orchard work was reserved more for the Anglo—the white farm worker. At that time, there were still a lot of white farm workers that had come from Oklahoma and Arkansas. They called them "Arkies" and "Okies" during the Dustbowl, the Depression. Some had moved on, but a lot had stayed. They were very poor, also, and they're the ones that worked in the orchards, because it was considered higher status work because you didn't have to be stooped over all day for low wages. So there was a real distinction between the Mexicans who did the stoop labor and the Anglos that did the orchard work—the pruning, the thinning, the picking. And orchard work was paid very well in comparison to today. It was done by piece-rate and people could make two, three times what the hourly wage was. So slowly, more and more Mexican workers started to come. I remember going to school and being one of a few in my school, but it would grow year by year.

Most of the work—at least the stoop labor—was either by piece rate, like in the asparagus, or by the hour, and the wage never was more than the minimum wage. It was just the minimum wage all the time. There were no benefits and at that time farm workers didn't have any unemployment or at least, in Washington, very few social services. So people worked, pooled their resources [and] tried to save money for periods when there was no employment. And it was hard work and there were a lot of indignities, because you could be fired at any time. There were no toilets in the fields or water provided for the workers. The worker basically had no say. So that's the background—a lot of hard work [and] very low pay. If the grower didn't like the work you were doing, he wouldn't pay you and you'd be fired.

Very few people went on to college. The farm workers had their Mexican culture; Anglos had their culture and social events and there was very little mixing of the two. Most farm workers dropped out of school, like my family, and became farm workers. It was in this type of background that we first started hearing about Cesar Chavez and the organizing efforts that were going on in California.

This was in the '60s. I was just finishing high school. I think I first heard about Cesar Chavez when I was [in] junior college, which would have been about '65, '66. At that time, it was the '60s, when the civil rights movement had started. Lyndon Johnson was president [and] the War on Poverty had begun in the Yakima Valley because it was a poor area.

So I graduated from my high school in Sunnyside, and I was one of maybe ten or fifteen Latinos, and I remember I went through from first to the eighth grade in Outlook, which was a little town out in the country. It was a little country school. I remember in the sixth grade I had a very good teacher, a guy by the name [of] Mr. Williams. [He was] kind of an oddity. He was from out of town and used to drive a Volkswagen. I had never seen a Volkswagen in my life, but they were new at that time, in the '50s. So that showed he was pretty nonconformist. I really liked him and he really took an interest in me. I remember once him talking to me after school and asking me if I was planning on going to college and [I] said, "College—what's that?" because I had no idea what it was, you know, it just wasn't in my frame of reference. So he told me what it was. The reason he was asking was because at that time they started to track kids. You would put them in the smart classes or the vocational ed classes or the classes that are more academic to prepare you for college. He counseled me about going to college. Neither my father or mother had a single day of schooling when they were growing up. My father couldn't read [or] write and my mother could read but couldn't write in Spanish. She later learned when she was in her 60s how to write. My dad especially was always talking to me about the importance of having an education; because I hated school after I flunked the first grade. It was Anglo, hostile. But he was always telling me about the importance of going to school—that if you went to school you could get out of farm work and become a lawyer, a teacher, a doctor, and so I guess that stuck.

I didn't drop out. I kept going, and then I finally graduated and went on to junior college [at] Yakima Valley Junior College [YVC]. And it was at Yakima Valley College that I first met Tomás Villanueva, [with whom I] formed a long-term friendship and we both got involved with the United Farm Workers at the same time. He was an immigrant [but] more recent. I was born actually in Texas, in this country, and he was a recent immigrant from Mexico and had a real distinct Spanish accent, but a very smart guy. So then we met at YVC, and I started doing research on Cesar Chavez and writing papers about him. I remember going into the library and taking out *The Nation* and other leftist papers—I didn't know they were leftist at that time [laughter] and reading about the organizing efforts and the grape boycott—well, the grape strike—and the great organizing he was doing in California. So, both Tomás and I had a very deep interest in what was going on because of the situation of our families, and farm workers in general, and our own personal experiences and growing up and being cheated and being mistreated.

So we both got hired, we were both activists and we wanted to do something; so when the War on Poverty started, I believe in 1966, we both got employed by a War on Poverty program called Operation Grassroots, whose stated object was to go around interviewing people [to] find out why they were poor, you know, and what they needed to not be poor anymore [laughter]. It was very idealistic—that we thought that people were poor because they didn't know any better or needed a little fixing-up. Then people were saying, "Oh, we're poor because we don't get paid anything and our jobs don't last very long and we don't know how to speak English"— very hard problems to solve. But it was through the War on Poverty, actually, that we first made contact with the United Farm Workers of America in the person of an organizer by the name of Nick Jones—[an] Anglo organizer who had been sent from Delano to look for people who had struck a grape ranch—I believe either Giumarra or DiGiorgio, one of the two. After pressure through our campaign from the union, the company had agreed to a secret-ballot election, and part of the deal was that anybody that had worked during [a] certain period of time could vote in the elections. So they had sent out organizers following the migrant stream all over the country looking for the strikers—a very, very thorough organizing campaign. [Nick] came and addressed the meeting, an anti-War on Poverty meeting. By that time both Tomás and I were pretty fed up with the War on Poverty, because they never talked about organizing workers or forming unions or forming political power—just nothing but services and stuff. So he gave a presentation at the end of a meeting which was like a real breath of fresh air. He talked about organizing and getting better wages and better working conditions in addition to looking for the strikers and former grape workers. We talked to him afterwards, and he invited us down to California, saying there was going to be an election that summer and they needed some help.

Both Tomás and I went down there. Tomás at that time had a 1958 or 1959 Pontiac and we took off and drove all night and got to Delano and it was pretty interesting. We arrived in Delano looking for Cesar Chavez, and in my mind, because I had been so conditioned by living in an Anglo world, Cesar Chavez was going to be a light-skinned, tall, debonair-looking guy in a suit, with a fancy car and having a nice, big, fancy office. So we arrived in Delano looking for such a guy, and couldn't find him and eventually got directed to a little run-down house in the barrio on the edge of town, which was the union headquarters and eventually Cesar Chavez showed up—this small, dark-skinned, Indian-looking guy with jet-black hair, dressed in jeans and a flannel shirt, in the middle of a bunch of workers. It was pretty amazing the first time that we saw him. Actually, the thing that made the most impact on me was, well, in addition to Cesar and his charisma, was the impact that he had obviously had on all the workers there. They were all really transformed, from the beaten-down workers in this state that lived in despair and didn't think they could do anything, and had been conditioned that they were inferior because they were farm workers, to workers that had been involved (at that time the grape strike had already occurred). They were all real fired up and determined and knew that they could win. They stuck together. It was an incredible transformation, and it had a really lasting impact on me. It showed the possibilities of what could be done.

So we were pretty much hooked after that [laughter], and we got put to work looking for people that we thought were being taken to work so that they could vote in the election. I was put in a bus, and Tomás was going to follow me, because we thought the bus might go to this farm, but it turned out that the bus went to a tomato field, instead of Giumarra or DiGiorgio. But again that was very symptomatic of the union. There were no hangers-on or people that just talked. People were put to work immediately. Then the election was held, and the UFW won by a huge majority. And so we were in Delano, we met Cesar Chavez, we were involved in the organizing, [and] we took part in the weekly Friday night meetings at the Filipino community hall that the workers had, where a report was given as to what was going on and the activities. I think we were introduced as representatives/visitors from Washington State. We were treated very cordially, very gracefully, and I think we spent two weeks there.

And then we came back to Washington and by that time—as I mentioned, we were both college students. This was our summer break and by that time we had decided we wanted to do something. I finished my two years at YVC and went another quarter—the fall of '66—and then transferred to the University of Washington in the spring of 1967. By that time the draft board was after me, because it was the height of the Vietnam War, [but] I managed to stay out of it. Tomás was married by that time and he decided not to go on to college. His dream was to become a doctor, and he started working with the War on Poverty and then eventually left it because they weren't doing very much. He formed the first farm workers union [and] the first farm workers health clinic in the Yakima Valley, after much opposition from the local politicians and the local medical association. [He] also started a co-op called the United Farm Workers Co-op that was supposed to be the base for organizing later on.

So that was the nucleus—the start of the contact and the relationship that's persisted to this day between Washington State and California. . . .

We weren't getting very far through that winter and spring and then in the summer of I think it was '71, we were asked to go to California. The union had at that time—the United Farm Workers national office—had just moved into a new location called "La Paz." It was a headquarters in the foothills of the Tehachapi Mountains. It used to be a former TB sanitarium where they had sent people who had tuberculosis so that they could lie in bed and breathe the fresh country air, I guess, and the union had gotten it as a donation from one of the wealthy supporters. It was a big complex. It had over three hundred acres. So we went there and we were trained for about two or three—I think it was two days. Fred Ross, Sr., who is the person who trained Cesar on how to organize, and Cesar himself spent two days talking to us, just telling us the basics of organizing and giving us a history of how the organizing techniques that they had used very successfully in organizing farm workers had developed.

The main organizing technique that the union was using at that time and that we still use is called the house meeting—house meeting campaign drive, where you would rely on other workers themselves to help you organize a community. You would go and identify the leaders and then do a—we call them personal visit—explain to them what the idea was, what the concept of unionizing was and how you could help them and what the benefits potentially could be, economically and politically and then get them to buy in to agree it was a good thing. And then while they were excited, you would ask them then to hold a meeting at their house and invite four or five other people that they knew. That way the employers didn't know what was going on and the people would feel comfortable because it was at a friend's or relative's house. And then you would go in—you do reminding calls—and then you would go in and do your presentation and at the end—the main thing to get out of that meeting was to get other people to have other meetings. It was like a chain. So then you went to that person's and then you got two or three other meetings, and before too long, you covered a wide spectrum of the community. So Fred Ross demonstrated that for us how he did it and explained how Cesar had used it when he was first organizing and at the same time gave examples [and] gave a history of the union and got people involved in the whole process. It was very, very much like the popular education that's being used throughout Latin America now.

So we came back and you know then you would have meetings every morning. The people would go out in pairs for the first month or so and then they would do critiques afterwards and people would make suggestions on how to improve the presentation. So then we came back and then by that time Fred Ross, Jr., the son of Fred Ross, Sr., was assigned to work also in Washington State. So there were three of us then instead of just two and we started the house meeting campaigns and they worked. We no longer held the big meetings where nobody would come but instead had a series of meetings. And then at the end then we would call a big meeting and then everybody would come because they were people that we had organized and that knew each other and we used the networks to mobilize these other people, so in the space of a year, we had turned the thing completely around, and we were having actually a lot of success in terms of getting people involved. . . .

Source: Seattle Civil Rights and Labor History Project, University of Washington, interview by Anne O'Neill, April 9, 2003, http://depts.washington.edu/civilr/gGamboa-transcript.htm.

Testimony of Eliseo Medina before the Senate Subcommittee on Immigration, April 30, 2009

In 1965 Eliseo Medina, a 19-year-old grape picker who had come to the United States when he was 10 years old, joined Cesar Chavez's grape strike in Delano, California. Recognizing the dynamic potential of Medina to become a leader, Chavez gave the youngster the opportunity to hone his organizing skills in a number of important assignments. He eventually became the UFW's national vice president. Along with a number of Chavez's closest advisors, Medina left the UFW amidst a period of internal dissension. Medina became one of many individuals who took their organizing skills learned in the UFW to other campaigns. He joined the Service Employees International Union (SEIU) in 1986 and helped revive a local union in San Diego. Later, he was a key strategist in a strike by building service workers of Los Angeles Local 1877. In 1996 he became the union's international executive vice president. SEIU became the nation's largest union of health care workers and the union with the largest membership of immigrant workers. At a congressional hearing in 2009 on the issue of comprehensive immigration reform, Medina spoke about the need to achieve legislation that secures equal labor and civil rights protections for workers, improves their wages and work conditions, and provides legal channels and a path to citizenship.

My name is Eliseo Medina and I am a very proud immigrant today. To address a U.S. Senate subcommittee is a great honor and I thank you for the opportunity. My family and I came to this country in the '50s. We worked in the fields harvesting grapes, oranges and other crops. We worked long days, without breaks, for very low wages and terrible working conditions. To ask for better treatment was asking to be fired on the spot. But, as difficult as the work was, we also knew that if we worked hard we had an opportunity to claim our own little piece of the American Dream. Because of my history, the issue of immigration reform is very personal to me.

Today, I am an executive vice president of the Service Employees International Union, one of the largest unions in America. I am honored to be here today to represent the 2 million homecare, janitors, security officers and other SEIU members who live and work throughout the United States, many of them immigrants who came to this country from all over the world.

Regardless of where we came from, we wake up and go to work every day with the same goal—to work hard, contribute to society and achieve our own American Dream. I believe that to achieve that dream, we have to finally address our broken immigration system. The status quo is simply unacceptable and works only to the benefit of those who break the rules.

That is why the two largest workers organizations in the country—the Change to Win Federation and the AFL-CIO—have come together around a unified proposal for comprehensive immigration reform that consists of five components, each of which depends on the others for success:

- Rational control of the border;
- A secure and effective worker authorization mechanism;
- Adjustment of status of the current undocumented population;
- Improvement, not expansion of temporary worker programs; and
- An independent commission to assess and manage future flows, based on labor market shortages that are determined on the basis of actual need

This proposal will allow millions of undocumented workers to come out of the shadows, relieving them of the fear of arrest and deportation and of leaving behind their families and dreams. It will stop unscrupulous employers from taking advantage of their lack of legal status to exploit them and violate existing wage and hour and health and safety laws. Guest workers fare no better because they are tied to their sponsoring employer, with no effective redress because to complain is to lose your visa and be deported.

I saw this system firsthand with my father and brother and later as an adult working with sugar cane cutters in Florida under the H2A program. These workers are not treated as "guests" in our country but more like indentured servants.

The current broken system has given rise to a three-tier caste worker system in America—citizens, guest workers and undocumented workers. This onerous system depresses wages for all workers because, unfortunately, too many employers seek out the cheapest, most vulnerable workers in order to gain a competitive advantage. This helps no one, not American workers, not immigrants, not businesses that play by the rules and certainly not taxpayers who wind up paying for an ineffective enforcement system focused on arresting nannies, farm workers and gardeners instead of stopping drug smugglers, gang members or other larger threats to our national security.

Real reform will allow us to focus our resources on our priorities instead of our prejudices. It will solve many problems at one time instead of the current band-aid approach.

Since we unveiled our proposal, the portion that has received the most attention—and been the most misunderstood—has been the independent Commission. The men and women of the labor movement have long believed that our current system for bringing in permanent and temporary workers simply does not work effectively.

The key to designing a sustainable workplace immigration system is that the flow of future workers must be rationally based on the always-evolving labor market needs of the United States.

The Commission would act in two phases. First, it would examine the impact of immigration on the economy, wages, the workforce and business to recommend to Congress a new flexible system for meeting our labor needs and set the number of employment visas. Next, the Commission would set and continuously adjust future numbers based on a congressionally approved method.

We believe our proposal will give all stakeholders a seat at the table to build a system that works for the long term that is based on sound public policy not politics, and will have lasting political support.

We hope you will give it your consideration. Thank you.

Source: Testimony of Eliseo Medina, http://judiciary.senate.gov/hearings/testimony. cfm?id=3793&wit_id=7857.

Glossary

Agricultural Labor Relations Act (ALRA) A 1975 law passed by the California state legislature and signed by Governor Jerry Brown guaranteeing, among other things, the rights of California farm workers to organize for collective bargaining purposes.

Agricultural Workers Organizing Committee (AWOC) An organization composed mostly of Filipino workers and sponsored by the National AFL-CIO for the purpose of organizing farm workers. The AWOC called a grape strike in Delano, California, in September 1965, prompting Cesar Chavez to encourage his own infant union to join the protest.

Boycott To refuse to have dealings with a person or organization and/or refuse to buy a product as a protest or means of coercion. Soon after its inception, the farm workers union engaged in a number of national boycotts of table grapes, wines, and lettuce.

Braceros A U.S. government–sponsored worker importation program, begun in 1942, under which Mexicans entered the United States to labor temporarily in the agricultural fields. The program ended in 1964.

California Migrant Ministry A Christian religious ministry founded in the 1920s to serve the nation's impoverished migrant worker families. By the late 1950s, the organization became involved in fostering programs on behalf of minority citizens and community organizers dedicated to promoting social well-being and political power.

Campesino Spanish word for farm worker.

Coachella Valley An agricultural area located in the area of Palm Springs, California, that produces the first table grapes of the season.

Community Service Organization (CSO) A Mexican American self-help organization. Cesar Chavez became one of the CSO's most successful organizers.

De Colores   A traditional Spanish folk song dating from 16th-century Spain. It became a popular song among farm workers and the UFW.

El Cortito   A short-handled hoe that farm workers were forced to use by growers. An instrument whose use from a stooped position caused much physical pain and injury, it was also seen by many as a symbolic sign of peonage. The dreaded implement was outlawed in California in 1975.

El Malcriado   The farm worker newspaper started by Cesar Chavez during the early years of the NFWA.

El Teatro Campesino   Theater group founded in 1965 by Luis Valdez after joining Cesar Chavez in the Delano grape strike and boycott.

Forty Acres   Area on the west side of Delano, California, where Cesar Chavez and his associates first built union headquarters.

House Meeting   The primary foundation of community organizing as developed by such pioneers as Saul Alinksy, Fred Ross, and others. Small meetings in homes lead to others in the community and the resulting momentum leads to organizational growth.

La Causa   Spanish word for "The Cause."

La Huelga   Spanish word for "strike." Striking farm worker protesters often carried banners with the words "*La Huelga.*"

La Paz   The headquarters of the United Farm Workers in Keene, California. Originally built as a tuberculosis sanitarium, the UFW began using *La Paz* as its main administrative facility in 1971.

National Farm Workers Association (NFWA)   Labor union of farm workers founded in 1962 by Cesar Chavez and Dolores Huerta. The NFWA held its first convention in an abandoned movie theater in Fresno, California, on September 30, 1962.

National Labor Relations Act (NLRA)   Legislation enacted by Congress in 1935 to protect the rights of employees and employers, to encourage collective bargaining, and to curtail certain private sector labor and management practices harmful to workers. Farm workers were not protected under this legislation.

Nonviolence   The policy or practice of rejecting violence in favor of peaceful tactics as a means of gaining political objectives. Cesar Chavez learned nonviolence protest techniques from the writings of Indian spiritual and political leader Mahatma Gandhi and from the American civil rights movement.

Our Lady of Guadalupe Celebrated Catholic icon of the Virgin Mary dating back to the 16th century, also known as the "patroness of Mexico." The banner of Our Lady of Guadalupe was ever present during farm worker marches and demonstrations.

Peregrinación Spanish word for pilgrimage or journey to a sacred or devotional place. The farm workers union preferred to use the Spanish term to characterize its protest marches.

Radio Campesino A radio station founded by the NFW to inform farm workers on key issues such as health care, education, consumer affairs, and other issues. Since its advent in the 1980s, it grew to include stations in three states—California, Arizona, and Washington.

Salinas Valley America's so-called salad bowl, stretching approximately 50 miles inland from the central California coast and an area of much UFW protest activity.

Scab Labor Workers hired as strikebreakers to replace regular workers who go on strike.

Si Se Puede Spanish phrase meaning "It can be done." The motto became the rallying cry of the UFW.

Synanon A therapeutic and counseling social movement primarily for drug addicts founded by Charles Dederick in 1958. Its unconventional counseling style, called "attack therapy," generated much controversy. The name is a combination of the words "symposium" and "seminar." When Cesar Chavez was attracted to the movement in the late 1970s and asked UFW members to participate in its activities, many union leaders rebelled.

United Farm Workers of America (UFW) In 1972 the UFWOC was chartered as an independent affiliate by the AFL-CIO and became the United Farm Workers of America (UFW).

United Farm Workers Organizing Committee (UFWOC) A 1966 merger arranged by the National AFL-CIO between the AWOC and the NFWA.

Annotated Bibliography

Bogater, Jillian. "King, Chavez Shared Social Justice Spirit on Road to Change." MLK Symposium, University of Michigan. The University Record Online, January 22, 2009. http://www.ur.umich.edu/0809/Jan19_09/20.php.

At a symposium at the University of Michigan in 2009, Julie Chavez Rodriguez, granddaughter of Cesar Chavez, delivered a lecture on values shared by Chavez and Martin Luther King Jr.

Broyles-Gonzales, Yolanda. *El Teatro Campesino: Theater in the Chicano Movement*. Austin: University of Texas Press, 1994.

In the early months of the Delano grape strike, Luis Valdez, a young playwright, joined Cesar Chavez on the picket lines, lending a vital cultural element to the movement—an acting company called *El Teatro Campesino*.

Chavez, Cesar. *An Organizer's Tale*. Edited by Ilan Stavans. New York: Penguin Classics, 2008. http://www.farmworkermovement.org/essays/essays/Gringojustice.pdf.

Ilan Stavans, one of the preeminent scholars of Latino history, edited Cesar Chavez's own reflections on the tactics and goals of the farm workers' movement.

Cohen, Jerry. *Gringo Justice: The United Farm Workers Union, 1967–1981*. The Papers of Jerry Cohen, Amherst College Library. https://www.amherst.edu/media/view/85629/original/Gringojustice.pdf.

Lawyer Jerry Cohen, as head of the United Farm Workers' legal team, participated in many of the most critical courtroom and legislative battles of the union. He wrote reminiscences of those battles in an unpublished tract called "Gringo Justice" that is housed in his papers at Amherst College Library.

Dunne, John Gregory. *Delano: The Story of the California Grape Strike.* New York: Farrar, Straus & Giroux, 1967; Reprint, Berkeley: University of California Press, 2007.

Early in his estimable career, novelist and screenwriter John Gregory Dunne, who lived in California during the Delano grape strike, wrote a first-hand account that is still riveting in its depiction of the fast-moving events of the labor struggle.

Farmworker Movement Documentation Project. Compiled by LeRoy Chatfield. http://www.farmworkermovement.org/.

LeRoy Chatfield was one of Chavez's close associates who had come to the farm workers' movement from a Christian religious organization. Many years later, he created the Farmworker Movement Documentation Project, gathering oral histories, personal correspondence, published works, and other materials to provide an essential source for those researching the history of the UFW.

Federal Bureau of Investigation. File on Cesar Chavez and the United Farm Workers. http://foia.fbi.gov/foiaindex/chavez.htm.

From the early days of his organizing activities, the Federal Bureau of Investigation gave Cesar Chavez special scrutiny. Was he a member of an anti-American, subversive organization? The files on Chavez are now open online and provide valuable insight into the suspicions of the government investigators and what they actually found.

Ferriss, Susan, and Ricardo Sandoval. *The Fight in the Fields: Cesar Chavez and the Farm Workers Movement.* New York: Harcourt Brace, 1997.

Containing many personal narratives from farm workers on the front lines of the union's struggles and many photographs, this book is a lively general history and standard reference work.

Ganz, Marshall. *Why David Sometimes Wins: Leadership, Organization, and Strategy in the California Farm Worker Movement.* New York: Oxford University Press, 2009.

One of Chavez's closest political strategists, Marshall Ganz played a leading role in planning many of the marches, legislative fights, boycotts, and other battles of the movement. One of those who left the UFW after internal strife, Ganz later worked in the presidential campaign of Barack Obama in 2008. This book traces the tactical approaches that led to the surprising success of the drive toward a union of farm workers.

Jourdane, Maurice "Mo." *The Struggle for the Health and Legal Protection of Farm Workers:* El Cortito. Houston: Arte Publico Press, 2005.

The fight against *el cortito*, the infamous short-handled hoe that farm workers were forced by the growers to use in the harvest fields, was one of the signal victories of the farm workers' movement. California Rural Legal Assistance lawyer Maurice "Mo" Jourdane, along with the UFW, fought an aggressive legal and legislative war against those who would continue to force farm workers to use a tool that produced debilitating back injuries. This firsthand account chronicles Jourdane's decade-long work to research and successfully advocate for a California state ban to protect the rights of field workers.

Levy, Jacques E. *Cesar Chavez: Autobiography of* La Causa. Paperback edition with foreword by Fred Ross Jr. Minneapolis: University of Minnesota Press, 2007.

In 1969 journalist Jacques Levy met Cesar Chavez with an idea for a book on the farm workers' movement. Reluctant at first, Chavez finally agreed to participate in the project, thus granting the writer unprecedented access not only to Chavez but to other United Farm Workers members. The book is largely composed of first-person accounts from those most directly involved in the union's struggles.

Martin, Philip. *Promise Unfulfilled: Unions, Immigration, and the Farm Workers.* Ithaca, NY: Cornell University Press, 2003.

Despite the successes of the farm workers' movement, especially the passage by the state of California in 1975 of the Agricultural Labor Relations Act (ALRA), granting field workers the right to organize, the plight of those workers in the 21st century remained grim. Wages remained low, working conditions barely tolerable, and only a small fraction of workers in the field unionized. This book examines the reasons that the movement and the ALRA left many challenges remaining.

Matthiessen, Peter. Sal Si Puedes: *Cesar Chavez and the New American Revolution.* New York: Random House, 1969; reprint, Berkeley: University of California Press, 2000.

The noted writer Peter Matthiessen spent three years working with Cesar Chavez. This account, featuring the author's elegant prose, is one of the most gripping firsthand looks into the many sides of the nonviolent movement for the rights of farm workers and the tactics of strikes, boycotts, marches, fasts, and community organizing that made real the improbable dream of a union for farm workers.

McWilliams, Carey, and Douglas C. Sackman. *Factories in the Fields: The Story of Migratory Farm Labor in California.* Berkeley: University of California Press, 2000.

Longtime journalist, editor of *The Nation* magazine, and author of books and articles exploring pressing social issues, McWilliams first published *Factories in the Fields* in 1939. McWilliams's book was the first broad exposé of the economic and environmental damage ravaged by corporate agriculture in California. Republished in 2000, the book remains a valuable source for understanding the origins of the farm workers' fight for a union in the 1960s.

Pawell, Miriam. *The Union of Their Dreams: Power, Hope, and Struggle in Cesar Chavez's Farm Worker Movement.* New York: Bloomsbury Press, 2009.

In 2006, *Los Angeles Times* reporter Miriam Pawel published a four-part series charging that the United Farm Workers had strayed from its original mission of helping farm workers and had suffered grievous decline not only in membership but in influence. Her subsequent book focuses on eight individuals who had clashed with Chavez over internal matters and left the union.

Prouty, Marco. *Cesar Chavez, the Catholic Bishops, and the Farmworkers' Struggle for Social Justice.* Tucson: University of Arizona Press, 2008.

Like the black civil rights movement, the drive for a union of farm workers employed strong religious elements in its marches, writings, fasts, and use of religious symbols. Although Cesar Chavez and most of the farm workers were Catholics, it was not until 1969 that the American Catholic hierarchy responded to the movement by creating the Bishop's Ad Hoc Committee on Farm Labor. Its creation was a welcome victory for Chavez and a vindication of his personal beliefs in nonviolent social change.

Ross, Fred. *Conquering Goliath: Cesar Chavez at the Beginning.* Keene, CA: El Taller Grafico Press/United Farm Workers, 1989.

Community organizer and founder of the Community Service Organization (CSO), Fred Ross became a close mentor, friend, and associate of Chavez.

He gave Chavez, along with cofounder of the UFW Dolores Huerta, invaluable training in organizing that led to their drive and determination to found a union of farm workers. He was with Chavez and Huerta at the beginning and offers a unique perspective.

Shaw, Randy. *Cesar Chavez, the UFW, and the Struggle for Justice in the 21st Century.* Berkeley: University of California Press, 2008.

Countering some recent studies that doubt the long-term impact of Cesar Chavez's work in establishing a union of farm workers, this book emphasizes the enormous influence that the movement brought to a wide-ranging number of activist enterprises and the rise of Latino economic and political empowerment.

Southwest Research and Information Center. "Voices from the Earth, An Interview with Dolores Huerta." October 29, 2003. http://www.sric.org/voices/2004/v5n2/huerta.html.

In October 2003, Dolores Huerta was in Albuquerque, New Mexico, to announce the launching of the Dolores Huerta Foundation, dedicated to train a new generation of grassroots organizers fighting for social change. While in Albuquerque, Huerta granted an interview to the University of New Mexico's Southwest Research and Information Center.

"The Story of Wendy Goepel Brooks, Cesar Chavez and *La Huelga*." www.farmworkermovement.us/essays/essays/...007%20Brooks_Wendy.pdf.

A young activist named Wendy Goepel, who had majored in sociology at Stanford, briefly worked for the California Department of Health, and who had also been a consultant to Governor Pat Brown on the antipoverty VISTA program, joined the farm workers' movement in its early days. Her recollections give extraordinary insight into the motivations and inspiration that led many young students to follow Chavez, Huerta, and the other leaders of the UFW.

United Farm Workers. "Veterans of Historic Delano Grape Strike Mark 40th Anniversary with Two-Day Reunion in Delano and *La Paz*." *El Malcriado*, Special Edition, September 17–18, 2005. http://www.ufw.org/_page.php?menu=research&inc=history/05.html.

In 2005, the United Farm Workers held a reunion in California commemorating the 40th anniversary of the Delano grape strike. The various speeches and reminiscences delivered by such early participants in the farm workers' movement as Dolores Huerta, Luis Valdez, Chris Hartmire, and others are unique personal perspectives.

Wells, Robert. "Cesar Chavez's Protestant Allies: The California Migrant Ministry and the Farm Workers." www.farmworkermovement.us/essays/essays/cec.pdf.

From the beginning of Cesar Chavez's quest to form a farm workers' union, the California Migrant Ministry and its leaders Jim Drake and Chris Hartmire gave the movement a powerful religious presence. At synods, conventions, and other religious gatherings, they spoke of the rights of farm workers in terms of the ideals of Christian charity. Members of the Migrant Ministry remained staunch allies in the movement's drive for social justice, and, as this article shows, Chavez gave great credit to the CMM for the creation and survival of the union.

Index

Acuna, Roberto, 87
AFL-CIO, 40, 53–54, 77, 79, 80, 110, 111. *See also* United Farm Workers of America
Agribusiness/growers: Bracero program, 2–3, 15; intimidation by, 32–34, 40–42, 80; legal actions by, 38; lost revenue due to boycotts, 41, 70; noncompliance with ALRA, 101–3; and short-handled hoes, 86–88; signing of contract with NFWA, 68; and Teamsters Union, 73–77; ties to Republican Party (*see* Republican Party); use of scab labor, 3, 25, 41, 111; use of undocumented immigrants, 24, 25, 38, 110, 111; violence by, 24, 75, 81, 99–100. *See also specific growers and companies*
Agricultural Labor Relations Act of 1975 (California), 91–94, 101–3, 105, 110–11
Agricultural Labor Relations Board (California), 101–3
Agricultural Labor Relations Initiative of 1972 (Proposition 22, California), 78–79
Agricultural Workers Organizing Committee (AWOC), 29–35, 53–54

Alianza Federal de Pueblos Libres ("Federal Alliance of Land Grants"), 85
Alinksy, Saul, 9–10, 109
American Civil Liberties Union, 41, 55
American Friends Service Committee, 40
Annual Chicano Youth Liberation Conference, 85
Antle, Lester "Bud," 75
Arizona, political gains in, 77–78
Arrests. *See* Law enforcement
Assassinations, during 1968, 65–67

Back-of-the-Yards Neighborhood Council (BYNC), 9
Baez, Joan, 77
Bardacke, Frank, 56
Barr, E. L., Jr., 67–68
Begley, Ed, Jr., 114–15
Bernstein, Harry, 32
Bird, Rose, 92
Black Panther Party (BPP), 68–70
Boycotts: artistic communications during, 36–38, 47, 106; of DiGiorgio Fruit Corporation, 52–54; extension into Europe, 82–83; of Gallo Brothers wines, 82; of Giumarra Vineyards

Corp., 54–57; of grapes, 38–44,
  57–58, 62, 63–65, 67, 70–73, 82,
  105–7; of lettuce, 82, 103, 106–7;
  of Safeway, 69–70, 82; of Schenley Industries, 38–44, 45, 48;
  of strawberries, 109–10; threat
  to under Proposition 22 initiative, 78
Boyle, Eugene, 81
Bracero program (1942), 2–3,
  14–15
Brecht, Bertolt, 36
Brown, Jerry, 83–84, 88, 91–93, 99,
  110
Brown Berets, 85
Bruce Church Inc., 101, 107
Bustos, Roberto, 46

California: Bracero program, 2;
  ethnic prejudice in, 4, 7; inves-
  tigation of DiGiorgio election
  fraud, 53; Latinos as political
  force in, 53, 79, 116; Proposition
  22, 78–79; Supreme Court of, 75,
  88. See also specific governors
California Farm Bureau, 65
California Grape and Tree Fruit
  League, 67–68, 70
California Migrant Ministry, 23,
  34–35, 49
Campbell, Joan Brown, 113
Campbell Soup Company, protests
  against, 107
Campos, Francisco, 80
Carmichael, Stokely, 43
Carmona v. Division of Indus-
  trial Safety, 88
Castro, Raul, 78
Catholic Church, 7–8, 35
Cesar E. Chavez Foundation, 112

Chatfield, LeRoy, 33, 51, 52, 77, 84,
  96
Chavez, Cesar: assassination
  threats toward, 75, 76; on Black
  Panther support, 69; and community organizing, 9–17; on
  dangers of pesticide use, 105;
  death of, 107–8; on death of
  Contreras, 99; on death of
  Lopez, 102; early life, 5–8, 107;
  family life, 58, 68; fasting by,
  59–63, 74, 77–78, 105–7; FBI
  harassment of, 12–13; on GOP's
  agenda, 102; imprisonment of,
  7, 75; later management style
  and staff dissension, 95–99;
  legacy of, 109–17; meetings
  with Brown, 91–92; meetings
  with Marcos regime, 97; meeting with Pope, 83; on nonviolent
  tactics, 56, 60, 61–62; overcoming of health issues, 67; photos
  of, 6, 11, 20; on Reagan, 102;
  relationship with Cohen, 55, 96;
  relationship with Huerta, 16–17,
  21, 24; relationship with Ross,
  11–13, 15–17; relationship with
  Valdez, 35–38, 47; response to
  letter from Barr, 67–68; role of
  religion in life's work, 7, 34–35,
  38, 40, 44–48, 59–63, 65, 83, 114;
  on short-handled hoes, 88; and
  SNCC, 42–44; speech at Commonwealth Club, 115; speech
  at Harvard University, 100; on
  Teamster sabotage, 74; traveling
  to Europe, 82–83; vision of center, 51, 96. See also specific initiatives and actions; specific
  union entities

Chavez, Helen, 7, 17, 19, 25, 30, 32, 33, 58, 60, 68
Chavez, Linda, 80, 109
Chavez, Manuel, 22
Chavez, Richard, 22, 51, 72, 86, 108, 110
Chicago, boycotts in, 9–10, 57–58, 69
Chicano movement, 84–86
Civil rights movement, 15, 39–40, 44, 73, 80–81, 109
Coastal Berry, 110
Cohen, Jerry, 54–56, 60–63, 71–72, 74, 84, 91, 93, 95, 96
Colson, Charles, 79–80
Commonwealth Club in San Francisco, 115
Community organizers, 9–17. *See also specific organizers*
Community Service Organization (CSO), 10–13, 15–16, 35
Congress of Racial Equality (CORE), 42
Contreras, Jose, 99–100
Contreras, Rufino, 99–100
Corona, Bert, 111
Court injunctions, 21, 38, 54, 60–61, 74, 75, 78, 80–81
Crusade for Justice, 85
Cruz, Philip Vera, 96–97

D'Arrigo Bros., 110
David Freedman & Company, 70
David Sometimes Wins (Ganz), 95
Day, Dorothy, 81, 82–83
Day, Mark, 64
Dederich, Charles, 96
"Definition of a Strikebreaker" (London), 30, 32

de la Cruz, Juan, 81
Delano grape strike, 29–49; AFL-CIO support, 40; American Friends Service Committee support, 40; boycott of Schenley Industries, 38–44, 45, 48; and *El Teatro Campesino*, 36–38, 47; and Great March to Sacramento, 44–49; nationwide intensification of, 57–58; SNCC support, 42–44; UAW support, 40
Democratic Party, 12, 65, 73, 79, 83–84
Deukmejian, George, 100–103
Diaz, Porfirio, 47
DiGiorgio, Giuseppe, 52
DiGiorgio Fruit Corporation, boycott of, 52–54
Dimas, Magdaleno, 55–56
Dispoto, Bruce, 40
Drake, Jim, 23, 25, 34, 61–62, 77, 99, 114
Dunne, John Gregory, 1–2, 33

E&J Gallo Winery, 81, 82, 91–92
Economist, on living conditions of farm workers, 110
El cortito ("the short one"), 86–88
Election fraud, 53
El Malcriado newspaper, 25, 26, 37, 57
El Plan Espiritual de Aztlan (The Spiritual Plan of Aztlan), 85
El Teatro Campesino, 36–38, 47
Environmental Protection Agency, 104
Ethnic prejudice, 4, 7, 84–86
Europe, boycott support in, 82–83

Fabela, Helen. *See* Chavez,
  Helen
Farm Security Administration
  (FSA), 3, 10
Farmworker Cooperative Inc.,
  51–52
Fatalities, of farm workers,
  99–100, 101–2, 110
Federal Bureau of Investigation,
  12, 47, 56, 76
Federal Marketing Service Com-
  modity Report, 41
Fernandez, Roberto, 56
Filipino farm workers, 29–33,
  45–46, 52
Fitzsimmons, Frank, 93
Flournoy, Houston, 83
Flowers, Dickie, 43
"Forty Acres, The," 51–52
Franco, Carolina, 45
Fresno, California, 81

Galarza, Ernesto, 6
Gallo Brothers. *See* E&J Gallo
  Winery
Gallyen, LeRoy, 32
Gandhi, Mahatma, 8, 59, 109
Ganz, Marshall, 43, 53, 54, 64,
  65–66, 73, 77, 95, 96, 97, 99,
  116
Gines, Ben, 29
Giumarra, John, Jr., 70–72, 110
Giumarra Vineyards Corp., 54–57,
  70–71, 81, 110
Goepel, Wendy, 30–31, 32
Gonzales, Rodolfo (Corky), 85
Govea, Jessica, 54, 64, 99
Grant, Allan, 65
Grape boycotts. *See* Boycotts; Del-
  ano grape strike

Grapes of Wrath (Steinbeck), 10
Great March to Sacramento
  (1966), 44–49
Gregory, Dick, 105
Growers. *See* Agribusiness/
  growers; *specific growers and
  companies*
Growers Exchange, 101

Hampton, Fred, 69
Hartmire, Chris, 20–21, 32, 34–35,
  49, 51, 65, 99, 114
Hartmire, John, 21
Havens, David, 32
Henning, Pat, 113–14
Hernandez, Julio, 23
Hoover, J. Edgar, 56
"*Huelga* Priests," 37–38
Huerta, Dolores: on boycott of
  Giumarra Vineyards Corp.,
  54; as community organizer,
  13–17; as contract negotiator,
  48–49, 75–76; and Delano grape
  strike, 30, 32–33; on fasting by
  Chavez, 59–60; on influencing
  elections, 79; as leader of New
  York City boycott, 63, 67; as
  leader of NFWA, 21–27, 77, 78;
  legacy of, 109, 111–12; on
  Medina's leadership role, 97;
  on nonviolent tactics, 34;
  police attack on, 106–7; preparation of wage contract for
  Schenley Industries, 48; and
  R. F. Kennedy, 61, 66; on slave
  labor wages of strawberry
  workers, 109; as speaker at
  Capitol, 49; traveling to Europe,
  82–83
Humphrey, Hubert, 65

"I am Joaquin/*Yo Soy Joaquin*" (Gonzales), 85
Illegal immigration, growth of, 3, 111
Imperial Valley, California, 99–100
Imutan, Andy, 29
Imutan, Luming, 32
Industrial Areas Foundation, 9, 114
Injunctions. *See* Court injunctions
InterHarvest, 75–76
International Brotherhood of Teamsters Union. *See* Teamsters Union
Itliong, Larry, 29, 30

Jackson, Jesse, 106
John Pagliarulo & Son (farm), 31–32
Johnson, Lyndon, 65
Johnson, Rafer, 75
Jourdane, "Mo," 88

Kennedy, Ethel, 75, 105–6
Kennedy, Joseph, 77
Kennedy, Kerry, 106
Kennedy, Robert F., 26, 43–44, 53, 59, 61, 65, 66, 106
Kennedy, Ted, 62
Kern County, California, 81
King, Coretta Scott, 75, 77
King, Martin Luther, Jr., 8, 34, 59, 66
Kircher, William, 46

Law enforcement: alliance with growers, 40–41, 54, 80–81, 102; arrests of farm workers/picketers, 21, 24, 32–33, 41, 56, 64, 75, 80–81, 93; deaths of farm

workers by, 99–100; violence by, 81, 99–100, 106
Leo XIII (pope), 7
Lettuce strike (1979), 99–100, 106–7
Lira, Augustin, 36
Lopez, Rene, 101–2

Mahony, Roger, 35
March to Calexico (1985), 102–3
March to Modesto (1975), 91–92
March to Sacramento (1966), 44–49
March to Salinas (1979), 100
Marshall Field Foundation, 9
Martinez, David, 107
McCarthy, Eugene, 65
McDonnell, Donald, 7–8
Medina, Eliseo, 54, 57–58, 69, 96, 97, 99, 112–13
Mexican Americans. *See* Chicano movement
Mexican American Youth Organization (MAYO), 86
Mexico, and Bracero program, 2–3
Miller, Mike, 42
Mississippi Pulpwood Cutters Association, 114
Monsanto, 110
Mount Arbor (company), 25
Munoz, Marcos, 54, 63
Murphy, George, 44

National Farm Labor Union, 6
National Farmworker Ministry, 20
National Farm Workers Association (NFWA, 1962–1966), 19–27; concessions with, by Schenley Industries, 48; Constitution of, 23; and Delano grape strike,

30–35; flag of, 21–22, 27; grower
skepticism of, 21; membership
of, 24–25, 29–30; merger with
AWOC, 53–54; motto of, 21;
services of, 25; strike actions,
25–27. *See also* Boycotts;
Strikes; *specific leaders*
National Farm Workers Service
Center Inc. (NFWSC), 51–52
Native Americans, politicization
of, 77–78
Newsweek, on "Cesar's Triumph,"
94
Newton, Huey P., 69
New York City, boycotts in, 63, 67
Nixon, Richard, 12, 67, 79–80
Nonviolent tactics, 51–88;
Chavez's appeals for, 31, 34; of
civil rights movement, 15; during Delano grape strike, 41–43,
57–58; fasting by Chavez,
59–63, 74, 77–78, 105–7;
against violence of Texas Rang-
ers, 55–57. *See also* Boycotts;
Strikes

Obama, Barack, 116
Olmos, Edward James, 105
Our Lady of Guadalupe, 35, 46, 47

Padilla, Gilbert, 19–20, 23–24, 25,
55, 69, 82, 98
Paul VI (pope), 83
Peregrinación, 44–49
Pesticides, 72, 76, 103–5
Phillips, Lou Diamond, 105
Pic N Pac, 76
Plan de Delano, 47–48
Plan of Ayala, 47
Plan of the Barrio, 85

Police. *See* Law enforcement
Poor People's March (1968), 85
Protests, 5–6. *See also* Boycotts;
Nonviolent tactics; Strikes

Rangel, Hijinio, 65
Raza Unida motto, 86
Raza Unida Party (Texas), 86
Reagan, Ronald, 63, 73–74, 83, 102
Religion and religious leaders, in
Chavez's movement, 7, 21, 33,
34–35, 37–40, 44–48, 59–63, 65,
81, 83, 114. *See also specific
religious leaders*
Republican Party, 12, 62, 67–68,
73–74, 76, 78, 100–103, 106
Rerun Novarum (1891), 7
Reuther, Walter, 40, 43
Rodriguez, Arturo, 107, 109, 111
Rodriguez, Conrado, 82
Rodriguez, Julie Chavez, 112
Rodriquez, Richard, 47
Ross, Fred, Jr., 113
Ross, Fred, Sr., 10–17, 30, 51,
53–54, 63, 64, 69–70, 109
Roybal, Edward, 10, 53

Safeway, boycott of, 69–70, 82
Saikhon, Mario, 99
Sanchez, David, 85
S&W Fine Foods, 52
San Francisco Police Department,
106
Santillano, Cecilio, 2
Schenley Industries, boycott of,
38–44, 45, 48
Schneider, Chris, 101
Schwarzenegger, Arnold, 110
Seale, Bobby, 69
Sheen, Martin, 105

Short-handled hoes, 86–88
Shroyer, John, 39
Sí, se puede (Yes, we can do it), 77, 116
Sikkema, Fred, 101–2
Sikkema Dairy, 101–2
Social justice, 7–8, 34–35, 60–62, 109–17
St. Clair, Jeffrey, 64
Steel union, 82
Steinbeck, John, 10
Steinberg, Lionel, 70
Strikes: by AWOC, 29–35; and coordination with grape boycotts, 67; against DiGiorgio Fruit Corporation, 52–54; grower use of scab workers during, 38; against Guimarra Vineyards Corp., 54–57, 81; against labor camp rental increases, 25, 27; against lettuce growers, 73–76, 99–100, 106–7; by melon pickers in Texas, 55–57; by NFWA, 25–27; against Sikkema Dairy, 101–2; against Teamster/grower contracts, 80–81. *See also* Delano grape strike
Student Nonviolent Coordinating Committee (SNCC), 42–44
Sun Harvest, 101
Sweeney, John, 110
Synanon, 96, 111

Talisman Sugarcane Company, 113
Teamsters Union, 52–53, 73–76, 79–83, 93–94
Texas Rangers, 55–57
Tijerina, Reies Lopez, 85

Townsend, Kathleen Kennedy, 105
TreeSweet Products, 52

United Auto Workers (UAW), 40, 55
United Farm Workers of America (UFW, 1972–present): as affiliate of AFL-CIO, 77; and California elections, 79; and conflict with Teamsters, 79–83, 93; contract with D'Arrigo Bros., 110; endorsement of Brown's campaign, 83–84; five-year agreement with Teamsters, 93–94; on immigration, 111; legacy of, 109–17; loss of contracts under Deukmejian, 101; membership of, 95; paid union reps, 98; Rodriguez as leader of, 109; staff dissension, 95–99; Wrath of Grapes campaign, 103–5. *See also* Boycotts; Strikes; *specific leaders*
United Farm Workers Organizing Committee (UFWOC, 1966–1972): contracts with grape growers, 68; expansion of grape boycott, 63–65; *La Paz* headquarters, 76; major contracts (1970), 70–73, 76; membership of, 58, 76–77; merger with AWOC, 53–54; support for Kennedy's presidential campaign, 65–66. *See also* Boycotts; Strikes; *specific leaders*
United Packinghouse Workers Union, 9
Uranday, Esther, 31–32
U.S. Justice Department, 12

U.S. Supreme Court, 55
U.S. Treasury, 75

Valdez, Luis, 35–38, 47–48
Valley Interfaith (Texas), 114
Vazquez, Alfredo, 41–42
Villaraigosa, Antonio, 114
Voter registration drives, 10, 12,
    65–66, 77–78

White, Kevin, 63
White Rose (company), 52

Williams, Jack, 77
World Council of Churches, 82
Wrath of Grapes campaign, 103–4

Ybarra, Richard, 69–70
Young Citizens for Community
    Action (YCCA), 85
Ytom, Felix, 45

Zambrano, Aristeo, 98
Zapata, Emiliano, 30, 47
Zermeno, Andy, 26

About the Author

ROGER BRUNS is a historian and former deputy executive director of the National Historical Publications and Records Commission at the National Archives in Washington, D.C. He is the author of many books including *Icons of Latino America: Latino Contributions to American Culture*; *Preacher: Billy Sunday and the Rise of American Evangelism*; and *Almost History: Close Calls, Plan B's, and Twists of Fate in America's Past*. He has written several biographies for young readers of such figures as Martin Luther King Jr., John Wesley Powell, and Thomas Jefferson.